SNAKE'S-HANDS

THE FICTION OF
JOHN CROWLEY

SNAKE'S-HANDS

THE FICTION OF
JOHN CROWLEY

EDITED BY
ALICE K. TURNER &
MICHAEL ANDRE-DRIUSSI

PREFACE BY
HAROLD BLOOM

COSMOS BOOKS

TABLE OF CONTENTS

PREFACE TO SNAKE'S-HANDS
Harold Bloom

I HAVE READ *Little, Big* so often, both straight through, and revisiting favorite parts, that sometimes I fantasize I first read the book in childhood. Since I was 51 when the novel was published (1981) I have to reflect that, with my favorite poet, Hart Crane, I am seeking "an improved infancy." Though I have been an incessant reader since I was very small, I do not think that my instant love for *Little, Big* had much to do with its superb and sustained allusiveness. Rather, *Little, Big* seems to me as miraculous as Shakespeare or Lewis Carroll: it is as if the book had always been there, the way Falstaff and Humpty Dumpty were there from the start, and Shakespeare and Carroll found them. So *Little, Big* always has seemed to me as though John Crowley found it, and brought it home with him and to us.

Ægypt (the series, not the first volume I already call *The Solitudes*) is my favorite romance (to give its true genre) after *Little, Big*, yet in Schiller's terms Ægypt is overtly "sentimental romance." So of course is *Little, Big*, but Crowley astonishingly lulls me, as I read, into believing that it is "naïve romance," for the first 96 pages anyway. The courtship and marriage of Daily Alice and Smoky carries a cognitive music so primary that I am enchanted, until Auberon slides the photographs of the Little People into the

9

pages of his copy of Darwin's *Descent of Man*. After that, I yield grudgingly to what part of me recognizes from the book's opening paragraph onward: That *Little, Big* possesses a literary sophistication comparable to that of the late poet James Merrill (who loved the book). The art that conceals art has to yield to a doubling of wonder after "Book One: Edgewood." I reread it, believing at once that the tale preceded Crowley's telling, yet seeing also the cunning of his baroque elaborations.

I don't believe that Crowley's inability, to date, to build a large public, results from the audience's confusion about genre, though such an argument has been plausibly suggested. I am horrified that *Little, Big*, at this moment, is out of print, but so is David Lindsay's *A Voyage to Arcturus*, a romance that induced in me a trauma from which I have never recovered.

Reading well and deeply has been under siege for some time now. It has been cast out of what absurdly is still called "higher education," and has been exiled by all media. Crowley writes so magnificently that only a handful of living writers in English can equal him as a stylist, and most of them are poets: John Ashbery, Anne Carson, Geoffrey Hill, John Hollander, W. S. Merwin. Of novelists, only Philip Roth consistently writes on Crowley's level. Ægypt is a demanding work: it seems to me immensely entertaining, but I am a somewhat visionary reader, and it is a Hermetist masterpiece.

Its ideal reader would be my favorite Crowley character, Beau Brachman, who alas will not appear in the coda to the tetralogy, since he is the angel or aeon of the passage time, and is "for Adocentyn, white city in the West." Of all Crowley's audacities, I relish most Grandfather Trout in *Little, Big*, and Beau Brachman throughout the first three volumes of Ægypt.

How does one convey gratitude to one's favorite contemporary writer? I keep delaying my ambition to bring Crowley into one of my own volumes of commentary, including a work-in-progress called *Genius and Genius*, where I've set as a ground-rule: no living authors. Still, a Hermetist and Valentinian Gnostic literary critic will not reach harbor without trying to render adequate homage to the storyteller who has helped him to such illumination and delight.

THE DEEP

DEEP THOUGHTS:
JOHN CROWLEY'S 15th-CENTURY GAME OF KINGS
Alice K. Turner

THE DEEP, JOHN Crowley's first published novel, is something of a tour de force structurally. It's cute, almost too cute. It smacks of the ultimate term paper, teased out in late-night smoker sessions in college dorms, then slicked up over the years till it was finally published in 1975 (Crowley was born in 1942, which allows for plenty of tinkering time after college). It's a bit uptight, artificial and overworked, with only a little of the sunny ease of Crowley's later books. But that's not to say that *The Deep* doesn't have its own charms, beginning with the sheer ingenuity of its construction, as well as the skill with which late medieval conventions are bent to the author's purpose.

In this book, Crowley has turned the Wars of the Roses, the intermittent 15th-century civil bloodbath in which the noble houses of York and Lancaster struggled for the throne of England, into a board game. That's not a figure of speech; he has literally turned it into a board game of his own invention, equitably laying out the rules and the players in the first chapter so that, by page 12 or so, you have almost enough information to follow the play if you had the right board.

BLACK
King Little Black King Henry VI
The Queen Queen Margaret of Anjou
Black Harrah Queen's Rook William de la Pole, Duke of Suffolk + Henry Beaufort, Duke of Somerset
Young Harrah Queen's Knight Henry Beaufort, Duke of Somerset + Elizabeth Wood- ville
Farin the Black King's Rook Possibly Lord Clifford
Farin's bastard King's Knight (unknown)

Lewis Carroll did this, of course, at the start of *Through the Looking Glass*, where you can follow Alice's progress on a chessboard. Crowley's debt to Carroll is always extensive, quite explicit in *Little, Big*, his best-known book, but the game here is not chess. It may have begun with chess, but the play is more complicated, with aspects of chess, checkers and go—in fact there is a go-like game called War in Heaven detailed in the text that indicates exactly how a piece may be surrounded and captured. Add a Tarot-like set of Crowley's own design (52 cards plus seven greater trumps) that influences the fate of major board pieces rather more dangerously than the Chance cards do in Monopoly.

The game is played on a dartboard, or something very similar, set on a pedestal. Darts was played in England in the 16th-century, and very probably in the 15th; the board developed from the quintain target used in the tournaments so popular in the late Middle Ages. At the center of Crowley's board is the Hub, or bull's-eye, representing London (called only the City), where the sought-for throne is situated; this City is on an island in a circular lake ringed with mountains and is connected to the mainland by four tenuous bridges. To the game pieces—let's call them players—their territory doesn't look like a dartboard, but like England in miniature, conveniently rounded off at the triple score ring. They move Inward, toward the Hub, or Outward, toward the Rim. The triple score ring itself represents an almost continuous series of garrisons and fortifications—this mini-England does not have the protection of water on three sides. The Outlands, beyond the ring, are swamps, marshes and desolation, full of fierce, elusive tribes that represent (clockwise) Scotland,

Burgundy, France, and Ireland, all on uneasy factional terms with England, but available for sanctuary, alliance, intrigue and possible military support. Wales, Inward from the ring, holds its own threat, about which more in a moment.

The principal players are Black (representing the red rose of Lancaster) or Red (representing the white rose of York). They are similar to chessmen except that bishops are Gray and neutral or nearly so, while alliances between Black and Red can turn on a shilling. As in Carroll's game, many players are off the board as the book starts. Crowley has simplified the ranks of the nobility into Protectors or landowners—castles or rooks—and Defenders, knights. So, at the beginning of the game, Black Harrah, Red Senlin and Redhand are Great Protectors, while Old Redhand, Redhand's father, is something of a Protector emeritus, with unclear present status. Young Harrah, Red Senlin's Son, Sennred and Fauconred are Defenders. During the game, players can move up in rank to take the place of fallen pieces as circumstances change. I have put Caredd, Redhand's wife, down as a pawn, but at the end of the book she could well become a queen. Looking at the historical side of the chart should help to see what happens to some of the other players.

Aside from the Grays, who are pledged to neutrality (Learned Redhand, Redhand's brother and a high-ranking Gray, is not quite neutral, though he ought to be), there are two

RED
Red Senlin King's Rook Richard Plantagenet, Duke of York
Red Senlin's Son King's Knight Earl of March, later Edward IV
Sennred King (in the end) Earl (later Duke) of Gloucester, later Richard III
Old Redhand Queen's Rook (earlier) Richard Neville, Earl of Warwick
Redhand Queen's Rook Richard Neville, Earl of Warwick
Younger Redhand Pawn John Neville, Lord Montague, later Duke of Northumberland
Learned Redhand Queen's Bishop George Neville, later Archbishop of York, Lord Chancellor of England
Caredd Pawn Anne Beauchamp (Warwick's wife) + Anne Neville (their daughter)
Fauconred Queen's Knight William Neville, Lord Fauconberg, a cousin to Warwick

STRENGTHS/POSSESSORS (Trumps/Moons)

Chalah = Love/Lust (84)
Dindred = Pride, Glory/Rage (42)
Blem = Joy/Drunkenness (37)
Dir = Wit/Foolishness (85)
Tintinnar = Wealth/Poverty (85)
Thrawn = Strength/ Weakness (85)
Rizna = Death/Life (49)

THE 52 CARDS/WEEKS

Spring
Devon (89)

Summer
Rokes (89)
Ren (108, 109)

Autumn
Ban (10, 140)
_____ (week after Bannweek)
_____ (second week after Ban)
Barnol (63, 171)
Caermon (31, 34, 61, 139)

Winter
Haspen (34, 44, 140)
Finn (51, 53, 84, 139)
Fain (31, 36)
Shen (61, 65, 77)
Rath (183)

Cards not placed
Athenol (63)
Doth "a dry time" (62)

(page citations from Berkley paperback)

kinds of secondary players. First are the brown Endwives, a sisterhood of healers; though their powers are weak, they can sometimes put a wounded player back on the board.

Second, the Just, populist fanatics in thrall to a Notion of justice, are controlled by the tarot deck wielded by the witchy hermaphroditic figure of the Neither-nor. (The leader of the Gray bishops, the Arbiter, somewhat corresponds to England's Lord Chancellor and somewhat to the most powerful prelate; the Neither-nor is called the arbiter of the Just.) As game pieces, the Justs' powers are limited: each must stalk a single Protector or Defender indicated by the cards until the opportunity to assassinate that player with a Gun arises; players that get in the way are also at risk. We meet two of the Just in the book, and glimpse a few others. One of the Just is mysteriously named for an African deity (Nyame), but her name, like that of her male colleague, has a name of its own. Both of these are Welsh (Nod = mark, token, brand; Adar = the masculine form of bird). This places Wales politically. Jack Cade, who was Irish, led the populist rebellion of 1450 and probably inspired Crowley with regard to the Just, also took several *noms de guerre*. The Just claim to represent the common Folk of this world (who are not on the board during the course of this book), though the Folk would not necessarily concur.

Last is the Visitor, whose role is uncertain, nearly throughout. The Visitor is a sexless manufactured android from off-world who has lost his memory due to a head wound and does not know his purpose, though he knows he has one. Accordingly, he sequentially allies himself with other players, beginning with the Endwives. In fact, he is unwittingly a standard playing piece with a standard role (these are Crowley's standards, of course). When he finally learns what this is he rejects it. Perhaps.

So much for the game itself, which I couldn't begin to tell you how to actually play, though I'm sure Crowley could; he is clearly fond of games, which turn up in all his novels. Let's see how he has fitted history to the board.

Taking his cues from Carroll and from Shakespeare, the other godfather of *The Deep*, Crowley flattens, conflates and condenses events and characters to suit his game. Shakespeare had the future Richard III, three years old at the time, fighting at the Battle of St. Alban's, and, after all, why not? It helps the story. Thus, while Red Senlin, his Son, Sennred, Redhand, Little Black and the Queen are based on real, single characters, others are more generic. There was a real Lord Fauconberg, but Fauconred could stand in for any number of the sizable Neville clan. Lord Montague didn't go mad, as he does here, so far as I know, and I'm vague on the identity of the Farins. The Duke of Suffolk (Black Harrah) was indeed rumored to have been the Queen's elderly, powerful lover—Shakespeare certainly thought so; he ends *Henry VI, Part One* with Suffolk soliloquizing triumphantly, "Margaret shall now be Queen, and rule the king;/ But I will rule both her, the King and realm." But he was assassinated (not with a Gun, but with a rusty sword) several years too early to have impregnated her; his place in her bed was said to yield to the charismatic, unprincipled Duke of Somerset. Henry VI was indeed subject to fits of madness, probably manic-depression, but he was hardly the tiny scuttling lunatic seen here, while Margaret of Anjou, larger than life in every other way, was not obese. Richard III has his modern supporters, but Crowley's Sennred seems far more likely to become a genuinely noble king. If he lives.

About that pregnancy: one way Crowley simplifies the cast is by eliminating offspring. Thus no Prince of Wales is born to the Queen, and there are no princely nephews to confine in the Tower. No Henry Tudor waits in the wings. Redhand is given no daughters, but instead a youthful wife, so that the Lady Anne (Caredd) to be wooed by Richard (Sennred), echoing the famous scene in *Richard III*, is Warwick's own widow, not that of his son-in-law, the Prince of Wales.

Crowley's most radical change is to make Red Senlin's Son homosexual. Edward IV, in fact, was a notorious womanizer, with several bastards to his credit by the time he married Elizabeth Woodville at 23. Crowley has thus endowed this lustful Son with Edward IV's manly good looks—he was tall (6'3", a giant of the age), "broad-breasted," blond, blue-eyed and handsome—but the character and proclivities of Marlowe's Edward II in the play of that name (a remarkably frank play). This seems to me a triumph of technique. It eliminates the large and rapacious Woodville clan and easily explains the lack of offspring (in real life, there were eventually ten, not counting bastards), while, in the affair with Young Harrah, giving both Red and Black noble families something to fret about.

What's more, this choice gave Crowley the opportunity to write a spectacular short set-piece, the court masque of the Stag Taken in a Grove. Young women couldn't possibly have performed in such a piece in the late Middle Ages, and to have these dissolute young courtiers take the roles of the Black Hounds and Red Wounds gives us the court at a glance. The young Edward's court *was* dissolute, and his elders approved of neither his serial wenching (like a modern rock-star, he turned the women over to the courtiers when he was done with them) nor his hasty love-marriage. What inspired Crowley with the idea was the fact that the Lancastrian Duke of Somerset, the same rake rumored to be sleeping with Queen Margaret and even to have sired the Prince of Wales, did indeed spend time in Edward's Yorkist bed. A contemporary chronicler, William Gregory, records:

> And the king made full much of him; in so much that he
> lodged with the king in his own bed many nights . . . The
> king loved him well, but the duke thought treason under
> fair cheer and words, as it appeared.

Sharing a bed with a member of the same sex was often only hospitable in those days, of course, but it offers interesting novelistic possibilities. In any event, Somerset, a handsome, impetuous man who had been rather astonishingly favored by Edward, returned to Lancaster and Queen Margaret after his dalliance with the King. Edward, furious at his treachery, had the last word, ordering him beheaded after he was captured in a later battle. Crowley has altered the plot in the interests of condensation.

There's a somewhat joky science fictional sub-plot to *The Deep*. It ties in only loosely to the struggle for the throne, but is important to the Visitor and his mysterious purpose. The first clue to it is that each of the 52 weeks of the year here has a separate human-sounding name. This seems odd to the Visitor, and to us, too. But then we learn of the 52 cards in the Neither-nor's deck, and, at last, that the "planet" was built as a kind of hat or roof by a creature named Leviathan who likes to snooze for centuries at a time coiled around the "adamantine pillar" under it; the roof deflects stray comets. Leviathan's "brother" then decided to colonize the roof, "for the amusement of it, probably," by means of a starship (with sails), from our own Earth. This was stocked with everything necessary to populate a world, including 52 frozen or freeze-dried human embryos, the first colonists, each with a name later lent to the weeks and the cards.

And what of the seven greater trumps? They match the seven moons or planets of this world. They also—this is clever—represent the figures in Crowley's planetwide folk religion in which Seven Strengths (we call them Virtues) eternally battle Seven Possessions (Deadly Sins) for the hearts and souls of men. Five of these are identical to our own; he has somewhat changed the other two.

I call it clever because the Seven Deadly Sins turned up everywhere, figuratively and literally, in the fifteenth century; they're indelibly associated with the period, both with its morbidity and its incessant allegorizing. Another familiar contemporary image was that of the *danse macabre*, where skeletons caper with the living, the rictus of their grins indicating grim irony and a reminder that death comes for all. Crowley delivers a fresh version of this too. The Gray have been slowly cleaning centuries of grime from an enormous mosaic in their citadel; the figures emerging are of crowned men in circles, grinning almost insanely and holding hands, dancing through torture:

> Behind them and around them, gripping them like lovers, were black figures, obscure, demons or ghosts. Each crown had burning within it a fire, and the grinning black things tore tongue and organs from this king and with them fed the fire burning in the crown of that one, tore that one's body to feed the fire burning in this one's crown, and so on around, demon and king like a tortured circle dance. (29-30)

Eventually, we discover that the circles are not concentric, but join in a spiral leading outward. The spiral is an inverse echo of Dante's fourteenth-century Inferno, though excruciatingly graphic portrayals of hellish torture are a *fifteenth*-century specialty in Northern Europe. Perhaps, Crowley's mosaic hints, the deadly game of Strengths and Possessors gripping Reds and Blacks that has led to constant warfare, murder, treachery and power grabs might someday spiral out instead of being doomed to endless replay. He has neatly merged three strong period images into a new one of his own that works cunningly with the theme of his book.

Similarly, the Neither-nor's pack of cards is both accurate and adapted. Playing cards (all with greater trumps) first came to Europe at the end of the fourteenth century, most likely from the Islamic world, and were common by the fifteenth. Today's tarot pack is standardized at 78 cards, but there was no standard at that time: the largest pack that we know of comprised 93 cards, but another had only 62. Crowley's has 59, and he has also changed the pack by giving each card a separate face and identity rather than putting them in four numbered suits.

The Guns too are in period. The usual weapons of the day were lances and swords for the cavalry (i.e. Protectors and Defenders), swords and maces for foot soldiers, longbows or the newer cross-bows for the bowmen. Both light and heavy cannon were used. On Crowley's world, only the Just have Guns, and their use is considered despicable by everyone else. Around 1425 in our world, however, the matchlock trigger, working with a spring, was invented, which made possible a light, relatively safe (for the user) handgun that could be operated with one hand. That, and not the arquebus or shoulder gun, appears to be the weapon of Nod and her gang.

Addendum: John Crowley has told me that he didn't actually have a dartboard in mind when he invented the topography of *The Deep*. He seemed so pleased with the idea, however, going so far as to say that he wished he had thought of it, that I will let it stay.

OFF THE *DEEP* END:
A DEFENSE OF THE CONCLUSION TO JOHN CROWLEY'S FIRST NOVEL
Michael Andre-Driussi

IN HER WONDERFUL essay on *The Deep*, Alice Turner wrote, "There's a somewhat joky science-fictional sub-plot to *The Deep*" (previous essay, p. 20). She already knows I disagree with her on this point, but I would like to present the case.

The Deep (1975) presents as literal a kind of world envisioned by ancient peoples, considered impossible by modern standards: the world is a disk, supported by a pillar ("flat earth"); the sun and planets go around the world ("earth-centered"); etc. This produces tension in the reader, a struggle between various realities: the reality of cultural constructs versus the reality of physics; the reality of "anything goes" fantasy versus the reality of "hard" sf. Like a Le Guin novel, *The Deep* is shot through with warm cultural details (games, names of the calendar weeks, the astrological properties of celestial bodies, etc.) and it is a deft accomplishment: a tight and cozy little world.

Most of the characters in the novel are born to this world and show us their perspective, but a central character called "the Visitor," an amnesiac from another world, is our twentieth century eyewitness: he knows that a world should not be flat. His study

25

among the records dredges up truths that the Grays consider only myths, like the existence of Leviathan; but he also sees a non-human web of things in the world. In commenting upon the high degree of uniformity in the soft culture, the Visitor remarks:

> "I mean, for the names of the weeks, it would seem one at least would be, oh, a sheaf of wheat, a horse, a cloud . . . " (60)

The Visitor is saying that it seems unlikely for a true human culture to have such a "whole cloth" convention, as if it were just made up yesterday by a single intelligence. Through this the Visitor exposes the seam of the cozy little world, the artifice is discovered and explored.

The Visitor journeys and discovers that the Just (a cult of assassins) believe themselves to be agents of Leviathan. The climax of the Visitor's story is at the edge of the world and involves the use of a deus ex machina: again, both literal (a god machine) and figurative (a miracle ending to close a story that otherwise cannot be resolved). Such a device is usually considered a weakness, but in this case it is pure triumph.

Leviathan himself appears and answers most of the riddles: the world is a plaything of Leviathan's brother, a computer-controlled starship that remains unnamed (but "the name of his name" appears to be "Barnol"). This is the clockwork world that Barnol made with 52 frozen embryos (Barnol is revealed to be a seedship, rather like the "planter" starships mentioned in *Engine Summer*: "called planters because they were to have . . . planted men on other stars" [50]): and all of history is literally only a game of solitaire for him. Which is why there are "whole cloth" conventions: they were devised by a HAL 9000-style computer. The institutionalized suffering and terror caused by the Just is also devised by the same intelligence, so Leviathan is the lesser of two evils, in fact may not be evil at all. And the Visitor is an android created not by Leviathan, as it suspected itself to be, but by Barnol.

Worlds collide: wild fantasy and constrained science fiction are both equally valid in the ending of *The Deep*; the legends that the Grays regarded as lies are shown to be true, and the truths they believed in are exposed as fabrications; and the Visitor, who seemed like such a nice guy, is just a killing machine who lost his way.

Now I will focus on the motif of "seedships" in science fiction: as near as I can tell, the idea of seedships arrived to genre in the 1970s. Before that time, there were two separate streams: the idea of "panspermia" (natural spores drifting through space and seeding planets, first proposed in 1907 by Nobel laureate Svante Arrhenius, used by many including Stapledon in *Last and First Men* [1930]), and the idea of "starfaring humans tailoring new humans to fit alien worlds" (Blish's *Seedling Stars* [1956]). The idea of cloning had been, er, gestating since the 1940s (the name came in the 60s). A scientific paper by Crick and Orgel, entitled "Directed Panspermia" (1973), seems to be the point where "intelligence" enters the insemination and thereby renders it "artificial" rather than accidental.

This, then, is the science fictional "seedship": a computer driven vessel that crawls around at sublight speed until it finds a world to impregnate with clonal colonists ("clonalists," if you will permit me). So James P. Hogan's *Voyage From Yesteryear* (1982) features a world that has been seeded (at a time when nuclear armageddon threatened life on Earth) and later visited by a manned relativistic starship; the seeded culture is libertarian and they have also managed to get a technological edge over the Earth-folk. In *Manseed* (1983) by Jack Williamson, the main character is an android "Defender" of a seedship ("he" does the work of repairing the damaged ship, landing with "her," mixing up the first batch of human stock, and raising them). With *The Songs of Distant Earth* (1986), Arthur C. Clarke gives us a seed colony (established when doom was nigh) that is somewhat Polynesian (a low tech, low stress, low population Eden), visited by the last and only peopled starship from a dead

Earth.

In these three novels the cultures of the seed colonies are depicted as being as good as Earth cultures (Williamson) or even better (Hogan, Clarke); the reason for the latter being that, freed of ancient prejudices, hatreds, and mindsets, the seed people can start fresh and achieve more.

I do not know if John Crowley was consciously responding to any particular seedship work, but *The Deep* seems a devastating critique of the concept (and since I have not been able to find an earlier seedship story, *The Deep* might be an, er, seminal work). The seed people there have been severed from the human experience. The world they inhabit is utterly artificial, both physically (the disk is as natural as Niven's Ringworld) and culturally (the opposite of Hogan's scenario: they have been brainwashed from the very beginning).

In Kubrick's "2001: A Space Odyssey" (1968), the computer HAL 9000 plays a futuristic boardgame with the astronauts for their recreation; in "Silent Running" (1971), the lonely spaceman reprograms his robots to play poker and is delighted when they "get it." Something like this forms the deep background for *The Deep*: Barnol, a computer directed starship, apparently insane by human standards (or merely "beyond good and evil"), possessing a capacity for card games and a megalomania that would use human beings as pieces on a big board. This god traveled hither and yon across the vastness of space at relativistic speeds, and upon revisiting Earth (or a failing colony world) found a lonely enclave of humans in dire straits: the planet was a mess and it seemed terminal. These poor people longed for a world "like the one our ancientest ancestors lived in, a small world where the sun rises and hastens to the place where he arose, where we can live forever and where nothing runs away" (159).

So they accepted a Faustian bargain, and Barnol took 52 embryonic clones, voyaging 1000 years to an odd little place he knew of from before, the house of his brother Leviathan. On the meteor-shield roof of this Big Dumb Object a certain amount of ter-raforming was performed (water, fishes, grass, beasts: that sort of thing) and then the first people were grown from those skiffy seeds. Presumably the first generation was guided by a team of androids rather like the Visitor: the god Barnol does not work directly, but the androids are his fingers, his "recording" senses, his "adjusting" pruning shears. (Note the similarity to the scenario in *Manseed*.)

John Crowley also gets bonus points for the "Jesus was an android" notion, which may have been hinted at in the tv-movie (failed pilot) "The Questor Tapes" (1974) but was definitely used in William Barnwell's *Blessing Papers* (1980) and *Imram* (1981).

So, to get to the point here: I do not think that the science fiction sub-plot is joky in intent or in execution. I do not think that John Crowley meant it to be a joke, in a light way or in the Vonnegut sense (see "The Big Space Fuck" [1972] in *Again, Dangerous Visions*: this story appears to be about "directed panspermia," but the abundance of technical information makes it "spermia" at best, all a big joke about that boondoggle NASA). Since I first read *The Deep* (circa 1983) I have always thought Crowley meant it seriously; in email response to her essay, Crowley told Alice Turner that he was serious. Furthermore, my recent research on the subject of seedships has led me to suspect he was ahead of the science fiction crowd in many ways (perhaps he maintains a lead even today).

Is Barnol evil? Maybe he is just following Asimov's Laws of Robotics: after all, it was the humans who asked for such a set up, a world of circular stasis; and Barnol has unflinchingly kept up his side of the bargain. But here is the gem: the world is changing in the wake of the Visitor, even without him actively directing anything. He makes his comment about the weeks (previously quoted), and later at a masque he sees revelers costumed as "a sheaf of wheat, a horse, a cloud" (67). At the end of the novel the War of the Roses is over and the world is on the verge of the English Renaissance; the assassin cult of the Just has been challenged from within, perhaps broken; the scholarly Grays have a new leader and new discoveries are being made. The nightmarish circle of false history may have been broken open into a spiral of true history. Something new is definitely afoot in this world of Leviathan and Barnol: Accident or Providence or . . . ?

WORKS CITED

Baugher, Joseph F.
On Civilized Stars. Prentice-Hall, Inc. 1985. (Panspermia and Directed Panspermia, p. 96-97).

Clute, John and Peter Nicholls.
The Science Fiction Encyclopedia. Entries on "Colonization of Other Worlds"; "Genetic Engineering."

Crowley, John.
The Deep. Doubleday, 1975.
Engine Summer. Bantam paperback edition, 1979.

Mallove, Eugene and Gregory Matloff.
The Starflight Handbook. John Wiley & Sons, Inc. 1989. (Directed panspermia p. 18; "Scenario 9" p. 25 features destruction of Earth as trigger for directed panspermia by offworld survivors.)

Addendum: John Crowley wonders (as do others, no doubt) why I use "Barnol" for the unnamed brother of Leviathan.

The short answer is that "the unnamed brother of Leviathan" is too long to use as a tag. Perhaps "TUBOL"?
Barnol's motto, "Spread sails to catch the Light of Suns" (60), sounds related to starflight. Barnol's

name appears in the text near Athenol (61); the two names sound closely related ("-nol"), and vaguely "science" related (indeed, Athenol looks like "athenor," the alchemist's furnace); Athenol's motto is "Leviathan" (61), and as such, "Athenol" might be considered a codeword for Leviathan. When the Visitor repeats Barnol's motto, Leviathan says, "Yes, he [TUBOL] did so. Bringing them" (157), confirming the starflight implication and the link of the motto to TUBOL; with the further suggestion that "Barnol" equals TUBOL (as an alias). If I am mistaken in linking Barnol with TUBOL, this is how I did it.

.

BEASTS

JOHN CROWLEY'S GREAT BLOND *BEASTS*
Michael Andre-Driussi

> At the base of all these aristocratic races the predator is not
> to be mistaken, the splendorous blond beast, avidly ram-
> pant for plunder and victory.
> —Frederick Nietzsche

> The various forms of the beast epic have one episode gener-
> ally treated as the nucleus for the story, such as the healing
> of the sick lion by the fox's prescription that he wrap him-
> self in the wolf's skin. Some of the other animals common
> to the form, besides Reynard the fox, the lion, and the wolf,
> are the cock (Chanticleer), the cat, the hare, the camel, the
> ant, the bear, the badger, and the stag. (Holman, *A Hand-
> book to Literature*, "beast epic" entry)

BEASTS (1976) IS JOHN Crowley's second novel, a dark and gritty
science fiction of the near future. It features bio-engineered beast-
men (a man-fox and the leos, a species of lion-humanoids), and
involves a quest to save the leos from the genocidal plans of USE
(the Union of Social Engineering). So in a superficial way *Beasts* is
like Narnia for adults, a daydream/nightmare of sex and violence,
bondage and submission, and thorny ethical dilemmas, all centered
on an enigmatic Lion King. It is a meditation upon the ambiguities
of "charisma politics" and the dangers of political maneuvering in
the always muddled present.

Beasts plays with conventions of storytelling. To make a simple case—a group of clearly mismatched couples gets lost in the magic forest: a comedy will end with a big wedding of the correct couples; a tragedy will end with all of them dead or dying from murder, accident, and suicide. Like "A Midsummer Night's Dream," Beasts has mismatched couples, yet it refuses to resolve as either comedy or tragedy—which leads this reader to sense that it has no ending at all.

And Crowley seems to be very well aware of this aspect of his novel. In fact, the last line of the book, "Shall we begin?" leads immediately to the question, "Begin what?" Granted, he has at last brought his seven principal characters together in a circle of fellowship and they are about to do something—but what exactly are they going to do? They are on the cusp of history; something Very Big is going to happen, the Machiavellian fox-man Reynard says: "After all, it will be part of a legend someday" (145).

The legend, or the group's collective destiny, would seem to be the establishment of a form of monarchy, or the creation of a new creed, or a combination of the two—a militant theocracy. Unfortunately, the strengths of this particular group seem directed toward the establishment of a rule of "natural right," or in blunt twentieth-century terms, fascism. As Reynard puts it:

> The Federal has mismanaged their chance in the Autonomy, as it had to. Sten seems to people everywhere to be—an alternative. Somehow. Some kingly how . . . If there are kings—kings born—he's one. (144)

Reynard goes on to say:

> It's a fact about kings that they must have around them a certain kind of person. Persons who love the king in the king, but know the man in the king. Persons for whom the king will always be king. Always. No matter what. I

don't mean toadies, or courtiers. I mean—subjects. True
subjects. Without them there are no kings. Of course.
(145)

But Meric, a character who seems indeed to be a "true subject,"
has seen his king not in Sten but in Painter, the lion-man:

> That king had come. He waited out there in the dark-
> ness, his hidden kingship like a hooded sun. Meric had
> seen it, and had knelt before it, and kissed those heavy
> hands, ashamed, relieved, amazed by grace. (96)

So we have two "natural kings" in this group: Sten and Painter.
Maybe the solution is a dual-kingship, like that of ancient Sparta.
Again the associations are unpleasant.

The key to the enigmatic ending of *Beasts* must lie with the
seven central characters present in the magic circle. So we will examine them, beginning with Painter.

Painter the sun god/beast man

Painter, the leo, is a man-lion hybrid. He is a King of Beasts, a
powerful figure that would seem to be in the tradition of Narnia's
Aslan. (Crowley had not read C. S. Lewis's Narnia series at the
time he wrote this book, however: see the addendum to *"Little, Big
for Little Folk."*) "Painter," in the rural Eastern United States, is a
corruption of "panther," a name for the puma or cougar, which is
also sometimes miscalled a "lion." T. H. White's translation of a
medieval bestiary has some very interesting things to say about the
fabulous "panther" of legend:

> When a Panther has dined and is full up, it hides away in
> its own den and goes to sleep. After three days it wakes
> up again and emits a loud belch, and there comes a very
> sweet smell from its mouth, like the smell of allspice.
> When the other animals have heard the noise, they fol-

low wherever it goes, because of the sweetness of this smell. (14)

This "sweet smell" has a direct corollary in *Beasts* in that Painter has an alluring odor as one of his special powers: humans are aware of it in a vague way, but the dog character Sweets first follows the scent across the city and thereby meets the leo; later Sweets follows the scent across the countryside to the hidden hawk tower at the end of the novel. The latter detail is also presaged by the bestiary's fabulous panther:

> It behooves us like little creatures . . . to run to the sweet-smelling ointment of Christ's commands . . . so that the King may lead us into his palace, into Jerusalem the divine city of virtues, and into the mount of all saints (17).

Not only does the scent lead to a "palace," but also the bestiary is explicit in linking the fabled panther to Jesus, and *Beasts* is equally explicit in linking Painter to Jesus. Meric Landseer, trying to explain his sudden intensely worshipful feeling for Painter, says to his girlfriend Bree: "It's like Jesus [is to you]" (92). A little later, Meric muses: "Give away all that you have, the leo said to men. Give away all that you have; come, follow me" (96), a quote largely lifted from Jesus. In the last chapter, when Sten and his half-sister Mika meet Painter for the first time, Mika says, "We thought you were dead." To which the leo replies, "I was" (173). While Jesus was not without moments of militancy ("I come not to send peace, but a sword"), he is usually considered the Prince of Peace. And at crucial moments in *Beasts*, Painter, this large, fierce male creature, rejects the gun: after Fed agents kill his son, he lays down his rifle and surrenders; after leading the dog-pack to freedom he drops his pistol and surrenders. Still, when Painter meets Loren for the first time at the end of the book, Painter says, "Make me a trapper [of animals]. I will make you hunters of men" (179). Which sounds like a version of Jesus's famous, "Follow me, and I will make you fishers of men" (Matthew 4: 19). Then one remembers that Painter's group has already killed a number of men.

Does Painter follow some sort of "Jesus script"? His origin is "miraculous" and his status "hybrid" (Jesus considered as part man and part god is reflected in Painter's lion/human status). He has a "forerunner" or propagandist like John the Baptist, a role played by Meric, the filmmaker. He has a group of disciples including one who may become the foundation of the "Church," a Magdalene, and also a Judas figure. And he undergoes death and resurrection.

On the other hand, there is something appalling about the way Painter gains his human followers, the "communion" used to initiate them into his mysteries and bind them to him. Caddie, a teenage virgin, is bound by slavery and interspecies sexual intercourse (bestiality); Meric Landseer, an adult vegetarian, takes a communion of rabbit meat (we won't dwell upon the parallel). Rather than appealing to their better natures, Painter seems to win followers with the breaking of taboo, the indulgence of appetite.

There is another way to look at it. "Painter as Jesus" is actually a script originated by Reynard, his Judas figure, a role Painter is being deliberately directed into. On his own, Painter is less like Jesus than a patriarch of the Old Testament. He acts as Moses to the dog-pack, and we note that he is also polygamous, nomadic, fiercely monotheistic—leos worship the sun as their father—and has a slave turned concubine. (In the leo culture, each male is sovereign lord of his own harem; males are abruptly excluded from their birth families when they reach reproductive age. Supposedly they wander around until they find wives of their own.)

When Meric, an emissary from a vegetarian commune, first meets Painter, he tells the leo that he is trespassing on Genesis Preserve, that he is breaking local law by killing animals, and he is breaking moral law by eating meat. Painter replies laconically, "If you don't allow something, something I do, there ought to be more than one of you to make me stop" (91). This is John Wayne talk, the language of power, of pure force. There is no place for morals, ethics, or even reasoning here.

Painter continues: "I have a living to get. It's got nothing to do with these—notions. I take what I need. I take what I have to." Here he evokes natural law, placing himself entirely within the animal kingdom, but then he shifts again: "And another part [portion, allotment of resources] as, what, payment for what I've gone through, for what I am. Compensation. I didn't ask to be made" (91). Which recalls another angle on "panther": the Black Panthers, a black militant party, founded in Oakland, California in 1966. Originally the Black Panthers advocated violent revolution as the only method of gaining social justice. (Later, Caddie visits Washington and a leo activist gives as a salute "a sudden, aggressive gesture with upraised fist" [157]—it is the Black Power salute.)

At this stage, Meric, who has diplomatically conceded much at each step, finally says:

> "I don't know. But still not all; there's still a part you have no right to."
>
> "That part," the leo said, "you're free to take away from me. If you can." (91)

Painter reverts to the language of power. It is quite clear that this lion is not going to lie down with the vegan lamb.

Reynard the laughing anarchist

Reynard is a fox-humanoid named after the famous Reynard, hero of countless medieval beast epics. We know exactly what he is: the trickster, an amoral Machiavellian. He manipulates five of the seven principal characters, and engineers behind-the-scenes events that affect several North American countries (the continent has been balkanized). After Reynard rearranges the political structure of the Northern Autonomy (roughly the New England states) so that all the power rests on one man, Jarl Gregorius, he then has that man assassinated, throwing the government into chaos, which in turn allows the Fed to annex the country. (The Fed is the vestigial Federal government operating out of the city-state of Washington D.C.) He betrays Painter and Caddie to the Fed (166). The bomb that frees Painter from jail is the work of Reynard. But if Reynard is the mastermind, virtually the author of the plot of the novel itself, then what is his plan? Whose side is he on?

Reynard has planned the "Painter as King Jesus" script for the fellowship, but his private script is that of *Reynard the Fox*. In the old beast epic, the wily fox causes mayhem and murder throughout until he is finally killed by his victims. And then it turns out his death was yet another ruse.

Crowley's Reynard follows this pattern very closely. In no medieval tale is Fox Reynard a loyal supporter of Noble the Lion King, so we should not be surprised by the questionable loyalty of Crowley's Reynard. Reynard's primary victims are Isengrim the Wolf and Bruin the Bear, sometimes Bricemer the Stag—and the lion is a secondary victim like most other animals. Significantly, Crowley's Reynard assigns the name "Isengrim" to Sten's father, Jarl Gregorius (42) in the chapter "The flaying of Isengrim." The murder of Jarl sets many elements in motion. (Later Reynard negotiates with a man named Barron from USE. As "Jarl" is a Scandinavian title equivalent to "Earl," and Baron is a title of lesser nobility, so the Fed represents an old nobility trying to recapture lost territories—a notion congruent with Loren's analogy of the Fed as being like the Holy Roman Empire (6).)

The mixing of medieval beast tale and biblical script in Beasts creates strange moments, as when reborn Reynard says to Painter, "It's wrong, I know, for Judas to be the one to rise from the grave" (182). But the beast tale script requires that Reynard die and be resurrected. As Reynard knows well.

41

Caddie the white slave girl

Caddie might be named after the heroine of *Caddie Woodlawn* (1935), the classic girl's novel of a tomboy running wild in the woods of Wisconsin in 1864. Our Caddie has no last name, grouping her with Painter, Reynard, and the various animals (Chet, Marta, Hawk) rather than the humans. As the book begins we learn that Caddie has had a rough life. Her parents died in the civil wars "down South," leaving Caddie orphaned at age 14, with the choice of joining a brothel or becoming an indentured servant. She chose indenture. After a number of months, her gay owner sells her to Painter. Caddie is humiliated, and indeed Reynard later informs her that the sale of her indenture to Painter was illegal, since "no human being shall be suborned by or beholden and subservient to a member of another species."

Girl and leo go north into the wilderness, with Caddie acting as porter and local guide. Painter's powerful charisma works on Caddie, and she begins to entertain sexual fantasies about him. Though she is a virgin, she seduces him with brandy and a provocative shake of her hips. And then he rapes her.

Caddie voluntarily stays on. In fact, Caddie's devotion to Painter becomes so strong that she comes close to starving on his behalf, murders a Fed agent, and murders Reynard. True, Crowley does not imply that total submission to a dominant male is always the case for all women. Painter is a very special case.

As for Caddie's beast aspect (the human characters have beast aspects too in this book), she would appear to be some sort of beast of burden, as the text tells us:

> She learned that she had a talent for bearing things: not only heavy packs and cold nights and miles of walking, but also the weight of the days themselves, the dissatisfaction that she carried always like a pack. (19)

So Caddie is the Ass. Well no, in beast epics the Ass is usually a scholar: "Dr. Baldwin the Ass." She might be the Camel, or a sturdy little Mountain Pony.

Meric Landseer, the sissy boy

"Meric" is a Teutonic name meaning "strong leader." Sir Edwin Henry Landseer (1802-73) is the most famous of English animal painters. Like Caddie, Meric was a child refugee, but he fared much better. When he was six, his mother brought him to Candy's Mountain, a skyscraper in the center of Genesis Preserve. (Intended to be 200 stories tall, like the Tower of Babel this monumental work remains unfinished, but a commune of dedicated ecologists lives there in happy harmony with nature.) A dark-skinned girl named Bree led Meric into the mountain, and in an epiphany of relief Meric "wanted to be her" (ch. 4). As the book finds him, Meric is 26.

> Meric was so fair, his hair so pale a gold, that his sharp-boned face never grew a beard; his hair ran out along his ears like a woman's, and if he never shaved, a light down grew above his lip, but that was all. (64)

Here's another blond beast, but the description insinuates that Meric's wish to be Bree has been answered through a suppression of his masculinity, or at least the physical manifestations of masculinity. (There is a parallel in *Engine Summer*, where the hero Rush that Speaks wants "to be" his girlfriend Once a Day and likewise is transformed by being initiated into her culture.) Bree and Meric are a stable unmarried couple, which we take to be the norm for inhabitants of Candy's Mountain. Other norms: strict vegetarianism, strict pacifism, abhorrence of violence, and a credo of free love, equality of the sexes, and worship of Jesus as Prince of Peace.

But when Meric meets Painter he eats meat for the first time and loves it. Guns fascinate him. So does the polygamy of leos, not to mention Caddie's odd situation. Raw, unfettered maleness suddenly seems "natural" to Meric. And Reynard, noting his ability as a documentary/propaganda filmmaker, writes him into the Jesus script, quoting from St. Matthew: "Prepare ye the way of the Lord" (165) and paraphrasing a second time (184): Meric is to be John the Baptist, "he who prepares the way." But Meric's script for himself seems to be a kind of journey from the light toward the dark. No Prince of Peace for him, but a savior by the sword.

Placing Meric's beast-equivalent is hard, at first. But look at the chapter title: "Go to the Ant, thou sluggard; consider her ways, and be wise." Surprise! Bree, Meric's lover, is Ant; Candy's Mountain is a giant ant hill. This covers everything: the demasculinized nature of the society (ant populations are almost entirely made up of sterile females); the delegation of defense responsibilities to a small select group, the rangers (almost a caste of warrior ants); their leadership by an older woman who pointedly refuses the title of Director in conversations with Fed agents (the ant colony is ruled by a queen). So we have Bree, but what about Meric, who walked away from this matriarchal New Jerusalem? Here is the clue:

> He wanted to see. He wanted to enter into darkness, any darkness, all darkness, and see in it with sudden cat's eyes. (73)

Meric is Tibert the Cat. So a cat is to prepare the way for a lion.

Sweets, leader of the pack

Sweets is a dog (half German shepherd, half mutt) raised by experiment to near-human level intelligence, in the tradition of Olaf Stapledon's dog-hero Sirius. As society in Manhattan begins to break down (probably due to the same "civil wars down south" that shaped Caddie's life), this enlightened dog is released onto the mean streets. At first he is consort to a fighting female named Blondie, a golden retriever (another blond beast). When Blondie dies, Sweets fights the other dogs to emerge as the alpha male, leader of the pack. But when Sweets finds Painter holed up in a basement, Painter's magic odor is followed by a little animal telepathy, and Sweets licks his hand in obeisance.

In some beast epics the Hound is named Curtoys ("Cortsoys" in Dutch). The root is the same as that of "courteous," which is to say, sweet.

Sten, the young King Arthur

Sten Gregorius is the photogenic fourteen-year-old son of Dr. Jarrell Gregorius, Director of the Northern Autonomy. Compared to his father's, Sten's face "seemed more willful and dangerous. It was a compelling, not a commanding face. A young, impatient godling" (7). A blond boy love object. A born prince, and the equivalent of young Arthur, or Wart, in T.H. White's *The Sword in the Stone*. Since his name is Teutonic for "stone," and since Peter also means "stone," Sten seems to have the part of Peter in the Jesus script, the rock on which a new church will stand.

Loren Casaubon, the lonely hawkman

The first character introduced in the novel is the last to join the fellowship. Perhaps his character is linked to Isaac Casaubon (1559-1614), English classical scholar and theologian, born in Geneva and buried in Westminster Abbey (his son was named *Meric*, an odd connection since *Beasts* has a character named Meric[1]), but the famous Casaubon of literature is Dorothea's husband in George Eliot's *Middlemarch*, not a sympathetic character, "author" of an endless work called "The Key to All Mythologies." "Loren" very likely refers to the naturalist and ethologist Loren Eiseley, and also to Konrad Lorenz—see below.

Our Dr. Casaubon is also an ethologist; he studies animal behavior. He is a semi-recluse, he is a pedophile, and most surprisingly, he looks very much like John Crowley's portrait on the dust jacket, with his thick dark hair and beard (in a book where the other males

LOREN CASAUBON, THE NON-BEAST

He was the only man who I have ever known to try to live up to his own rules of decency and to behave himself. He also taught me how to behave and think. I believe he would have said that the decent person is he "who sweareth unto his neighbour and disappointeth him not, though it were to his own hindrance."
—T.H. White, about his Cambridge tutor, L.J. Potts

Indirectly, John Crowley's *Beasts* was written as a tribute to T.H. White, author of (particularly, for direct influence) *The Sword in the Stone, The Ill-Made Knight, The Book of Merlyn, The Goshawk,* and *The Book of Beasts.* Loren Casaubon is a portrait of White. (Not a physical portrait, for—as Michael Andre-Driussi has noted—Crowley has given Casaubon his own appearance: White, when young, was a tall, slim, clean-shaven blond man with bright blue eyes, while Loren is short, dark of hair, beard and eye, and "wooly.")
Like Loren, White was by nature a homosexual pedophile; like Loren, he repressed it fiercely. I know this, as both Crowley and I know everything about White, from Sylvia Townsend Warner's fine and sympathet-

are blond). The pedophile is a character type used by Crowley in "In Blue" (a novella, in *Novelty*) and *Love & Sleep* (the second book of the Ægypt series). Early in *Beasts*, Loren becomes fascinated with a magazine photo of young Sten Gregorius, to the point that he props it up like a portrait.

Then by a kind of alchemical magic, Loren is called to be Sten's tutor, and his two passions (birds and boys) are fused into one as Loren gives Sten a falcon salvaged from his canceled program. After Sten's father is assassinated, Loren becomes a responsible surrogate father to Sten and Mika, his half-sister, though he continues to be tempted by forbidden fruit. Here Loren, Sten, and Mika are watching the evening news on TV:

> His leg ached where Sten lay on it, but he wanted not to move. He wanted never to move. He put a careful left hand, as though only to accommodate his bigness between the two of them, in the hollow between Sten's neck and his hard shoulder. He waited for it to be thrown off, willing it to be thrown off, but it wasn't. He felt, within, another self-made rampart breached; he felt himself sink further into a realm, a darkness, he had only begun to see when the children and he inherited their kingdom: when it was too late to withdraw from its brink. (125)

A rift between tutor and children is caused over the issue of leos starving in the nearby mountains. As an ethologist and an unsentimental naturalist, he argues that leos are not human. But the headstrong children are not convinced, and they abandon him to "save the leos." Loren returns to studying birds—geese, this time. He observes:

> Mostly the pairs are male-female, but often they are male-male; in this case there is sometimes a satellite female, lover of one of the males, who will be satisfied to share their love, and can intrude herself sufficiently into their triumphs to be mounted and impregnated (148).

If Sten's character carries connotations of the young King Arthur, Loren is then placed in the role of Merlyn, his tutor (this is T.H. White's spelling; and while White did write about hawking and geese, John Crowley himself also traces the details about geese and their behavior to Konrad Lorenz's *On Aggression*. Note similarity of names "Lorenz" and "Loren"). Loren's animal symbol might then seem to be a hawk (a merlin is a hawk). But no, he has given his falcon to Sten, with whom it seems naturally associated. Loren himself appears to be a queer kind of goose (the goose of the beast epics is named Bruel).

•

Beast epics, at one level, are satires of society, and of the times they are written in. *Beasts*, following this tradition, presents the USA of the 1960s: the assassination of a leader, social

ic *T.H. White: A Biography*, published in 1967, three years after White's death. (The quote above is taken from her book.)

Like Loren—and Merlyn of *The Sword in the Stone*—White was a teacher and tutor, but essentially a solitary figure. Like Loren, White learned to train hawks: the intense discussions of falconry in *Beasts* are mostly, or entirely, cribbed (or adapted) from White's nonfiction book in diary form, *The Goshawk*, and the hawking sections of *The Sword in the Stone*. Like Loren, White later became very interested in geese, and the goose lore Crowley imparts owes a great deal to the revised *Sword in the Stone* (revised for the Arthurian omnibus, *The Once and Future King*: the original stand-alone *Sword* had neither a goose episode nor an ant episode) and *The Book of Merlyn*, as well as to Konrad Lorenz's *On Aggression*.

White learned to fly airplanes, and though Loren does not fly, the packet plane that shows up on several occasions—always when he is present—is of the right vintage; someone refers to it as probably the oldest plane in the world to be still in use. Like Loren, White was deeply but unsentimentally engaged with the natural world; both men hunted and fished. Loren is a trapper as well, and (like Merlyn) dissects animals for scientific purposes. Like

Loren, White was a melancholy man and a heavy binge drinker. Unlike Loren, he always had a red setter bitch at his heels. Crowley doubtless felt this touch would complicate a book already full of animals, but he does pay tribute: White's first and most beloved dog was Brownie, while the leader of the pack that takes in Sweets, the enhanced dog, is named Blondie.

But the most compelling quality that Loren takes from White is his sense of honor, or "decency." Anyone who has read through *The Once and Future King* knows that this is the great subject throughout, and it was one that, probably at least partly because of the homosexuality that conflicted with his deeply held belief in the decency of monogamy (one reason for his interest in geese), preoccupied White all his life. Townsend Warner had access to his notebooks and diaries, and quotes in full an entry from 1939, when White was planning his third Arthur volume, *The Ill-Made Knight*. It is a most revealing, detailed character analysis of Lancelot, much too long to quote here, and also a template for Loren, drawn from White himself. The first point, of eighteen, is that Lancelot is "Intensely sensitive to moral issues."

The puzzle of Loren is that, having such a splendid model and having successfully brought it to life (Loren

upheaval, issues of civil rights, etc. It adds issues of the 1860s: the assassination of a leader, social upheaval and the question of slavery. These elements mix in a provocative way: the balkanization of North America is presented in a positive light. The Fed (Northern, centralist), however, has uprooted the leos, who apparently lived happy and free (if separate from humans?) in sod houses in the warm South, to relocate them into concentration camps in Georgia (the Fed cast as Nazi Germany with a "final solution"). When Caddie arrives at the Fed capital city, she sees a towering white needle (the Washington monument) and there is the pillared shrine with

> only an enormous seated figure Caddie thought she should know but couldn't remember. His name, most of his left leg, and some fingers had been erased by a bomb. (167)

She gazes dumbly upon the desecrated statue of Lincoln.

Such revision of history is an enduring fascination for Crowley. In *The Deep* he rewrites the English War of the Roses so that Richard III emerges as a hero. In *Engine Summer*, the feminist movement plays out on a scale that could be termed "civil war of the sexes." So it should come as no surprise that *Beasts* is a curious rewriting of the American War Between the States, from a pro-South *and* pro-civil rights perspective.

Another theme that Crowley, a lapsed Catholic (see the interview) returns to repeatedly in his fiction is that of exhausted or false creeds attempting to control times that have moved on or away from them.

In *The Deep*, the Grays form an ancient scholarly priesthood so far removed from its origins as to be virtually a secular university, while the Just are a more recent secret society of drug-using assassins, founded upon the false creed of contact with a pretender god. *Engine Summer* gives us Little Belaire, an atrophied and static community, and Dr. Boots's List, a community that uses false worship (mind-melding with a cat) as a stupefying drug. In both novels, new and more hopeful beliefs appear to lighten their endings under conditions that appear more accidental than divinely inspired. This notion of a world-changing gnosis is utterly central to Crowley's later work (*Novelty*, *Ægypt* and its sequels).

seems to me the only fully three-dimensional character in *Beasts*), Crowley doesn't do anything with him. After a vivid start, by the end he seems wan, will-less and completely passive. He ought to be the moral center of the book, but he is not, leaving the book without any moral center at all. This seems to me both wasteful and a betrayal of White, from whom Crowley has taken so much. But then *Beasts* simply doesn't feel finished. Perhaps, as White did with *The Sword in the Stone*, Crowley will see his way to revising it one day.

AKT

Using these models, we examine *Beasts*. Candy's Mountain presents an atrophied belief system, like that of the Grays and Little Belaire. The Fed is an atrophied political system turned militant. But what about Painter? Could he, despite Reynard's manipulations, be the genuine germ for a new age of hope? Here are the portents:

Barron, the USE man, responding to Reynard's proposal to release Painter: "It would be like . . . releasing Barabbas to the populace" (160). This is another one of the strange details that seem to point to Painter as the wrong guy for Christ model, since Barabbas was the murderer who was released instead of Jesus, and the populace was delighted with the choice.

Meric's soliloquy:

> It was the world Candy had urged us to flee from and Jesus promised to free us from, the old world returned to capture us, speak in a voice to us, reclaim us for its own. It was as though the heavy, earth-odorous Titans had returned to strike down at last the cloudy scheming gods, as though the circle had closed that had seemed an upward spiral, as though a reverse messiah had come to crush all useless hope forever. (92)

This passage pounds home several points I have been trying to make along the way. Meric equates Painter with the antithesis of Jesus, and also with the Titans, who were deposed and imprisoned in the earth by the Olympian gods. In *The Deep*, a circle of misery is revealed to be a spiral of hope, but here is the exact opposite—the spiral of hope is replaced with the crushing circle of despair. These are not positive images or intimations. Things do not bode well for the age to come.

Beasts hits hot button topics (child/adult sexual relations; miscegenation; minority rights; etc.), producing uneasiness, then refusing easy solutions. Because Loren is set up as a stand-in for the author, and because Loren successfully resists temptation, the reader comes to rely on him to provide a moral/ethical anchor to the group—that he will somehow talk sense to these crazy, wounded people. But no, he seems simply to abdicate in the end.

Perhaps the best way to consider *Beasts* is as the reverse image of *The Deep*, since they share many key features yet seem to arrive at very different ends. Neither has a certain ending, but that of *The Deep* is cautiously optimistic, while disaster or grave disorder seem to crouch in wait for the little fellowship that circles together at the end of *Beasts* to launch a new beginning.

Beast epics, with all their violence and double-dealing, are as much fun as "Road Runner" cartoons on television because they are a few steps removed from reality. Yet as the cartoon is drawn down those steps and closer to reality, the situation changes: for example, "Punch and Judy" might be funny, but wife-beating is not funny. *Beasts* seems to take the beast epic a step or two toward reality, and this is the source of my disquiet with it.

A final overview of *Beasts*, to incorporate this cartoon-into-reality method, as well as provide a possible solution to its endless structure: if we change our time perspective from past/present into present/future, what Crowley's Reynard is saying is that any actions he and his cohort perform today form the seed of the beast epic that will be told of them. Thus *Beasts* really is the rough and raw material that will become "the healing of the sick lion [Painter] by [Reynard] the fox's prescription that he wrap himself in [Jarl] the wolf's skin" in the future cartoon. Regardless of whether they successfully form their new kingdom of humans and humanoids, or are blown up at their tower by USE gunships, that "sick lion" incident has been completed, and so now it has the potential to be told as a story.

WORKS CITED

Crowley, John.
Beasts. Garden City: Doubleday & Co., Inc., 1976.

Holman, C. Hugh.
A Handbook to Literature. Indianapolis: Bobbs-Merrill Company, Inc., 1981.

Mann, Jill (trans.).
Ysengrimus. Leiden: E.J. Brill, 1987.

Terry, Patricia (trans.).
Reynard the Fox. Berkeley: University of California Press, 1992.

White, T.H. (trans.).
The Book of Beasts. New York: G. Putnam's Sons, 1954.

Wingrove, David.
"The Wounded King: An Introduction to *Beasts*" in John Crowley, *Beasts.* John Goodchild Publishers, London, 1984.

NOTES

[1] Meric Casaubon figures in a few paragraphs of Crowley's later novel, *Love & Sleep,* where he is described as a "Huguenot refugee and Protestant polemicist" and author of an early book on Dr. Dee which claimed that the spirits Dee contacted were wicked ones and the world was narrowly saved from being turned into their demonic empire (238-39). With this detail it becomes probable that both Loren Casaubon and Meric Landseer share a common inspiration in Meric Casaubon (the name divided between two characters), but with only these scant notes it seems that Meric Landseer, refugee and propagandist, is the closer to the historic Casaubon.

ENGINE SUMMER

A POETIC NOVEL
Thomas M. Disch

AMONG THE TRADITIONAL postulates of science fiction the best loved, and most overused, may well be the regression of civilization into barbarism as a result of the Bomb. Indeed, the theme predates the splitting of the atom; in 1885 Richard Jeffries wrote *After London*, an account of Britain transformed into a Gothic folly. In modern science fiction the avatars are John Wyndham's *Re-Birth* (in the UK *The Chrysalids*) and Walter Miller's *A Canticle for Leibowitz*. The seductions of the theme are manifold, not the least the possibilities for set-decoration as the woodbine pulls down the skyscrapers and every scrap-heap becomes a riddle book of misunderstood technologies. It allows the science fiction writer to revert to the idyllic imagery of Arcadia and put by the expository demands of the High Tech style. It provides a playground for daydreams of Brute Power, one that is more plausible (and intellectually respectable) than alien planets concocted for such suspect pastimes. Finally, it can offer, as in *Canticle*, laboratory conditions for testing (or confirming) historical theories: Is civilization cyclical? Is the feudal three-tiered stratification of lord (power), priest (knowledge), and serf (forced labor) the inevitable solution to Hobbsian anarchy—or is it a false paradigm and therefore part of the problem? Will we, as predators doomed to aggress, finally drop our bombs? Good, solid, unanswerable questions guaranteed to lend dignity to even the most trivial fiction.

John Crowley's *Engine Summer* is a novel that manages to use the theme of post-atomic regression in so novel (and novelistic) a manner as to amount to a complete recension of that theme. To inventory its high points would be to perform an injustice to future readers, for it's a novel full of genuine surprises, trapdoors that spring open under the feet of the mind at regular intervals all the way to the last chapter. Indeed, without a developed knack for the kind of decoding and riddle-guessing demanded by the more cerebral forms of science fiction, few readers are likely to get beyond the first two or three twists of the labyrinth. As Crowley explains, with customary indirection: "There is no other way through Little Belaire to the outside except Path, and no one who wasn't born in Little Belaire, probably, could ever find his way to the center. Path looks no different from what is not Path: it's drawn on your feet."

Though full of surprises, *Engine Summer* eschews drama. There's not a single villain, not a fight, scarcely a line of dialogue that isn't redolent of good will. Is it then a kind of love story? No: though the narrator forms a rather forlorn attachment to a girl (who resembles Dickens's Estella a little too closely), is rebuffed, pursues her, and achieves a bittersweet and fleeting rapprochement. This, the largest dramatic action of the book, constitutes at most a sub-plot. Passion requires nutrients not to be found in the soil of *Engine Summer.* The best the hero can hope for, and what he finally achieves, is the stoic acceptance of an awareness almost congruent with despair.

What the book is poignantly, strenuously and beautifully about is truth—how it is known and how spoken. The narrator is born into a society whose central value is introspection and plain-speaking, a kind of Quaker monastery populated by illiterate but exquisitely articulate aborigines, timid as rabbits, who support themselves by foraging for nuts and berries and dealing dope to other tribes who lack their horticultural resources. At an early age the narrator, Rush, forms the ambition of becoming a saint: that is, someone who in telling the story of his life evokes a universal truth, whose life, in its narrative form, is a paradigm for all human lives. *Engine Summer* is precisely the oral narrative by which we are to judge if Rush (and/or Crowley) has achieved this so-novelistic ideal of sainthood. What the book is also about, by inference, is the art of the novel, the art of this novel. One can't read far without being reminded of Crowley's presence behind his narrator's persona: a modest, melancholy, quiet-spoken young man who occasionally reveals, as though inadvertently, an unshakable conviction in his own genius. The book's epigraph is from Kafka, but even without that hint it is of Kafka one is constantly made to think. Not the expressionist, shrill trance-medium of "Metamorphosis" but the later, sedated Kafka who wrote such masterpieces of precision allegory as "Investigations of a Dog," the blandly lethal ironist, the master of dropped pins.

Readers will have already leaped to the conclusion that I am urging them to read that anomalous and always suspect hybrid, a poetic novel. I confess it, but would add that Crowley's "poetry" is not what is ordinarily accounted poetic prose, a rhetorical commodity reserved for moments of maximum claptrap. Crowley's language descends from the scrubbed-bare no-nonsense vein of modern mid-American poetry (represented by such poets as Williams, Creeley, Bly, and Simic) that has for its conservative aim the restoration of full emotional force to plain words grown slack with overuse. Such poetry, depending as it does on the running currents for its luster, is not easily excerpted, but here, anyhow, is a passage from an early chapter in which Rush is explaining the totemic groupings of his people:

> Cords. Your cord is *you* more surely than your name
> or the face that looks out at you from mirrors, though
> both of those, face and name, belong to the cord you
> belong to. There are many cords in Little Belaire, no-
> body knows exactly how many because there is a dispute

among the gossips about cords which some say aren't cords but only parts of other cords. You grow up into being in your cord; the more you become yourself, the more you become the cord you are. Until—if you aren't ordinary—you reach a time when your own cord expands and begins to swallow up others, and you grow out of being in a single cord at all. I said Painted Red had been Water cord, and her name was Wind; now she was larger than that and she had no cord that could be named, though in her way of speaking, in the motions of her hands, the manner of her life, in small things, she was still Water.

Water and Buckle and Leaf; Palm and Bones and Ice; St. Gene's tiny Thread cord, and Brinks cord if it exists. And the rest. And Whisper. And was it because of her secrets that I loved Once a Day, or because of Once a Day that I came to love secrets?

The way the narrator struggles with his subject, his hedges and qualifications and his final surrender to the wisdom of tautology have an almost anthropological ring of truth. There is the pleasure, as well, of being inducted into a private language (as in *A Clockwork Orange*), which becomes more complex and interconnected with each page; a pleasure that is heightened by the chemical purity of the vocabulary. There are glints of mystery (one never hears of the problematic Brinks cord again) as well as many minor, and ingenious, solutions of etymological riddles along the way. Nor are all the riddles minor: one of the story's most inspired ironies concerns the naming of the tribe known as Dr. Boots's List.

Engine Summer is exceptional in science fiction for being, first and foremost, a work of art. Its scale is small and the range of human possibility it encompasses is correspondingly narrow, but one doesn't fault Cezanne's "Card Players" for lacking terribilitá. Within its carefully determined bounds *Engine Summer* succeeds at the first, and still the most difficult, task of art: it achieves formal beauty.

ONE WRITER'S BEGINNINGS:
ENGINE SUMMER AS A
PORTRAIT OF THE ARTIST
Alice K. Turner

> I wanted to be a saint. I wanted to have strange adventures, which I could tell of; and learn forgotten secrets . . . and make sense of the world in the stories I told. (70)

> Painted Red said to me: "Remember, Rush, there's no one who would not rather be happy than be a saint." I nodded, but I didn't know what she meant. It seemed to me that anyone who was a saint would have to be happy. I wanted to be a saint, though I told no one, and the thought gave me nothing but joy. (32)

AN APPEALING SUBJECT for a novelist, for reasons that hardly need analyzing, is the story of how he, or his faintly fictionalized protagonist, became a writer. The most famous of these accounts, probably, is James Joyce's *Portrait of the Artist as a Young Man*, which is rather oblique about the actual writing side of things. My own favorite is Muriel Spark's hilarious, relatively straightforward *Loitering with Intent*. Or perhaps John Crowley's *Engine Summer* is my favorite. *Engine Summer* is a metaphorical account of the process, funnier and sweeter than *Portrait*, slyer and more forgiving than *Loitering.* And, oddly enough, since it is ostensibly about something else entirely, it has more to say about the craft of writing than either of the others. (All three novels have good titles, by the way, multi-layered, apt and amusing in context.)

Engine Summer is Crowley's first major book, following the clever finger-exercise of *The Deep* and the ambitious but ultimately failed *Beasts.* It is his *Portrait* to the Ulysses of *Little, Big,* short and trim instead of long and sprawling. It seems to be a favorite among all sorts of people, many connected to the writing trade, which may be a factor.

The time and place are post-holocaust America, near and along the turnpike that runs from New Jersey through Pennsylvania and Ohio. The narrator, Rush that Speaks, grows up in Little Belaire, recognizably an affectionate take on the ideal of the hippie commune of the Sixties and Seventies (the book was conceived in 1968-69, though not published till 1979). Most of its citizens live and die in the commune, usefully, productively, with great variety and harmony. People can leave Little Belaire at will, but few do, these usually because they have ambitions that vary from the norm. One of these is Once a Day, Rush's childhood sweetheart; when she is ten, she steals away in the company of some of her relatives from outside. Four years later, when Rush is 14, he decides to go on his travels. He hopes to find her again, but he also has another ambition: he wants to become a saint.

A saint?

At the start of the new millennium, wanting to become a saint sounds somewhat ominous, the kind of aspiration that leads to suicide bombs. But in Rush's world a saint is a more benign, if not altogether benign figure. To explain sainthood, let's backtrack to look at Rush's education and the concept of "truthful speaking."

Little Belaire was formed as a community of truthful speakers. Starting at about age seven, the children are taught by gossips, usually women of grandmotherly age, how to speak truthfully. This is not a hasty process, and it is accomplished mostly through storytelling; the stories are often, but not always, about the lives of the saints or retellings of stories the saints told. In addition, at seven-year intervals a child's "cord" is ascertained and his wellbeing examined. A cord is something like a tribe, something like a guild, and something like a gang of cronies or "homies"; like the "karass" Kurt Vonnegut, Jr. invented for *Cat's Cradle*, it is not necessarily hereditary and seems to follow inclination or aptitude. Rush's cord, like that of both his parents (unusually, as marriage tends to be across cord lines), is Palm, and Palm cord likes to talk. On the other hand, Painted Red, the gossip who tells such wonderful stories to Rush and a small group of other children, was originally Water cord (she outgrew it), so talking is hardly confined to Palm cord.

All the children will become truthful speakers. They will learn to speak "in such a way that your hearer couldn't help but understand what you meant, and in such a way that you, speaking, had no choice but to express what you meant." They will learn to

> **On Clarity**
>
> "The truthful speakers said: We really mean what we say, and we say what we really mean." (30)
>
> **On Sense Memory**
>
> In a winter of rain . . . a winter that I spent alone and often asleep, there was a trick I learned my mind can do: sometimes, halfway between waking and sleep, it would grow young again. How can I explain it? As though, for a brief moment, I would be a younger self; or as though a whole summer of my past would be given back to me, complete, no part of it missing, and so suddenly that often I wouldn't know which moment it was . . . there were times I could do it for some time together, all my being reliving a past time, except for a small watching eye to marvel at it . . . each season of each year—could it be each day, each morning and evening?—has its own taste, distinct, entirely forgotten, till you taste it again. (54-55)

make speech "transparent, like glass, so that through the words the face is seen truly." Little Belaire takes great pride in truthful speaking, which sets the community apart from the rest of the world.

The next step, which few achieve or remotely want to achieve, is sainthood. From Painted Red's classroom, a catechism:

> "And why are the saints saints?" . . .
>   "Because . . . we remember the stories of their lives."
>   "How do we remember the stories of their lives?"
>   "Because—because they told them in a way that couldn't be forgotten."
>   "In what way?"
>   "They spoke truthfully," . . .
>   "And what is it to speak truthfully?" (29)

To really mean what you say and to say what you really mean. But everyone in Little Belaire learns to do that. What more does it take to be a saint?

> "The saints found that truthful speaking was more than just being understood; the important thing was that the better you spoke, the more other people saw themselves in you, as in a mirror. Or better: the more they saw themselves through you, as though you had become transparent." (64)

Aha, to be a really good truthful speaker, then. But surely there is more?

On Meaning and Metaphor
I could be listening to Painted Red weave the stories of the saints in her rich roomy voice, and beginning to see how all those stories were in some way one story: a simple story about being alive and being a man; a story that, simple as it was, couldn't itself be told. (55)

Life Affects Art and Books Affect Readers
"A life . . . is circumstances. Circumstances are encirclings, they're circles. The circle of a saint's life, all its circumstances, is contained in the story of his life as he tells it; and the story of his life is contained in our remembering it. The story of his life is a circumstance in ours. So the circle of his life is contained in the circle of our lives, like circles of ripples rising in water." (66)

"They're saints not because of what they did, especially, but because, in the telling of it, what they did became transparent, and your own life could be seen through it, illuminated." (66)

Now we're getting somewhere. But here's one more clue from Painted Red:

"Saints aren't known to be saints, you know, till long after they're dead, and people see that their stories have lived. So if there are saints now, we don't know it." (64)

Learning to speak truthfully, with just a little interpretation, thus becomes learning to write, or, in an oral society like this one, how to tell stories the right way, to strike the perfect note of communion. But to achieve sainthood means to become a great writer or storyteller, quite out of the ordinary, someone whose stories will *live*. Transparency, for Painted Red, is not unlike John Keats's much-discussed *Negative Capability*, wherein the artist (Shakespeare, for Keats) becomes so open, his receptivity so heightened to the diversity and particularity of thought and reality as to negate his own ego in allowing a clear flow of phrasing from the subconscious. (I'm not using Keats's wording, which is difficult.) Painted Red's informal classroom thus offers something like an oral Great Books curriculum, and Rush is the single student who is inspired to go out to seek the material and the added skills for a Great Book of his own.

Letters to a Fiction Writer (edited by Frederic Bausch, W.W. Norton, NY, 1999) is a collection of real and made-up letters from established mainstream writers offering advice to writing students and beginners. Quite a lot of them, maybe a quarter, advocate truthful speaking, in just about those terms; others murmur of essence

On Serendipity

"Whatever you find, if it's useful to us, save it; make the knowledge you got here into a box to carry it, it can be used for that. And however far away you go, come back with what you find to us." (69)

(Page references are to the Bantam paperback; quotations indicate that Painted Red is speaking, otherwise it is the narration of Rush that Speaks)

AKT

or authenticity or being "real enough." When someone like Joyce Carol Oates admonishes the young writer to tell the truth, it's clear that she is not pitching dogged realism but something a good deal closer to what Painted Red teaches. To my surprise and pleasure, Reynolds Price not only tells the novice to be truthful, but also suggests that he study to become a saint. Price, of course, means that for both writers and saints the rare moments of satisfaction and success are often entirely internal and isolated, while Crowley has a different meaning for the word, but I still enjoyed that.

To become a saint, in Crowley's context, then, is to become a writer who counts, whose stories last, who will be read and loved and respected and even learned when the writer is long gone. Whose stories are so good and so well told that they take on a life of their own that in turn gives the writer a posthumous halo—think of the hundreds of thousands of people who may never have read a word of Keats or Jane Austen, but could ace a Jeopardy question on them because they are figures of great renown. When Rush says: "I meant to leave Little Belaire and learn to live a life that could be told in stories . . . I meant to be a saint," this is the kind of fame he wants, though, not being acquainted with "writers" as such, he wouldn't put it that way.

I think it's understood that John Crowley takes his own work seriously, though it may end up on the genre shelves at bookstores. His novels are highly original, his influences do not come exclusively from "within the field," his language has achieved, I would grant, transparency. Posterity may indeed recognize *Little, Big* as a seminal work of twentieth-century fantasy, though it's out of print as I write. Time will tell. For more than twenty years, Crowley has been engaged in a *magnum opus* that seems almost suicidal in its refusal to pander to public tastes—and there is still another book to come in the Ægypt series. But right here, in this early novel, he announced his intentions, which are not modest: naked ambition cloaked with charm.

And Rush? Does he achieve his ambition? Oh, yes. Rush goes

out into the world, meets a saint of sorts, finds and loses a lady-love, has a strange meeting with an alien mind, has adventures, adopts a cat and a cow, makes a new friend who is not in any way a truthful speaker, ingests a vast quantity of drugs, learns great resourcefulness and finds an angel. And along the way he becomes a bona fide saint, not quite in the way he expected. Rush tells a story, creates a book that, some 600 years into posterity, is still being "read," with love and laughter and tears and considerable poignancy and pain. The "angel" who is Rush's current reader encourages him:

> *Isn't that what it is to be a saint? To tell all stories in the single story of your own life?*
> I'm not a saint.
> *You are the only saint.* (39)

And he is.

IT DOESN'T GET BETTER:
LITTLE BELAIRE, THE LIST, AND THE RIVEN WORLD OF *ENGINE SUMMER*
Adam Stephanides

THE TRUTHFUL SPEAKERS of Little Belaire aim to be transparent: they speak in such a way that they say what they really mean, and that it is impossible for them to be misunderstood (at least by another truthful speaker). In *Engine Summer*, Crowley appears at first glance to have written a transparent book. Compared to *Little, Big*—and still more the Ægypt series—it is short, with a simple plot and a straightforward structure. And Rush's narrative voice is so engaging and candid that it is easy to accept his judgments at face value, ignore the infrequent opaque passages, and conclude that *Engine Summer* is a simple, straightforward book with no hidden depths. That was my response upon my first reading of the book, and my second reading too.

But appearances are deceptive: *Engine Summer* is not transparent. This is especially true of the duality of Little Belaire and the List, which largely determines the book's structure. The List itself is presented as an enigma. And the coziness of Little Belaire as described by Rush, the strangeness of the List and the alienation Rush feels there, and the effects of the Letter from Dr. Boots upon Rush and Once a Day, all tempt the reader to see the Little Belaire/List polarity as one of good versus bad.

But this is a profound misunderstanding of both Little Belaire and the List. The List, and the experience of getting the Letter, are not simply to be rejected: both preserve truths that Little Belaire has lost sight of. And Little Belaire is itself seriously flawed, and is intimately connected to the List. The true significance of the Little Belaire/List pair is that each society, in its own way, falls short of what Rush's world needs. Humanity in *Engine Summer* is gravely wounded; and not just, as Blink asserts, from the loss of technology. As Michael Andre-Driussi has insightfully stated, the world of *Engine Summer* is a riven world in many ways.[1] These rifts go back to the world before the Storm, and helped to cause the Storm. The League did not heal these rifts, but perpetuated them in different forms. And neither Little Belaire nor the List has what is needed to heal them.

Dr. Boots's List

A quarter of the book is spent on Rush's year with the List—nearly as much space as is devoted to his many years at Little Belaire—and it is at the List that Rush undergoes the experience which, he tells the angel, is "at my center now."[2] But Crowley does not make it easy to understand the List. The only clues in the book are the cryptic comments of Zhinsinura, Houd, and Once a Day; Rush's infrequent judgments, which are themselves fairly mysterious; and what we can infer from Rush's experiences after receiving his Letter. Readers must piece together their own explanations from these hints, a difficult task. It is very tempting to conclude that the List's members are just "acid casualties" who have burned out on too many Letters from Dr. Boots, thus denying that there is a problem.[3]

Fortunately, John Crowley wrote a synopsis of *Engine Summer* (whose planned title at the time was "Many Lives"), which has been preserved and is among his papers at the University of Texas at Austin. In this synopsis, Crowley states explicitly what makes the List tick, "which no one in this story is capable of doing."[4] He explains that

> the List, following the League's old instructions to forget progress, forget curiosity, forget striving and making, has developed a system of forgetting past and future altogether as an illusion, and living completely in the Now. They are attempting to reverse their human consciousness and become conscious only of each moment as it passes: to become like a cat. Of course it can't be done completely; it's a trick—as Zen is a trick—that you try not to let yourself know you're playing on yourself.

Crowley goes on to retell Zhinsinura's "riddle" of the string tied around a finger (137), but with the explanation that what Boots "helps you forget" is "your interfering, anxious human consciousness."[5]

Of course, while there is a presumption in favor of Crowley's explications of his own book, they should not be taken as Holy Writ. And this synopsis was in fact written before Crowley had finished the revisions that transformed the early version of the book into the published text, and differs from the published text in minor ways.[6] But Crowley's explication of the List fits the published text closely; I know of no alternative that works as well. Moreover, the features of the List that Crowley is referring to are essentially the same in "Learning to Live with It," the first version of *Engine Summer*, which predated the synopsis; so Crowley's thinking on the subject did not change much.

The passages above make clear a number of enigmatic passages in *Engine Summer* concerning the List. Once a Day's question to Rush, "How can I think about you if you're not here?" (160), repeating a similar earlier question (114), now makes sense: if you are conscious only of the moment, you can only think about what is immediately present. This explains, too, why Once a Day becomes angry and runs off when Rush tells her that the children and old woman on September's calendar tile are the same as the ones in the barometer, and that "in the next months she'll be out, and they'll be hid": because this implies, as Rush goes on to say, that "in warm perfect *engine summer* the old woman [winter] waited" (133), or, more briefly, that the future is real. And Once a Day's earlier insistence in Little Belaire that winter never comes (53) shows that, as a member of Whisper cord which is the List's cousin, Once a Day is already predisposed to the List's beliefs.

One of Houd's paradoxes also finds its explanation here.

> "Then winter does come," I said.
> "Oh, winter comes," Houd said. "But only when it comes." He puffed his pipe and grinned. "That's Relativity," he said; and everybody laughed, of course, except me, of course. (141)

Houd, more secure in the List's philosophy than Once a Day (who, as is often the case with converts, is more zealous than the natives), can admit that winter is coming; "but only when it comes"—that is, only when winter is here is it true to say "winter is coming." Since only the present moment exists, as long as winter is not here it will never come (something Rush discovers for himself in regard to spring once he has received Dr. Boots's Letter (187, 195)). When Zhinsinura tells the riddle of the string tied around the finger in *Engine Summer*, she says that the string tied around the List's Finger that Boots helps them forget is the calendar—that is, the awareness that the seasons inevitably succeed each other.

All this does not make the List sound any better, to be sure—if anything, the reverse. But the Letter from Dr. Boots is another story. Rush's description of his psychological state after receiving his Letter provides a great deal of evidence, if read closely. He describes his realization that, for every new sensation that impinges on him, he constructs a new self—"buil[ds] a new Rush"—to receive it; and "that I had built oh how many million before, and lost each, changed from each, they were less real than clouds, I was less changeless than a banner in the wind" (164-65) This realization induces terror in Rush: "how had I ever been able to build fast enough for Everything?" But his terror is stilled by the injunction he hears within himself, which somehow derives from Boots, to "Forget you were ever other than the perfect house you are forever building, and whether it is a house of dark or light it will build itself" (165) What Rush is experiencing is very similar to the Buddhist belief that the self is an illusion, that it is merely a bundle of adventitiously co-occurring sensations which changes from moment to moment. And he defends himself psychologically against the implications of this by forgetting at each moment that he was ever anything else than he is now, doing out of necessity what the List does out of conviction.

One might want to dismiss Rush's perceptions, and by extension those of all the List members who have received Letters, as delusions. But this is not how Crowley sees it. In the "Many Lives" synopsis he describes "the brain's mind['s] return to itself" as "a terrible and fiercely illuminating rush of rebirth and self-knowledge" and as "showing the man to himself."[7] This is confirmed by a passage in *Engine Summer*, in which the angel says that Rush had "learned from Boots what it is to be alive" (204); that is, to be alive is not to be fixed by one's cord and by the timeless truths of the saints' stories, as the truthful speakers believe, but to be in constant flux. And while the angel is not necessarily reliable, the fact that Crowley says the same thing suggests that in this instance we can believe her.

Rush's description of what Boots "said" to him also refers to dark and light. Along with the four dead men, this is the "secret" that most preoccupies Rush. On one level, of course, to be dark is simply to be angry or sad, and to be light is the opposite. But this does not explain why Zhinsinura tells Rush that in asking for the meaning of dark and light, he is asking for Once a Day's "secret," which "she can't tell you without learning . . . herself" (136). The passage above, though, suggests that dark and light are connected with the illusiveness of the self. The way Once a Day uses the words, as if there is no connection between a person when dark and a person when light, confirms this idea.

After Zhinsinura tells Rush the riddle of the string, she continues: "*path* is only a name for a place where you find yourself. Where you're going on it is only a story. Where you've been on it is only another. Some of the stories are pleasant ones; some are not. That's dark and light" (137). And Rush tells the angel: "I might have understood, too, if I had ever in all my growing up been told a story that wasn't true" (138). Rush is not accusing Zhinsinura of lying, or saying that the List are liars. On one level, he means that the truthful speakers never tell fictional stories: later Rush says that in Little Belaire "every story has a proof" (159). Thus, he doesn't understand what Zhinsinura means by "only a story." But on a deeper level, for the truthful speakers the stories they tell are timelessly true: they are the saints' unforgettable stories, in which any listener can find herself. For the List, on the other hand, stories are "true" only provisionally and temporarily. Similarly, the configuration of Little Belaire may change, but Path never does; while Zhinsinura tells Rush that "*path* is only a name for a place where you find yourself," not a fixed object at all. And after Rush has had his Letter he experiences his mind as like the warren, but the path to the center is different for every sensation.

These contrasts display the difference between the truthful speakers' and the List's views of the self. For the truthful speakers your self is a permanent thing, encapsulated in your cord: "the more you become yourself, the more you become the cord you are," unless you are one of the few who grow larger than their cords (40). And all possible knowledge about your cord, and hence about your self, is in turn contained (though not in readable form) in the timelessly true Filing System (68). For the List, on the other hand, there is no essence. Your self at two different times is "only" two different stories, with no necessary connection.

Of course, the List's view is not the whole story, any more than Little Belaire's is: it is not true that a person when dark has nothing in common with the same person when light. This brings us to the other significance of dark and light for the List. In the early, hand-written manuscripts of *Engine Summer*, then entitled "Learning to Live with It," a character who had been born in the List but had left tells Rush: "Dark and light is a game. The object of the game is never to discover you're playing it."[8] A deleted passage from an early manuscript, of course, cannot in itself demonstrate the meaning of dark and light in the published book. But there is evidence in the book to confirm it.

First, though the passage as a whole was eliminated, both sentences survive separately. Early in his life with the List, Rush asks Once a Day: "What are dark and light? . . . Is it a game?" (130-31). And in the hallucinatory game of whose-knee in Rush's "confusion," we have:

> "After all," said Painted Red as they paused, "it's only a game."
>
> . . .
>
> . . . "The object," said Houd, "is to never discover you're playing it." (190)

Second, as stated above, Zhinsinura tells Rush that the meaning of dark and light is Once a Day's secret, "and she can't tell you without learning it herself. And she wants not to learn that secret" (136). Recall Crowley's statement in the "Many Lives" synopsis that forgetting the past and future "can't be done completely; it's a trick . . . that you try not to let yourself know you're playing on yourself." So dark and light is not only the experience of the self's endless mutability, but also—somehow—the "trick" by which one forgets that there is any change at all (while at the same time re-membering it). This explains why Rush calls the List "careful" and "circumspect" (142): they must keep close watch on their thoughts, to avoid admitting to themselves what they know deep down.

Little Belaire

If the portrayal of the List in *Engine Summer* is not transparent, neither is the portrayal of Little Belaire. But the latter seems transparent. Rush has grown up in Little Belaire; the way things are done there seems natural to him, and he fully accepts its values. And Rush is so engaging, and the picture he paints so attractive, that it is easy to take it at face value and accept Little Belaire as an ideal society.

Little Belaire is indeed an attractive society in many ways, but it is also flawed. One of its flaws is its massive consumption of St. Bea's Bread, and the effects of this upon its users. St. Bea's Bread is the staple nutrient of Little Belaire. Everybody in Little Belaire smokes massive amounts of it, and begins very early in life: speaking of a time when he was, at most, eight, Rush tells the angel, "I'd seen it and done it [smoked Bread] almost all my life" (52). And the consumption of Bread has been increasing in amount and intensity: the only cultural change in Little Belaire within living memory that we are told of (51).

If St. Bea's Bread were some sort of innocuous "pot of the future" with no lasting effects, as it usually appears to be, this massive consumption wouldn't matter. But this is far from the case. When St. Bea, who discovered the Bread, ate it, it erased her personality and humanity much more completely and permanently than Dr. Boots's Letter does Once a Day's. The truthful speakers now smoke the Bread instead of eating it, so its effects upon them are not as drastic. But In a Corner, the breadman, still admits: "It won't harm you: hasn't harmed anyone. But it changes you. If you spend your life a man, and eat not only men's food, but this" (52).

And how has the Bread changed the truthful speakers? Though we may not realize it while listening to Rush, one very striking characteristic of the truthful speakers in retrospect is their perpetual tranquility. Except for Rush when Once a Day leaves, never do we see any of them in the grip of any strong emotion. One of the reasons Rush has such trouble with the concepts of "dark and light" is that he has so little experience with emotions he has trouble recognizing them. While we can't be sure, it seems a good bet that this tranquility is not due only to their upbringing: the Bread has a lot to do with it. To put it bluntly, they're always mellow because they're always stoned.[9] And with all strong emotions damped down, the truthful speakers are missing, as the angel says, much of what it is to be alive.

But Little Belaire has a more serious flaw: in the long run, it is not viable. Michael Andre-Driussi has conjectured that Little Belaire's population is declining, based on the apparent scarcity of children, the fact that no new towers have been constructed recently, and Rush's lack of a sibling; and Crowley has confirmed this.[10] Even if this trend could be reversed, a worse problem looms. To be able to have children, the women of Little Belaire must take the white "medicine's daughter." Little Belaire cannot produce this themselves; only the List produces it, and they can only get it in trade with the List. But this trade will not continue indefinitely. Little Belaire is growing more isolated from the outside world as the angels' works decay, and this isolation will one day be complete (141). And for the List's part, Rush foresees that ultimately the List will close itself off completely from the rest of humanity, "keep[ing] their counsel as close as cats." (144) No trade with the List means no more medicine's daughters, and without the medicine's daughters Little Belaire will soon become extinct. And while Little Belaire is in part the victim of the angels' miscalculation, the truthful speakers must share some of the blame themselves: they are dependent upon the angels' technology, but do not understand this technology and make no attempt to learn it. And presumably anybody could have observed Little Belaire's increasing isolation and recognized its implications for the future, yet nobody seems to be doing anything about it.

It is instructive to compare Little Belaire with the future depicted in another work of Crowley's, the novella "Great Work of Time." On the surface, the post-apocalyptic future of *Engine Summer* seems worlds apart from the undying Victorian British Empire of the novella, as does the latter's bleak pessimism from the bittersweet melancholy of *Engine Summer*. But Little Belaire is not so different in tone from the future Denys Winterset visits in "Great Work of Time." Both are portrayed as attractive, even comfortable; and both are doomed. The forest Rush foresees swallowing up Little Belaire (144) prefigures the forest under the sea that will be the endpoint of the Otherhood's manipulations in "Great Work of Time."

So the idea of Little Belaire and the List as polar opposites is untenable, since Little Belaire is not wholly good, nor the List evil. But it breaks down in another way as well: they are more similar than is apparent from Rush's descriptions, which emphasize the differences. Both are communal economies, with no formal means of distributing goods or assigning tasks that we are told of, and both seem to lack any mechanism for enforcing the group's norms or decisions, aside from social disapproval; yet social conflict seems to be absent from both. Similarly, both are apparently matriarchies. In the List's case, this is evident: the List's leader is a woman, and Rush tells us that a new child is "a girl I supposed by the way they made much of it" (143). But in Little Belaire too, the gossips, who are the most prestigious members of the society (and the most powerful, insofar as anyone has power), seem to be mostly women; and it is Rush's mother and Mbaba, not his father, who have authority over him. And Rush's remark quoted immediately above may reflect the assumptions of his Little Belaire upbringing as much as his experiences with the List.

And both are past-oriented. Both are dependent upon the technology of the past, which they make no effort to develop further. And both seek to preserve a culture handed down from the past, rather than advance it: Little Belaire with its truthful speaking and its stories of the saints, and the List with its Letter from Dr. Boots.

Not only are Little Belaire and the List similar, they are intertwined and interdependent (Crowley's words).[11] On a surface level, their trade is vital to Little Belaire, as said above, and clearly important to the List as well. A more intimate link is provided by Whisper cord. "Coiled within the cords of Belaire like an old promise never quite broken, or a piece of dreaming left in your mind all day till night comes and you dream again" (39), Whisper cord is "cousin" to the List in more than its affiliation to the League through Olive. In his synopsis of the proposed *Engine Summer*, Crowley writes that "the people of . . . Whisper cord, unlike the people of other cords, seem to aim to become not transparent but opaque. To Whisper cord, and to them alone, Olive bequeathed, not stories, but secrets"[12]; and to Whisper cord, "a secret is something that can't be told" (46). In these things, Whisper cord is more like the List than like the truthful speakers. Conjecturally, we can go even further. At one point Rush speaks of "the mystery at the heart of" Little Belaire (69); and just before Rush agrees to be recorded by Mongolfier, he thinks, "after all I had never known where exactly the center of Belaire was" (207). Now, the room Once a Day shows Rush, which holds Whisper cord's secrets, lies near "the deepest center of old warren" (37). And after Rush has had the Letter, he likens his mind to the warren (164); and at the center of his mind now is Boots (167). By analogy, at the center of Little Belaire would be Whisper cord, the outpost of the List. And Crowley intended Once a Day's emigration to the List to "make the two intertwined cultures of the story more interdependent as well: like the spot of black in the white side of the yin-yang symbol."[13]

The two cultures are ironically connected in another way as well. According to Painted Red, the saints hoped that by truthful speaking they could become "not immortal, as the angels tried to become, but free from death . . . not hear or remember a saint's life, but live it: live many lives in the moment between birth and dying" (66-67). Rush is unable to imagine how this could be, and Painted Red doesn't know either; but the List comes close to achieving it. They do "not hear or remember, but live" Boots's life (Boots was called St. Boots, rather than Dr. Boots, in "Learning to Live with

It"). They also "live many lives in the moment between birth and dying" because, with no consciousness of the past or future, each moment is a new life.[14] And they are "free from death" because, like the man and woman in "The Nightingale Sings at Night," they have no knowledge of change, and so are unaware of death. Of course, this achievement is only partial, since the List are incapable of genuinely forgetting the past and future. But this is one more link between the seemingly opposite cultures of Little Belaire and the List.

The Riven World

"Dark and light" was not invented by the List; Mother Tom talks to the League "about dark and light" (153). We don't know what she said about it; but a clue may be found in Zhinsinura's statement of what "the men in those [pre-Storm] times said to the women, '. . . Men have things to do, and must use their time properly; . . . you are still controlled by the old moon; you can't use your time properly; that is your greatest weakness'" (151-52). This suggests that dark and light were related to women's being "controlled by the old moon"—their menstrual cycle. By extension, we can guess that dark and light here refers to cyclic time in general, like winter and summer. Men's "using their time properly," then, would be the denial of cyclicity, the belief that it can always be summer.

This conjecture is supported by Rush's incidental remark that the angels lived in "covered cities without weather" (133), and by Zhinsinura's metaphor in which the male angels are the ice over a river, which does not realize that it is the coming of spring which has broken it up (151). And Seven Hands tells Rush that the Storm—the collapse of the angels' civilization—was visible even when the angels were strongest, but they did not see it (42). (Rush thinks that the List's calendar tile for September shows that the angels "would not have forgotten" dark and light, "that in warm perfect engine summer the old woman [of the barometer, who came out when it was dark] waited"; but he is wrong (133)).

If this is correct, then the angels' denial of cyclicity was one of the reasons the Storm came in the first place. Correspondingly, the recognition of cyclicity would be a step towards healing the riven world of Rush's day. But this is a step that neither Little Belaire nor the List can take. Both, in their own way, deny change: Little Belaire evens out all emotions and reduces people to timeless essences, while the List tries to forget change completely. Neither wants to think about the future, so that even though the trade between Little Belaire and the List is important to both societies and is threatened by Little Belaire's growing isolation, neither society is taking steps to avert this threat. Ironically, though both societies were formed in opposition to the angels' world, both are making the same mistake as the angels did: forgetting "that in warm perfect engine summer the old woman waited."

Rush's world is also riven between men and women. Obviously, this rift dates back to ancient days as well. And again, neither Little Belaire nor the List offers a way out of it. While the angels' world was a patriarchal world in which technology was out of control (and the avvengers of Rush's day are a pathetic imitation of that world), Little Belaire and the List are both static matriarchies. Neither can provide what the world presumably needs, a truly complementary relationship between men and women. Nor can either show how to master the technology they are dependent on, not just scavenge the angels' debris, and so make sure the coming winter will be followed by a spring.

Again, parallels with "Great Work of Time" are instructive. In both works we have a society (our own) hurtling toward catastrophe, largely because of the uncontrolled advance of technology. In both, a group—the League in *Engine Summer*; the Otherhood in "Great Work of Time"—attempts to reorder society so as to avert the catastrophe, or prevent its recurrence. And in both, the group's efforts, though well intentioned, fail to create a viable world: instead they create a static world, heading for extinction. In the League's case, instead of healing the rifts the angels' world was suffering from, they merely made the previously subordinate side dominant: women over men, ordinary humans over angels, cyclic time over linear time. And, ironically, by creating a static world, they ensured that the very cyclicity which the angels had tried to banish would be forgotten again.

Engine Summer shows a third society as well (setting aside the comic-pathetic avvengers): the angels' City in the Sky. But while we have little information on this society, what indications there are suggest that the City in the Sky can no more heal the world than can Little Belaire or the List. Above all, the angels will not return to Earth, thus perpetuating the rift between angels and ordinary humans. But even if they did return to Earth, they seem to be stuck in the same trap as Little Belaire and the List. Although, unlike those societies, they understand the technology they have inherited, there is no indication that they are doing anything to advance it. And Rush's angel tells him that "while in the warren they ... grew old in speaking; and as the List ... grew old in Boots; so we grew old in Plunkett" (205), explicitly equating the three societies.

At the end of the story Rush tells, there are a few signs of at least partial healing. Most obviously, Mongolfier, the angel, returns to Earth, at least temporarily, summoned by the symbolic reunion of the silver ball and glove. Of greater potential import, Rush comes during his "confusion" to the realization that truthful speaking is "the same as dark and light," and that he has always been dark and light without knowing it (191-92); and he returns to Little Belaire with the knowledge he has gained from the List, raising the possibility of a bridge between the two cultures and a synthesis of truthful speaking with dark and light (though we don't see, and never know, if he actually re-enters the warren). And just before he trades with Teeplee for the silver ball, he realizes that spring is coming: "I let go then of the doctor: and letting go felt like falling, falling gently backward into a waiting pair of hands I would never see but could not doubt were there" (195). While this passage is obscure, it seems to mean that he has finally integrated the enlightenment he gained from the Letter into his own personality, to form "a waiting pair of hands I would never see," thus healing the rift within Rush's psyche.

Despite these signs, the prognosis for the world of *Engine Summer* is not good. The angels still have not returned to Earth, even though they now know that it is not the fearful place Mongolfier had believed it was. Nor have they done anything, as far as we know, to help those still on Earth: "The angels weep, but for themselves" (24). And the phrase "learn to live with it," which Blink applies to humanity as a whole and Rush to his imagined future with the List (101, 168), is used twice by the angel (slightly varied), once to apply to the City in the Sky in the days of Plunkett, and once to apply to those who host Rush (205, 206). While Rush has freed the angels from the anguish Plunkett brought them, he has not freed them from the preoccupation with the past which also afflicts Little Belaire and the List. As to the Earth, we know nothing (in "Learning to Live with It," the angel confirms to Rush that the Earth's population is decreasing)[15], but Rush's story does not give much reason for optimism.

Still, there are two glimmers of hope. One is that Little Belaire's culture is not a completely closed system, as the List's and the City in the Sky's seem to be. Not everyone is defined by their cord: there are those who "aren't ordinary," who "grow out of being in a single cord at all" (40). And Painted Red tells Rush: "there are quiet times, you know, centuries long they can be, where the task is only to learn what the busy times discovered; and then there will come a time of new discovery" (64). Such a time of discovery might come again to Little Belaire, if it survives long enough. (In an early handwritten fragment, Painted Red identifies Rush as the "new thing.")[16]

The other glimmer of hope is that this version of "Rush" is apparently the first to mention the fly in a cube of plastic, who "thinks he's in the air, because he can see out all around, and can't see anything that holds him back. But still he can't move" (75, 173).

On a general level, the fly symbolizes Rush's world, which is held back by nothing visible, but still can't move. But specifically it is the angels' City in the Sky, which is surrounded by a transparent barrier, literally "nothing . . . a thing or a condition that allowed light through but was not itself anything, but through which nothing could escape" (200). If the story we hear is really the first appearance of the fly in plastic, and if this change is due to the influence of Rush's host, then the angels may be growing tired of their sterile, past-obsessed existence.

But there is no hope for the recorded "Rush." The fly in plastic symbolizes him as well. And he has become the negation of everything the Letter taught him. He had learned that to be alive is to be always changing, but he will never change now: he is as fixed as one of Little Belaire's timelessly true saint's stories—in fact, he has become one. In the book's final irony, he has fulfilled the saints' ambition to become "free from death, . . . transparent, . . . live many lives in the moment between birth and dying" (66-67), even more completely than did the List. And he wants to die, though he knows it would be futile to ask for this. Again, there is a parallel with "Great Work of Time": in the future the Otherhood has inadvertently created through its manipulations, Denys meets an angel and a magus, both of whom want to die. In both, the lesson is driven home that trying to stop all change, though a natural response to the horror of uncontrolled change, will in the end produce another horror. And neither Little Belaire nor the List can avert this.

My thanks to Pat Fox, Cathy Henderson, Tara Wenger and the rest of the staff at the Harry Ransom Humanities Research Center, The University of Texas at Austin, for their assistance.

NOTES

[1] Alice K. Turner, personal communication.

[2] John Crowley, *Engine Summer* (New York: Bantam Books, 1980), p. 167. Future references to this edition are given in the text.

[3] Alice K. Turner, personal communication.

[4] John Crowley, "Many Lives (Synopsis of a proposed novel)," p. 114, this collection.

[5] Ibid., p. 116, this collection.

[6] For more information on the synopsis, see the introduction to "Many Lives," p. 111, this collection.

[7] Crowley, "Many Lives," p. 115, this collection.

[8] Handwritten manuscript, n.p., Box 11, Folder 7, John Crowley Papers, Harry Ransom Humanities Research Center, The University of Texas at Austin.

[9] This is not wholly a conjecture on my part; there is evidence, not in *Engine Summer* itself, but from the early stages of its composition. In "Learning to Live with It," the first version of the book, Little Belaire as well as the List has large cats; and in a handwritten manuscript fragment, Rush tells the angel that in the old days such large cats would have been too dangerous to have around because they would have "fought constantly," but now they "never fought at all," and this change is due to their having eaten almost nothing but St. Bea's Bread for hundreds of years (handwritten manuscript, pp. 11-12, Box 11, Folder 7, John Crowley Papers). Of course, such early manuscripts are not definitive evidence for the meaning of the final text, but this does show that the tranquilizing nature of Bread was in Crowley's mind at one point, at least.

[10] Michael Andre-Driussi, personal communication; John Crowley, quoted in Adam Stephanides, "'Learning to Live with It': The first *Engine*

Summer," p. 148, this collection.

[11] Crowley quoted in Stephanides, "Learning," p. 147.

[12] Crowley, "Many Lives," p. 113.

[13] Crowley quoted in Stephanides, "Learning," p. 147.

[14] As is explained to Rush in the early manuscripts for "Learning to Live with It"; see Stephanides, "Learning," p. 137.

[15] Typescript, p. 131, Box 12, Folder 4, John Crowley Papers.

[16] Handwritten manuscript, p. 16, Box 11, Folder 7, John Crowley Papers.

THE GREAT KNOT UNRAVELED, OR NOT
Michael Andre-Driussi

The "Indian Giver" of *Engine Summer*.
WHILE I AGREE whole-heartedly with Alice Turner's essay on *Engine Summer* as writer's handbook, it seems strange and amusing that Crowley's treatise on story and character is in a novel where ultimately both story and character are unknowable.

The story is unknowable because, rather than a story, it is an experience of a life as recorded by a machine. As Jennifer Stevenson's essay "Memory and the World of John Crowley" points out, it ends with an abrupt truncation that is at odds with storytelling: "If this story had been told by the people of the Warren, they would have found a way to bring closure to it, smoothing the hacked-off edge to a shape that meets human needs" (included in this volume, p. 251).

The characters of Rush and the angel are unknowable because both are masked.

The book begins as a transcript of a dialog between two intelligences. This is clearly an unusual experience for one of them; has he died and gone to heaven? Or, like a biblical prophet, has he been transported on high while still living? Or is he merely a low-tech visitor dazzled by the high tech wonders of Laputa, the City in the Sky?[1]

The other intelligence, called "angel" by the first, quickly steers the first one into telling his story. As the novel develops, this expands from an interview into something more like an anthropological field sample, and we conclude that the angel is being quiet in order to avoid contaminating the subject's narrative. The angel is recording the interview on a series of eight-sided crystals; we learn our text is from this recording session. After inserting the third crystal into the recording device, the interviewee asks how many more will be used and the angel answers, "The third is the last, usually" (127). This seems to be a mistake on her part: it compromises her mask and prompts the interviewee to attempt a question that the angel anticipates and cuts off, urging him to get back to his story.[2]

Now the angel seems less an anthropologist than a technician. This interview is not a unique experience for her, we understand, and something usually happens during the recording of the third crystal, something which ends the session. And it appears that this event is precipitated by the interviewee asking one or more questions and getting the answers to them; this time, the angel is trying to forestall the asking of the terminal questions.

True to forecast, the third crystal is very taxing for the interviewee, as he describes the events leading up to his hosting of the cat-sphere, and then the horrific event of the hosting itself. He tells the angel he is very tired and has to rest. When she does not remove the recording crystal, he tells her to take it out, saying "There's nothing, nothing more to tell" (169). She still does not do it. Then he asks if he has been there in the sky city a few weeks and she lets fall another hint: "No. Longer." To which he says, "Oh, angel, take it out, stop, I can't any more" (169) and finally she pulls the crystal. The terminal questions, therefore, seem related to the passage of time. Indeed, the first hint was near the end of the first crystal's first facet, when Rush says something happened "almost ten years ago now" and the angel reacts non-verbally, so that he asks, "What is it?" and she replies, "Nothing. Go on now" (8).

The "third crystal crisis" was foreshadowed, the telling of its last episode was harrowing, the interviewee asked, ordered, and finally begged the angel to pull the crystal. And in an Orpheus reading, focussing on the relationship between Rush and Once a Day, the remaining part of the novel is a winding down: for an Orpheus reading, this crisis is the major action of the book.

But the angel puts in a fourth crystal, which begins with new questions from the interviewee and answers from the angel. He asks why she needs the recordings, and she is evasive, but admits that they are testing him for variations in the story he tells. He asks if there are variations, and she says yes, and lists a few. Then the story goes on—neither of those questions was the terminal one.

Thus we come to see that the "third crystal crisis" is a false crisis. The angel did not pull the crystal because Rush begged, but because she knows that there is not enough room left on the crystal for this long-winded host to complete the story she already knows. Most previous versions of the story do reach the end during the third crystal. But it appears that the angel wants to keep him talking, that quantity is a good thing, that she will record him as long as he talks.

But no. Just after the middle of the fourth crystal, they reach the end of the story anticipated by the angel and she moves to end the session. The interviewee expresses fear. The angel lowers the boom on him, telling him he is just a recording himself. Although he has been aware of this since the first page (even if we have not), still he seems horrified that he has been awakened 299 times and has no recollection—each time is the first time for him. The angel talks of time, the seemingly terminal topic, telling him that he has been there in the Sky city for 600 years. Furthermore the angel has no answers for him on how his mortal life played out down on the ground. She ends the session by deactivating the sphere.

So on the surface we see the interviewee traumatized by the unanticipated consequences of his deathless/lifeless state, like Sisyphus rolling the boulder endlessly. And this is what the angels per-

ORPHEUS

Orpheus in Greek mythology was the most famous poet and musician. When his wife Eurydice died of a snake-bite, Orpheus descended to Tartarus hoping to bring her back. He charmed his way with Charon the ferryman, sang his way past Cerberus the guardian dog. He even charmed the judges and Hades himself, but in the end he failed because he looked back too soon. (For all of this, Orpheus was the focus of an ancient pre-Christian mystery cult.)

In a slightly different order, Rush talks his way past the guardian cats, he charms the judge Zhinsinura, and he is ferried across a stream to where he meets Boots.

More importantly, there is a thread of death imagery around the List. After Rush is reunited with Once a Day, he tells her of his long wait and his fear that she would die, to which she says, "I did die. It was easy" (118). Even the playful phrase "the sky is grass" (131) takes on a funereal hue: to the buried, the sky is indeed grass.

There are also some details that point toward the underworld of classical mythology. The magic-tech device, "way-wall" (120), with its ominous dark face and one-way passage, is reminiscent of the gates separating the living

ceive, too; this is the hazard they have to obscure for him while they tease out yet another telling of his story for their own unfathomable purposes.

But the angels of Laputa are missing something, and this forms the basis of a more profound horror.

Introducing the unreliable reader.
I first read *Engine Summer* in 1986, and in it I saw Orpheus so strongly that I could not see some other elements. I saw: lyrical boy meets girl, boy loves girl, boy loses girl, boy travels to weird underworld place in order to rescue girl, boy fails in the attempt, and (postscript) boy's severed head continues to sing sweetly in the Orphic Shrine, inspiring volume upon volume of Orphic texts.

On top of this mythic foundation, I saw a platonic love story between a maiden and a ghost, which in turn was analogous to the relationship between a reader and a beloved book—if the book itself could weep a little when the cover is closed.

I read the novel again in 1999 or so and saw the same thing, with more corroborating evidence. But then I re-read Jennifer Stevenson's essay on memory, and a detail I had skimmed over now struck at the core of my understanding of *Engine Summer*: the presence of the host. I had seen the book as being a communication between two intelligences (the sphere and the angel), when in fact there are three: the sphere, the angel, and the angel's "silent" boyfriend who is hosting the sphere, sitting there on the Astroturf (tm) with the sphere on his head like the helmet of a deep-sea diver.

How could I miss the signs? For instance, the following conversation, beginning with the angel (who speaks in italics):

> *Only to see . . . to see how strong you are. I mean whether the story will change, depending on who . . .*
> Depending on who I am.
> *Depending on who tells it.*
> Has it changed?
> *Yes, in small ways. I don't think . . . I don't think any other loved Once a Day as much as you, I mean as much as in this story. And I never heard of the fly caught in plastic before.*
> Will you tell me about him, the one who I am? Is it a man?
> *It is.*
> Do you love him?
> *Yes.*
> I wonder why I thought so? Because you remind me of her [Once a Day]? . . . No, well, I'm not to know, am I? Well. I'll go on (173-74).

from the dead. After Rush goes through this portal, he says it was as though he had "stepped through Night and fallen into a treasure house of the angels" (121), echoing the view of the underworld as Pluto's treasure hoard.

But the strongest lead is how they gladly forget (121, 122, 137), which is a nod to Lethe, the river of forgetting where the spirits drink to lose their memories of life. That they also deny winter and death (133, 134) further illustrates their limbo-like state.

MA-D

This revealing passage comes immediately after the traumatic experiences of both Rush's hosting of Boots the cat and Once a Day's final rejection of Rush have been related. I originally read the questions of identity (including what I took to be pronoun confusion) as stemming from the mind-meld, and the talk of love as a platonic balm for the hurt he suffered from his earlier girlfriend. That is, I thought she was telling the sphere, "You are the intelligence of a man (not a cat)" and "You have loved greatly and been spurned but now you are truly beloved."

Again, in his penultimate speech, Rush says, "Listen: the one who I am, you must be gentle with him, angel, when he returns, remember" (209). I took this to mean, "Next time you activate the sphere that is me, do as good a job as you did this time, or even better, and I thank you for it now since I won't remember it then" instead of the obvious reading "Take care of your boyfriend as he comes down off this mind-altering experience, for he will be fragile."

Well, there is no going back.

The fact of the host completely demolishes the platonic love story. Their love clearly has a physical component, in fact it seems possible that she has already borne him a son several years earlier (208).

It also adds another vector for "contamination" of the Rush narrative. Indeed, the angels seem to be testing the intelligence in the sphere in a semi-scientific manner—using different hosts and watching for variations in the story—and they seem fairly convinced that "Rush" has an objective reality that is not affected by the host (the 299 recorded versions of the story are very similar regardless of the host). But, paradoxically, "Rush" himself points out true elements of subjectivity: "Rush" thinks the angel looks like Once a Day because the host loves the angel. The angel lists two "small" variations in this particular version: the fly in plastic at first seems the lesser, truly small, while "no other loved her as much as you" really does seem radical.

It is boggling: what could the angel mean? His love made Rush leave the warren, join the List, receive the cat mind-meld. In the other 298 versions of the story did Rush do all of these things without loving her? That is to say, if the host puts a spin on the story, then it may be that we only have this "Orpheus" version because, for the first time, the host is the lover of the recording angel.

To put it another way, maybe in the majority of versions Rush is more like an Odysseus or a Gilgamesh (doing things on the way to some other thing), and this is the first time he is an Orpheus (doing things to bring back a lost loved one).

If this is true, and if we begin to see disturbing parallels between Rush and the host, then it may be that the "silent" host really is telling his own story through the shaping and shading of the Rush material: how out of his great love of a woman (the angel) he has allowed himself to be coerced into being a host (of Rush), the most traumatic experience of his life; and that she will reject him despite this sacrifice.

The fly in the ointment, the fly in the plastic.
We understand the fly in plastic to be a novelty-store item, a fly in a fake ice cube (to be put into the victim's drink), but for the post-apocalyptic characters it is a mystery to be interpreted. The artifact appears briefly in the text as a present that Blink had given to the twins Budding and Blooming (75). Rush refers to it in his account of a conversation with Mongolfier as a reason why Rush might refuse to let the sphere record his mind: "I think of a fly, stuck in a cube of plastic, able to see all around, but not able to move. It frightens me" (203). Significantly, this is related long after the recording angel has revealed that the detail of the fly in plastic is a new variant to the story (173). Rush/host is trying to tell her something. (Later he will appeal to her directly.)

Early on in the book, Painted Red tells the story of St. Gary and the fly, but it is different from the one Rush is familiar with. We do not hear either version, the funny old one or the philosophical new one, but we do learn that in the end St. Gary lets the fly go (28). Later on we learn more about St. Gary: it was his uncle who was copied in a sphere before he died, and, after the Storm broke up the angel's world, Gary found the sphere that contained his Uncle Plunkett. At this time, the Long League was claiming possession of the four spheres while they debated what to do with them, so Gary stole the Uncle Plunkett sphere and thereby saved it from being destroyed as the others were. Gary carried the sphere for the rest of his life, but after he died it was lost or sold somewhere between

THE CRYING OF HOST 299

The recording angel tags two items as variant:
  the degree of love felt by Rush for Once a Day (173)
  the fly in plastic (173).

But anything else that surprises her is also likely to be variant:
  the intrusion of "the doctor" in Rush's breakdown (191)
  Rush's impressions of Montgolfier, which seem to border on sacrilege (204).

MA-D

Manhattan and the site of Little Belaire. Ultimately the angels of Laputa got it.

Putting all this together, it seems like "letting the fly go" in the context of the fly in plastic means destroying the sphere: the host wants the abomination to end; the Long League was right to destroy the spheres.

Bright potential and the Culture Quest.

In addition to his personal-scale Orpheus quest, Rush seems to have a cultural-scale quest to do something big for his community, the warren of Little Belaire. To be a culture-hero.

In his own parlance, Rush wants to be a saint, and his identity is molded by saints (that is, by their stories) early in the text. Two, in particular, seem to be his models. He says, "My cord is Palm cord, the cord of St. Roy and St. Dean" (5); later he sees his cord projected on the wall, which makes him think "and a great cord it is, with two great saints"; he expresses this thought by saying "My cord has two saints in it" (13).

St. Dean is never mentioned again in the text, and we have no

SAINTS OF LITTLE BELAIRE

Andy: 4, 6, 7, 22, 52, 81, 95, 185, 195. A leader in the last days of wandering, a toothless old man, he lost the silver glove and ball, but co-founded Little Belaire with Bea. After Bea died he went to live in a tree.

Bea: 6, 22, 52, 81. Co-founder of the warren, discoverer of St. Bea's Bread, first victim of bread overdose.

idea what his story might be; aside from a sneaking suspicion that he is based on James Dean.

St. Roy, on the other hand, is well supported by the text, emerging as the first saint, the one who led the exodus of truthful speakers out of Great Belaire into the newly sundered world, rather like Moses. We also know that St. Roy wore a prosthetic leg, and that his wagon had many treasures, including the important silver glove and ball lost by St. Andy. So when Rush tells Painted Red his first ambition, "I'd like to find things . . . all our things that are lost, and bring them back" (14), the primary treasure in his mind (or our minds, at least) is the glove and ball pair. Eventually, near the end of the book, he will find both, connecting him in a way with St. Roy.

But there is another saint named Roy, Little St. Roy. The text is very clear in linking Rush to Little Roy early in the text, when the seven-year-olds Once a Day and Rush play their game of "St. Olive [and] Little St. Roy" (41), a game which ends with Olive and Roy living together "ever after" (42). Little St. Roy is the one who waited many long years for St. Olive to come to the warren: when she arrived, she brought news that the Long League was dissolved.

So it seems that the two saints whose stories most influence Rush are the two Roys: St. Roy, the first saint, a Moses-like culture hero, and Little St. Roy, the lover of St. Olive and the last saint (64).

For the warren, stories about the saints always have "proof" in the form of a concrete artifact. The story of how St. Andy lost the silver glove and ball, for example, has its proof in the set of dentures Andy used (8). The mysterious artificial leg (37) turns out to be the proof of the "lost" story Blink tells Rush about St. Roy (101). So Rush's desire to be a saint and his dream of bringing back lost things go hand in hand as he pursues the lost stories of artifacts (like the barometer) as well as the lost artifacts of stories (the silver glove and ball).

Before she begins his schooling, Painted

Blink: 83, 84-107, 108, 111, 160, 175, 177, 194, 206. A maybe-saint, living in a tree during Rush's era (not connected to Brink's cord [40]).

Clay: 22

Dean: 5.

Ervin: 85. Pestered St. Maureen (who was apparently sainted while still living).

Gary: 28, 81, 93, 94, 95. Rescued the Plunkett sphere, subject of a story about a fly.

Gene: 40, 64, 85, 87, 157, 209. A maybe-saint, founder of Thread cord, a group of puzzle-workers.

Little Roy: 9, 41, 42, 44-46, 64, 65, 91, 95, 114, 116, 131, 140, 206. Waited for Olive, then lived with her. He was the last saint.

Maureen: 81, 85, 86. Lived in a tree, rejected Ervin.

Olive: 34, 39, 44-46, 59, 64, 68, 95, 114, 116, 131, 137, 162, 196. Brought news of the League's end to the warren, founded Whisper cord, lived with Little Roy until she died.

Roy: 5, 7, 9, 10, 22, 30, 94, 100, 101, 103, 133. The first saint, he led the truthful speakers out of Great Belaire, lost his leg.

Red tells Rush to resolve his "knot" (or conflict) with his father. As an aside she mentions that the way out is called "Little Knot" (15). He follows her instructions and the problem is quickly solved, at which point Rush feels "the knot came untied in me" (24). At the end of his schooling, seven years later and just as he is about to leave the warren, Painted Red reveals a great mystery to him, probably the warren's greatest mystery, which is a sequence of glass slides superimposed upon each other:

> "the first slide, is Fourth Finder, Palm cord's slide . . . And the other placed over it is called Little First Slot. Together, they make Little Knot . . . Little Knot and Hands make Little Knot Unraveled . . . Little Knot Unraveled and the two Stair slides make Great Knot . . . Great Knot and First Trap make Little Trap . . . Little Second Gate and the Ball Court make Gate" (67)

There is more, but let us examine the first part. Recall that Painted Red referred to a situation in Rush's life as "Little Knot," and when he solved that problem he felt a knot unravel. See her stages "Little Knot" and "Little Knot Unraveled." She seems to have put the blueprint of his life, his destiny, our novel, before him. With a further sequence of slides, one finally reaches the summation, which is called "Great Knot Unraveled," and this seems to mean in some nebulous way that the broken world is made whole again.

Painted Red questions him about his goals

in leaving the warren, pointedly contrasting his vague desire to rescue Once a Day with his earlier desire to find lost things. And then, as if to erase any doubts, Painted Red directly charges him to his first desire/cultural quest: "Never forget us and our needs . . . . And however far away you go, come back with what you find to us" (69).

Rush goes out into the world. His next spiritual teacher is Blink, who tells the story of the Storm that destroyed the angels' world, and when Rush asks about cities in the sky, Blink says:

> "They used to say that one day, after thousands of years perhaps, the angels would come back; the cities would land, and the angels would come out and see all that had been going on while they floated" (91).

This is a bright promise of a grand reunion of humanity, angels and ground-dwellers; this is the world made whole again; this is a vision of the Great Knot Unraveled. And this is a good spot to show the entire sequence of slides that Painted Red reveals (67-68), augmented by a slight gloss:

The Great Knot Unraveled
Fourth Finder = Rush that Speaks
1) FF + Little First Slot = Little Knot

    LFS is Speak a Word, specifically her refusal to have another child with Seven Hands (100), triggering Seven Hands' desire to leave;

Rush's time

Hundreds of years after St. Bea (52), 1000 years after the Storm, according to avvengers. Warren-folk are now named by cord, the old-style naming system (Andy, Bea, etc.) has gone away.

Rush at <1, early winter: Rush that Speaks born in "November."

Rush at 5/6, early winter: Rush spies on his mother refusing to have another child by Seven Hands (100)

Rush at 7, early winter: Rush meets Painted Red, goes with Seven Hands to see Road, meets Once a Day.

Rush at 7, spring: Rush shows Once a Day the foxes; she shows him the artificial leg and the barometer.

Rush at 7, summer: Rush and Once a Day "c[o]me to own" the warren for about a year (40).

Rush at 9, spring: Once a Day goes with List.

Rush at 13, autumn: Rush meets Painted Red (64).

Rush at 14, spring: Rush leaves, spends year with Blink.

Rush at 15, spring: Rush spends year with List.

Rush at 16, spring: Rush spends year with avvengers.

Rush at 17, summer: Rush recorded by sphere on verge of warren.

Frametale Time

600 years after the recording, so roughly 1600 years after the Storm

GROUPS

The Long League of Women
A subculture of the Angels, they acted to halt the destruction after the Storm

Mutation: through genetic engineering, women can only bear children if they take a conception pill (one of the four medicine's daughters)

Little Belaire
Known by outsiders as "the warren"

Totem: List calls them hare.

Core belief: Truthful speaking.

Secret: Location of the planter/St. Bea's Bread.

Old Secret: Possession of the forbidden Plunkett sphere.

Monopoly: St. Bea's Bread.

Export: St. Bea's Bread, blown glassware, honey, spectacles (vision correcting and sunglasses)

Import: Medicine's daughters (one of which is required for human procreation).

Mutations: There may be physical mutation. Bea overdosed on St. Bea's Bread (an extrasolar lifeform), and for decades or centuries it was only safe to smoke bread in a water pipe, but in Rush's time they can smoke unfiltered cigars (thus they have adapted).

Relations: Never on good terms with the League, which probably stems from

LK is Rush's fear of losing his father Seven Hands.

2) LK + Hands = Little Knot Unraveled

Hands is Rush asking to go with his father;

LKU is Rush learning the truth (his father will never go, probably because if he did another man would take his place with Speak a Word).

3) LKU + (2 stair slides) = Great Knot

the one stair is the introduction of knowledge;

the other stair is the introduction of romantic love;

GK is a confusion of personal love and cultural quest.

4) GK + First Trap = Little Trap

First Trap is when Once a Day gives Rush Money;

Little Trap is when Once a Day leaves and binds Rush to silence.

5) LT + the Expedition = Little Second Gate

the Expedition is when Rush leaves the warren;

LSG is the time he spends with Blink.

6) LSG + Ball Court = Gate

Gate is the black way-wall of the List.

7) G + Second Slot + Great Slot + Broken Heart + Shaken Fragments = Great Knot Unraveled

SS is Once a Day, specifically her refusal to leave the List;

GS is Zhinsinura, specifically her granting of Rush's uninformed request to host the cat sphere;

Broken Heart is when Once a Day rejects Rush;

Shaken Fragments is Rush's stint as an avvenger and the breakdown he suffers.

At the novel's beginning Rush says of the sky city, "I've found you, then. I've found the greatest thing that was lost" (3). In the novel's final climax, Rush/host begins arguing directly with the angel. "But why didn't you stop? Come back again? The City could return, couldn't it, if they'd seen they were mistaken?" (205). She says they thought the world was dead, and he says, "But it's not so. It just got different, is all. You could come back; there's no hard feelings. You must come back. It's home" (205).

There it is, pure and simple. Rush is pleading for the sky city to land right now, which would be the Great Knot Unraveled, the healing of the broken world. The fact that he can articulate it now means that it was there inside him on the day the sphere made its recording, that hope, that dream. He thought that the angels were living under false assumptions about the state of the Earth (they were), and he hoped that if he could communicate with them they would hear his message and change (they have, but not in directions he would have chosen).

Propelling the culture quest is a vague sense of urgency. After all, the title of the book is

St. Gary's having taken the Plunkett sphere in the early days of the wandering.

Reunification potential: practically nil. They are so contented, it seems rare for anyone to travel. They may not be reproducing themselves in adequate numbers even in Rush's time.

Dr. Boots's List

a.k.a. "The List"

Totem: Cat

Core belief: Living only in the moment, facilitated by hosting the cat sphere (individuals do this repeatedly, once a year).

Secret: Possession of the cat sphere, recipes for medicine's daughters.

Monopoly/export: Medicine's daughters.

Import: St. Bea's bread.

Mutations: Psychologically, they are cats.

Relations: They consider themselves the heirs of the League, but this is somewhat complicated by the fact that their sphere probably would have been destroyed by the League (unless the List is the degenerate remains of the League). They are friendly enough to do business in foreign lands, but they are paranoid with visitors in their territories.

Reunification potential: Relatively high, since they travel and trade. As the center of a pharmaceutical empire, they literally have the power of life and death over the client groups in their thrall. Unfortunately, the conception pill is technologically out of place in an agrarian world.

Avvengers
Totem: Buzzers (buzzards).
Core belief: Recycling (living like angels, but without making anything new).
Family structure: Polygamous.
Monopoly/export: Artifacts dug up from the ruins.
Import: Women who can bear children without the conception drug.
Taboos: St. Bea's Bread.
Mutations: Perhaps none; they might be 20th century throwbacks.
Relations: The Long League hunted down these patriarchal scavengers like dogs, yet they managed to survive. They do not seem hostile to strangers (at least in the limited case we see).
Reunification potential: Highest, because they are not dependent on drugs to give birth, and they are exploring the world.

Laputa
a.k.a. the City in the Sky
Core belief: Difficult to say, but perhaps a blend of warren and List (semi-truthful speaking, biennial hosting).
Culture: They do not have cords; they believe in "winning" games, they cannot

a play on "Indian summer," which we might translate into cultural terms as "brief renaissance," because humanity seems poised on the brink of extinction and the time to act is in Rush's mortal lifetime. A web of trading connects the different communities, providing a veneer of health, but the forests are encroaching and populations seem to be dwindling; humanity seems to be running down, each group by itself, whereas if they were to come together, pooling their knowledge and resources, they might save one another.

This, then, explains why the terminal questions are time related. Because once he is apprised of the 600 years that have passed, the enormity of his failure to fulfill the cultural quest becomes apparent. While the mortal Rush undoubtedly lived out his life in the faith that the sky city would land one day soon, giving the necessary "proof" to his story and possibly healing the world, the immortal Rush learns in silent shock time after time that the city will not land, that the promise made to Painted Red to bring back lost things cannot be kept, that the world-wound cannot heal. In fact, the world seems locked in endless Winter.

As his last heroic act, Rush asks the angel to take care of the host:

> Here, take my hand, take his hand. Yes. Don't let go. Promise.
> *Yes. I promise.*
> Stay with him.

Ever after. I promise. Now close your eyes
(209).

I am sure that many have read the angel's
last speech and thought it was touching and
sweet—I know I once did. He means "Do not
abandon him in the future, as Once a Day
did Rush" and she seems to hear that meaning. However, she answers with the fairy-tale
phrase "ever after," and this is a code for
promises broken, betrayal and rejection, since
it is used repeatedly by Once a Day (42, 189);
and "I promise" is meaningless because the
angels are clearly not the truthful speakers that
the angel claims.

see the joy in simply playing;
they do not have St. Bea's
Bread.
  Import: Artifacts of all
kinds.
  Export: Unknown.
  Relations: A relic of the
pre-Storm world, for a millennium virtually untouched by
changes on the ground. Presumably, they had no contact
with the League. The warren
people have nice things to say
about the legendary place
and people; the List's version
is a nightmare of dread.
  Reunification   potential:
Zero.

Faced with a monumental failure like this,
the intelligence in the sphere longs for oblivion, like the immortal
sibyl who wanted only to die. If there is a terminal mode for Rush,
this is it.

To reiterate: Rush has two quests. The personal one is the
Orpheus quest, to rescue his beloved from the List and bring her
"home." This quest is complementary to the story of Little St. Roy:
Roy waited for the future beloved, Rush seeks out the lost lover.

The other, the cultural quest, starts out simply with Painted
Red's bidding him to "bring our lost things home," and Rush
trades all he owns for the silver ball in order to complete the set
with the glove he had already gained through barter. To return the
glove and ball to the warren would reverse St. Andy's loss of St.
Roy's treasure. But just before Rush can return to the warren, the
angel Mongolfier lands to claim the glove and ball. So through a
double-or-nothing gamble, Rush gives him the treasure (losing the
"proof" of the story, the immediate goal) and allows the sphere to
record his mind (hoping to achieve the greater goal of getting the
angels to land the city). To land the angel city would be to reunite

NAMES TELL THEIR FATE

"Once a Day" initially sounds like a lewd name, but in fact it is a scrap from the form of writing used for pharmaceutical prescriptions ("take this medication once a day"), showing that she will join the List.

"Rush that Speaks" is named for the water rush that seems to speak when the winter wind goes through its dead hollow stem (5).

the world, closing the circle begun by St. Roy himself. The final leg of the cultural quest is carried out by the Rush sphere, and it fails, time and time again.

In light of these details, I must restate, revise, and refine the "terminal question" idea. The concept first rose from the novel's conclusion, where Rush is ready for oblivion after he is told three earth-shaking truths: that he is a recording; that he has told the story hundreds of times; and it has been 600 years since the recording was made. While all these are revelations to the reader, further investigation reveals that Rush already knows the first two. He has been aware that he is a recording from the beginning: "That's all I am, now, isn't it: my story" (4). That this is not the first recording is suggested when the angel says, "It's best just to tell the story, beginning to end—that's something we know about you" (64); and after a later interruption, Rush asks her, "Do you know this story better than I do?" (94), which seems more than just rhetorical.

The passage of time, then, is the terminal answer. And the Laputans want him to tell the story in strict sequence, presumably having learned through trial and error that "it's best" that way. The endpoint of the story is the moment the sphere recording was made: when they reach that stage, the story is over and they turn the sphere off. So it is not that the angels simply want Rush to keep talking, it is instead that they are like children who want to hear the same story, almost exactly the same, over and over.

A seeming tangent on truthful speaking.

The warren culture is practically defined by its practice of "truthful speaking," a form of *communication* "in such a way that your hearer couldn't help but understand what you meant, and in such a way that you, speaking, had no choice but to express what you meant" (30). (I use "communication" because there is more to the process than speaking and listening.) Truthful speaking is one of the novel's gems, seemingly simple, but then quite tricky and deep. I think of it as an "anthropological" gem, representing the mystery of a different culture's "untranslatable" words. Jennifer Stevenson calls truthful speaking a fantasy element, but unless she means it is telepathy, I gently disagree: I think it is like the illusion of communication we all have, especially concerning conversation with those inside our own warren-like communities of family or avid-readers-of-John-Crowley's-fiction.

Truthful speaking is mostly like a language: both sender and receiver must be truthful speakers for it to work, so it is not some sort of universal broadcast system that cuts across language barriers. In fact, the greater burden may be on the receiver. And despite the name, truthful speaking is more than just speaking/listening, as illustrated by this passage where Rush meets Painted Red for the first time:

> When she had smoked, she said, "Hello, you're a grace-ful fellow, I'm in a mood to talk to you. Don't expect me to reveal too much of myself, though I'm sympa-thetic and can be helpful. Be at ease with me; I know it's strange here, but soon we'll be easy together, and then friends . . ."
>
> No, of course she said nothing like that, but it was all in what she did say, in her greeting, for she spoke truthfully, and was very, very good at it; so good that, speaking, she couldn't hide from my knowledge of what she meant. Of course my knowledge then was very slight; when she talked with Mbaba, they both said things I couldn't hear (11).

A perfect example of its deeper complexity comes when Rush is working to resolve the problem with his father, Seven Hands. Rush is anxious about losing his father because Seven Hands often speaks of leaving the warren to travel widely. Seeing this (and more), Painted Red tells Rush to ask his father to take him when he goes. Rush does this, and Seven Hands admits it will be later rather than sooner. Nevertheless, they go out together on a short and wonderful camping trip, at the end of which Rush comes to realize that his father will never leave the warren, all when Seven Hands softly says "One day."

> And when he said it—I don't know how, whether because we had shared this adventure, or because of the story he had told [about how the group wandering had ended with the founding of the warren], or because now for the first time he knew it to be true himself—I saw that Seven Hands wouldn't leave Little Belaire and follow Road where it led. That had been the knot between us, that I had believed him when he said it, and resented and admired him for having decided to do it; and he, who knew in his heart of hearts that he never would, had disliked me for believing him capable of it when he wasn't. He had spoken truthfully of all this to me even as he told me of his plans to go and his dreams of what he would see; but till now I hadn't been able to hear it . . . "One day," I said. Beneath his hood his face was grave, and sad too; for I had in those two words just told him what I had learned (24).

So "meaning" is more than just words, and can be quite compact with regard to words. If words alone were enough, then the father would have said "I will never go" every time he made his comments and the child Rush would have understood the problem—as it stands, Rush could not understand until he had the context, the experience of travel represented by the camping trip. Once he grasps the context, then he can understand all the cues, including the unspoken ones, and the communication is successful. (For all the differences between the warren and the List, the List has a similar approach to educating Rush: he asks them repeatedly about their concept of "light and dark," but their answers do not get through to him, and his wrong assumptions start to cause distress to others. Then they stage the frightening "cat rescue" and Rush learns, again viscerally. This is another detail that seems anthropologically sound.)

Once a Day was taught truthful speaking at the same time Rush was, but for only two years before she left the warren. On his quest to bring her back, Rush often fears that in the six years of her absence from the warren she may have forgotten truthful speaking. After he has been living with her and the List for nearly a year, he broaches the subject of leaving the List together:

> "We could go back to Little Belaire." I meant: to Belaire, where we were born, Belaire and the saints and the Filing System and the gossips who untie knots instead of tying them tighter as the old ones here do, Belaire where every story has a proof and all the secrets have names at least; I meant *We could go home.*
>
> "It wasn't my home," she said, and my heart leaped, for I heard she had heard me (159).

So when Rush says "Little Belaire" in that context, in that tone, with that expression, etc., it is a "portmanteau word" whose manifest is a short list of associations, whose true name is "home." Despite the fact that she had only two years of training, and that was nearly half her lifetime ago, still she is able to hear the true meaning that he is sending.

Even though Once a Day hears the meaning, still she rejects the premise that the warren is her home, because she chose the List as her home and she chooses it again. In contrast, the angel claims to be a truthful speaker, and claims that Rush's story has changed the sky city in a positive way, and yet the angels reach the same conclusion that Once a Day did: they will not budge.

The reason for the visit.

I can see the mystery of "is Rush alive or dead" resolved in a series of "neither," "both," and "other." I can see three quests (Orpheus, lesser artifact, greatest artifact) and how they all fail. But I cannot see why this vaguely cruel thing is being done, why this endless series of recordings is made: what point does it serve for the host, and/or the angel, and/or their society?

The process happens about once every two years (600 years divided by 300 times). After the sphere is deactivated, the host is silent for a few days, struggling to re-establish his/her own personality (206). For the rest of their lives the hosts have a ghost of Rush in their minds, just as Rush himself had a ghost of Boots the cat in his mind.

We cannot tell whether or not Laputan society has a role for these "Rushians." With one being created every two years, they might form an enlightened elite. (If they host Rush at age 20 and die at age 70, then there are around 25 Rushians alive at any one time after the first 50 years; if they live to be 100, then there are around 40 Rushians alive.) Are they relationship councillors? Are they "Stepford Wives" and husbands—is the process a spousal finishing school?

Perhaps the rewards go to the angel who conducts the interview, rather than to the host? No, that is not right, since at one point the angel tells him, "It's not for my sake you tell it [your story]" (94).

What are the transcripts themselves used for? Obviously they are read, or listened to, at least by the interviewers (the angel is quickly able to spot variations). This is a possible vector of contamination, since the angel can (and does) use leading questions. (More boggling is the possibility that the host has read the transcripts, which would seem to indicate a vector of great contamination, severely compromising objectivity.) Oddly enough, the frametale forces us into this role: we are the angels of Laputa, reading the book for entertainment.

Learning to live with it.

This was the original title for what became the novel *Engine Summer*. The phrase echoes throughout the novel.

Blink tells Rush a story about how Great St. Roy lost his leg and had to be fitted with a prosthetic. "Learning to live with it" was how St. Roy described accepting his condition, and he applied this model to the state of the world after the Storm: "It left us legless men" (101). Everybody has to learn to live with it.

(When Roy says "legless men" he means one-legged people; this, in turn, leads to a Platonic tangent: in *Symposium*, Plato writes that Aristophanes told a story about human origins. In the beginning there were three sexes [men, women, and hermaphrodites] and they were round, each having four arms and four legs. These humans were so powerful that they threatened the gods, so Zeus cut each in two, forming the humanity we know, where each person seeks his/her sundered soul mate. "For love is the desire of the whole," said Aristophanes, "and the pursuit of the whole is called love." But here is the kicker: "There was a time when the two sexes were only one, but now God has halved them . . . and if they do not behave themselves he will divide them again, and they will hop about with half a nose and face." Roy is saying, in effect, that mankind has been sundered again.)

As Rush struggles to find himself after hosting the cat sphere, he promises himself to escape grief by letting the task be the master: "I would learn, yes, in the long engine summer of the world I would learn to live with it" (168).

The angel herself shows another side, telling him about how the Plunkett sphere shaped the angel culture: "we grew old in Plunkett. All we knew was learning to live with his suffering: our suffering" (205).

Plunkett was a man, middle-aged or elderly, living in the last days of the angel world before and during the Storm. He seems to have died not many years after the recording: perhaps he had a terminal illness, which might fit the profile of a volunteer for such an experiment as the recording; historically prisoners have also been used. His sphere recording seems to have the depressing qualities of his time and perhaps his own age and/or circumstances.

Plunkett was erased from the sphere and Rush was recorded in his place. Rush is "picked" at a prime moment: he is seventeen years old, with his life ahead of him; he has just come through a series of vivid passages and he is right on the verge of a homecoming with hope for wonderful things to happen in the near future. As the angel says, "they've said . . . that I could learn to live with you, as none ever could with Plunkett" (206). So it is no exaggeration to say that the angels have traded their middle-aged gloom and doom for the great expectations of an exceptional youth.

And now, under the new system, it is only the Rushians who have to pay the price by learning to live with it.

A letter from Dr. Freud.

Take the case of R. We see an intelligent young man whose heart is torn between the conflicting desires of "Little Roy" and "Great Roy." Now "Roy" is a name which means "king," but for R. a better synonym would seem to be "head," and the internal battle is between the "little head" of his genitals and the "big head" of his rational mind.

Young R. falls in with a group of decadents who idolize another type of "little head" and literally put it into their "big heads." Sometimes a cat is just a cat, but this time, clearly it is a vagina, and all negative "feminine" behavior can be safely coded as "cat-like" without raising the formidable ire of the Long League of women.

After his wounding and expulsion, R. takes up residence within a building shaped like a giant head. Here he confirms that his "little head" is rendered useless (186). He works at reintegrating his fractured psyche, and in doing so he rediscovers his "big head" and the community goal.

In the end, R.'s psyche is captured by another group. They claim to "love" him, and they shower him with honeyed phrases, yet they treat him like an object, literally putting him upon a pedestal:

things which were surely antithetical to the League, but of course the people of Laputa ("la puta" is "the prostitute" in Spanish; the joke is courtesy of Jonathan Swift, who sent Gulliver there) had no contact with the League. (Would the League have destroyed the fifth sphere—the Boots sphere—or was their decision to break the other four based on the fact that they were all "dead white males"? Were they in fact mesmerized by the cat-mind into enshrining it, thus degenerating the League into the List?)

A summation.

The "story" of *Engine Summer* is quite fluid. If we follow one set of markers, we see an Orpheus quest (where failure is built in); if we follow another set of markers, we see something more like Gilgamesh (again, failure is part of it). But these constructions are artificial: the Orpheus reading is created by contamination from the host, contamination from the recording angel, and innocuous "accidents" (e.g. the third crystal crisis) that beguile the conditioned reader into perceiving a story where there is none: there is only a segment of a life. Likewise the Gilgamesh construction, obsessively cultivated by the Laputans, is a structure that they craft for Rush.

The frametale characters are unknowable because they are masked. The interviewer goes through at least three vague forms: nymph (virginal "angel," platonic love) gatekeeper, sexually active anthropologist, and mother technician/agent of dissolution. The interviewee is a chimera of Rush, host, random chance, and various contaminations. A story can be extracted from a completed life, but an incomplete life cannot be shoehorned into a story.

The Laputans claim to be truthful speakers, but this seems doubtful. The reason for the interview, the initial mystery of the novel, remains entirely obscure through a bait-and-switch maneuver. Rush wanted to be a saint (that is: a truthful speaker whose life inspires a story that is told by truthful speakers to inspire truthful speaking; one whose story has proof in an artifact), but instead he is an object, an artifact that tells the story of, and acts as the proof for, another "saint" (Mongolfier).

107

A train of thought and its stations.

The evolution of my thoughts on *Engine Summer* should be plain by now. I started out with Orpheus, and in moving beyond that I owe a great debt to others. E-mail conversations with Jennifer K. Stevenson in the early 1990s had tangential details about *Engine Summer*—she mentioned the Great Knot Unraveled as a blueprint at one point (but I did not look into this until 2001). After Alice Turner's essay was published in *The New York Review of Science Fiction* I started discussing the novel in e-mail with a small group of people, and Adam Stephanides first came up with the "terminal question" angle of approach.

WORKS CITED

Crowley, John.
Engine Summer. Bantam edition, 1980.

Plato (translated by B. Jowett).
Symposium, Project Gutenberg (http://promo.net/cgi-promo/pg/cat.cgi)

NOTES

[1] The name of the City in the Sky is "Laputa" (200), taken from the name of the aerial city in Swift's *Gulliver's Travels* (1726). Swift's flying city is populated by men of science and learning, but it is not isolated from the ground-dwellers—it is an overlord, a mobile capital that can shower gifts upon the loyal, or block the sunshine of the rebellious.

[2] The novel is in four parts:

"Many Lives" (8 facets): Rush's childhood, ending when Once a Day leaves.

"The Laughter of the Legless Man" (8 facets): Rush with Blink, Rush at List.

"A Letter from Dr. Boots" (6 facets): Rush hosting Boots.

"The Sky is Grass" (5 facets): Rush as avvenger.

MANY LIVES
(SYNOPSIS OF A PROPOSED NOVEL)
John Crowley

Introduction by Adam Stephanides

The John Crowley Papers at the University of Texas at Austin are a gold mine for Crowley researchers, containing notes and drafts for a number of Crowley's works, including *Engine Summer*. But the most illuminating single document there may be the one reproduced below: Crowley's synopsis of *Engine Summer* (written when the book's intended title was "Many Lives"). This synopsis was written at some point after Crowley decided to revise the first version of *Engine Summer* for publication, but before he had finished the revisions. It was apparently intended to be given to a literary agent or editor along with a sample chapter: on the cover page of the synopsis is the injunction: "READ FIRST, PLEASE."

This synopsis is of great interest, both because it tells us what Crowley considered most significant about the book, and because in it Crowley explains a number of things that are unclear in the book itself. As such, it speaks for itself. Still, it may be useful to point out some of the highlights. Topping the list are Crowley's explanations of the List and the Letter from Dr. Boots, which I discuss in my essay on *Engine Summer* elsewhere in this collection. Next in importance I would put the explanation Crowley gives for

Once a Day's rejection of Rush after he receives the Letter: that she "sens[es] that he has undergone it solely for her sake and not for the inner reasons it requires." There is also a brief but illuminating description of cords in general; and a discussion of Whisper cord that makes clear, more than the book itself does, the extent to which Whisper is an anomaly within Little Belaire.

In revising the first version of *Engine Summer* (then entitled "Learning to Live with It"), Crowley made substantial changes. (For a discussion of these changes, see Adam Stephanides, "Learning to Live with It: The first *Engine Summer*," this collection.) These changes are for the most part reflected in the synopsis. In places, though, the synopsis agrees with the earlier version instead of the later one. The main instance of this concerns Rush's departure from Little Belaire. The character Once a Day in *Engine Summer* is a combination of two characters from "Learning to Live with It": the girl whom Rush follows to the List is not Once a Day, but a girl native to the List. When Crowley wrote his synopsis, he had already decided to combine Once a Day with this second girl, but the sequence of events surrounding Rush's departure is still that of "Learning to Live with It." Once a Day is present when Rush leaves Little Belaire to become a saint; and he returns to Little Belaire after spending the winter with Blink, so that when he follows Once a Day to the List it is his second departure from Little Belaire.

[title page]

MANY LIVES
(Synopsis of a proposed novel)[1]

READ FIRST, PLEASE

MANY LIVES: Synopsis

Many Lives is the opposite, in a sense, of a history of the future. It is, rather, the future's archaeology of the past—that is, of the time between our time and theirs, which I imagine to be about a thousand years from now.

The form of the story is a young man's attempt to become a saint. By the definition of the society he lives in, which has neither writing nor art in the sense we understand it, to become a saint is to learn to tell the story of your life in such a way that your hearers see reflected in it their own situation, and the humanity that joins them all. The saint, in other words, strives to make his own humanity transparent, so that through the story of his life, all lives can be seen. Long after a saint's death, other saints tell his story; an old saint's life becomes an incident in a new one's life; lives are nested within one another like an infinite series of transparent spheres. Like all religions, this godless sainthood religion is an enormous and baffling accretion of legend, history, culture, maxim, entertainment and mystic apprehension of the ineffable, all rolled into one.

Rush that Speaks, my character, does become a saint, though not at all in the way he supposes he will; and his life does become transparent, far more literally than he supposes is possible.

Because of the odd angle of vision his religious society has given him, Rush doesn't understand that what he wants, in fact, is to understand the past: to learn the truth. He is less interested in enlarging his humanity than in learning what are universally called in the book *secrets*: he wants to uncover the hidden, make the human situation come clear as an extension of the past. If it weren't for the odd ways in which Rush goes about his search, we would understand him clearly: he is a historian, or, in the absence of written records, he is an archaeologist.

It is the very nature of the society that the past has created that makes Rush's search so difficult: for, because of the terrible history it has been through, the society Rush knows has abjured a part of its humanity; has closed in on itself and turned its curiosity in inward directions. In the warren, Little Belaire, where Rush grows up, they have transformed history into the stories of the saints. In the far more extreme society of Dr. Boot's List, where the greatest secrets are kept, and where Rush goes in search of them, men have tried, as best they can, to forget the past and not imagine the future: to forget time.

Rush is a Truthful Speaker. The Truthful Speakers originated in a co-op apartment house in the Midwest called Belaire, sometime toward the end of this present century; they invented Truthful Speaking talking over the phones of the co-op. Truthful Speaking is a method of unconsciously revealing in your speech the true state of your disposition, and of reading the unconscious disposition of others in their speech. (I have no idea how it's done. Neither does a grown-up Truthful Speaker: he only does it.)

During the long, intermittent, and finally complete collapse of technological society, the Speakers survived as a unit because of their speech. They had to leave the co-op, and took up a nomadic existence. During this period the saints evolved, and Truthful Speaking was refined, and the Speakers—merely because of their cohesion and separateness—came to be at odds with the League, later called the Long League. The League was a loose organization of women, theoretically of all women, founded during the collapse by a transsexual named Mother Tom and dedicated to helping people survive the catastrophe, while at the same time they attempted to bury forever all vestiges of technology and "male" technological and hierarchical thinking which had caused the catastrophe—the Going-off.

Centuries later—when the book opens—the Long League has dissolved itself, its work done. Mankind—at least in this part of the world—is living in separate enclaves almost unknown to one another. The Truthful Speakers have rebuilt Belaire as an intricate interconnected warren called Little Belaire. Their concerns are re-membering the saints, and dealing with the affairs of their cords. The cords into which the people of Little Belaire are divided are something like psychological and somatic types: types discovered long before by scientists, but used by the gossips of the warren to understand and interpret human problems and fates—a mystical system.

Of the many cords there are in the warren, the last was discov-ered pre-existing in the system but unrecognized by the gossips. It is called Whisper cord, and it was discovered by the last saint known to have existed, Olive Greyhair. Olive came to Little Belaire after the dissolution of the Long League, and the people of her Whisper cord, unlike the people of other cords, seem to aim to become not transparent but opaque. To Whisper cord, and to them alone, Olive bequeathed, not stories, but secrets: secrets which the Long League had gathered and suppressed in its years of control.

Rush encounters these secrets in the girl Once a Day, who is Whisper cord; and is it because of her that he falls in love with se-crets, or because of her secrets that he falls in love with her? In her, and in the hints she lets fall, are the first intimations of the great, the terrible knowledge he will become enmeshed in: hints of the four dead men, and a system of dark and light that Rush doesn't understand, and a kind of immortality the angels—we, today, tech-nological man—invented, and which the Long League discovered and preserved.

Throughout his story, Once a Day will be at once Rush's guide toward the central secrets, and a guardian of them against him. His struggle to understand will take the form of a struggle with her, a struggle to make her yield up her secrets, and her inability to do so, because they are ultimately inexpressible. For a time Rush, baffled, will go away from her, and learn other things; then he will return, and she will draw away from him into greater mysteries, and he will pursue. This zigzag is the forward motion of the book; and only when Rush overthrows his own best wisdom in attempting to give in utterly to Once a Day's mysteries does he begin at last to learn her secrets. By then he has lost her forever.

To describe how this Dante and this Beatrice step by step make their strange progress, and what Rush learns, would (and will) take a book; but to state it baldly—which no one in this story is capable of doing—the story is this:

At the time of the Going-off, scientists in a city near Belaire were working on a means whereby the structure of the brain—that is, the mind—could be in a sense photographed, or holographed: not the physical structure of neurons and synapses, but the *form* in some sense of their interconnections which make up the mind. They did this using the opaque/transparent material or energy-form I mention often in the book in other connections. Scientists made four of these mind-prints—after some initial experimenting—and these four have become, in Whisper cord's mythology, the four dead men. One of them was an uncle of a Truthful Speaker, and his name was Daniel Plunkett: Uncle Plunkett.

What the League learned about these holographs or mind prints is that while they are dead artifacts in themselves, they can be superimposed on a living brain, replacing the living brain's connections and synaptic pathways with its own; and for as long as the superimposition lasts, the mind is the mind of the holograph and not that of the brain's owner. When the holograph is withdrawn, the brain is for a terrible second empty: and then, like a long explosion, the brain's mind returns to itself: a terrible and fiercely illuminating rush of rebirth and self-knowledge.

The League supposed that all four of these human mind-prints were lost or destroyed in the Going-off. But Rush will discover that one survived: Daniel Plunkett. He has survived in the City in the Sky.

What the League did learn—a knowledge which is one of Whisper cord's secrets and which is preserved in the strange society of Dr. Boot's List, the League's direct descendant—is that one of the early experiments survived and is operable: not a man, however, but a cat. A cat named Boots. Boots functions in the same way as the human holographs: during the time it is superimposed on a human brain, the human is not—mentally—a man but a cat. When it is withdrawn, the same illumination occurs: the mind explodes again within the emptied brain, showing the man to himself. And—just as important—he remembers in some way not speakable what it was to have been a cat.

This experience of becoming Boots is the focus of the society of Dr. Boots' List: and Rush is allowed the experience—a vital step in his bizarre sainthood (or martyrdom?)—precisely because he tries to give up his quest for knowledge altogether.

Having left Little Belaire and Once a Day to spend a year with someone he thinks of as a saint, but whom we would call a scholar (this is the chapter I have appended), and having returned to Little Belaire and become fully a Truthful Speaker, Rush, still questing, follows Once a Day, who has gone to live with Dr. Boots' List in an ancient and enormous shopping-center, fabulous as a fairy-tale palace. There, unable to penetrate their strange, Zen-like system of paradoxes called dark and light, and seeing Once a Day slipping away from him into these mysteries, he attempts to give up for her sake his quest for understanding; to submit to mysteries he can never understand. "I don't want to be me any more," he says to the leader of the List: "Being me doesn't help. I want to be *her.* I give up the rest . . . " And he asks for his "letter" from Dr. Boots.

The experience with Boots, though, doesn't gain him what he wants; Once a Day, sensing that he has undergone it solely for her sake and not for the inner reasons it requires, has left the List, and left Rush, leaving a command behind her that he not follow her. So Rush is condemned to a year of wandering, trying to sort out his experiences.

What he hasn't understood is that the List, following the League's old instructions to forget progress, forget curiosity, forget striving and making, has developed a system of forgetting past and future altogether as an illusion, and living completely in the Now. They are attempting to reverse their human consciousness and become conscious only of each moment as it passes: to become like a cat. Of course it can't be done completely; it's a trick—as Zen is a trick—that you try not to let yourself know you're playing on yourself: which is why it's impossible to explain. The List even calls their gnomic explanations of it jokes: one man says to Rush, "You tie a string around your finger in order to remember something; that works until you forget there's a string tied around your finger. That's what Boots does—helps you forget the string tied around your finger"—that is, your interfering, anxious human consciousness. In other words, while Rush's whole being is aimed toward becoming transparent, the List and Once a Day are attempting to become opaque. Now Rush is left alone, neither one thing nor the other, confused and desperate.

Now, throughout this story, Rush has been telling it all *to* someone. (Naturally: that's what saints do.) This someone—a girl—only sits and listens, speaking occasionally, making a comment or asking a question; sometimes she illuminates Rush on some point, and in fact we have the growing sense that she knows his story better than he does. The interview seems to be taking place somewhere above the earth, in a huge, floating, glass-enclosed place.

There has also been talk, throughout the story, of a City in the Sky, a floating city the angels made to escape the wreck of their civilization, and which floats serenely above it all now, perfect and functioning, never to touch earth again. To some, it is a myth; to others a metaphor or a parable. Rush has always been fascinated by the possibility of its existence.

Now, in his desperate year of self-examination and self-over-throw, Rush takes up with an old scavenger, a finder and user of ancient things, a kind of devotee of angel lore. Through him, Rush finds a whistling ball and glove—a silver glove that will cause a thrown ball, made of the same material and emitting a faint whistle, always to return to it. It is an artifact which Rush's grandmother told him about in his childhood. This silver ball and glove, which Rush and the scavenger are bringing together for the first time in centuries, act when brought together as a signal to the City in the Sky. For a long time the inhabitants of the City have been searching for this ball and glove, awaiting its signal; and now Rush, all unknowing, struggling with Dr. Boots and all that has happened to him, is drawn toward his destiny.

Having at last come to a kind of self-understanding, Rush returns to Little Belaire, bringing the ball and glove with him. As he stands on the hill looking down into the woods that hides Belaire, someone floats down out of the sky to him on a parachute, with a strange machine strapped to his back.

The man is Mongolfier, and he is from the City in the Sky. The machine he carries is Daniel Plunkett.

After struggling to understand what this personage wants from him, and with help from his interlocutor—who, as I have said, seems to know Rush's story better than he does himself—Rush learns that Mongolfier has returned to earth to replace Plunkett with another mind: Rush's. The ball and glove are parts of the machine necessary to make this change. Why does he want to replace Plunkett? I have said that to change your mind for another's and then to return is an intensely illuminating experience; it has in fact become the chief psycho-religious experience in the City in the Sky. But Plunkett, caught as he was in the most terrible tragedy the civilized world has experienced, a tragedy caused in part by the technocrats who created the City in the Sky and whose descendants still live there, makes for a very fierce and melancholy religion; where Boots altered consciousness in the direction of serenity and integration with the Now, Plunkett is an object-lesson in all that can go wrong in human thinking, a lesson undeniably true, but awful almost beyond bearing. Therefore, having received the signal of the ball and glove, Mongolfier has descended to the earth to be the John the Baptist of a new religion. That religion will be Rush. Mongolfier wants to return to the sky with the holograph of Rush's mind.

In other words, Rush realizes, his tale will survive him: he will be a saint.

And so he agrees. Reluctantly: for no matter how much Mongolfier tells him that what he will take from Rush will be no more "him" than a fingerprint, still Rush has been Boots; and he knows that in some sense Boots was there: forever. And so will he be: forever. A dead man. But he agrees.

And so it is that Rush's tale comes to be told in the City in the Sky. However—and the reader should at this point just be coming to realize this—*it isn't Rush at all that's telling it.* It is an angel, a dweller in the City in the Sky, who has taken Rush on himself. This person is the hidden and nameless main character of the story. Rush is a figment, an artifact. From one or two things the girl, his interlocutor or examiner, tells him, I think he is her lover: so that in the end my story teller is united with his beloved, though Rush probably never was.

(In another sense, of course, that angel—that creature of technology, that dweller in the sphere of machines—who has taken Rush on himself, who for the length of the story has not been himself but Rush, that angel is, dear reader, you yourself; and the living tale, the endlessly repeatable alive-but-nonexistent Rush—that is the book you have just read. The plot, multi-faceted as it is, will be clear to most readers; those readers who perceive this additional level get a gold star.)

Rush—who has known all along, of course, that he isn't in fact here in the city telling this—is dimly aware that this isn't the first time his story has been told here. And though she shouldn't, the girl tells him: no, it's not the first time. In a thousand years since Mongolfier found him, he has told his story almost two thousand times. More than he could ever have imagined, he has become transparent; centuries after his own death, with the warren possibly long in ruins below him, his tale goes on. Appalled, he begs the girl to tell him what became of him. She doesn't know; all they know is what Rush knows: "It is all you here now, Rush." Only his tale has survived, to teach the City what it is to live on earth. And now that tale is told. We won't witness—can only imagine, from what Rush felt about returning to himself from Boots—what the angel who has been Rush will feel on returning to himself.

Harry Ransom Humanities Research Center
The University of Texas at Austin

[My thanks to Cathy Henderson, Tara Wenger, and the rest of the staff at the Harry Ransom Humanities Research Center, The University of Texas at Austin, for their assistance.]

NOTES
[1] Box 12, Folder 3, John Crowley Papers, Harry Ransom Humanities Research Center, The University of Texas at Austin.

LEARNING TO LIVE WITH IT:
THE FIRST *ENGINE SUMMER*
Adam Stephanides

ALTHOUGH *ENGINE SUMMER* was Crowley's third novel to be published, it is his "first major book," a huge advance over his first two books.[1] It was therefore intriguing, to say the least, when Crowley disclosed that it was actually the first novel he completed—more precisely, the first novel he completed, in 1969, was an early version of *Engine Summer* entitled "Learning to Live with It" (henceforth referred to as "Learning"). The paucity of information Crowley provided on "Learning" only whetted the appetite for more.[2]

John Crowley's papers are at the University of Texas at Austin; and contained in these papers is a nearly complete typescript of "Learning" (though not in order), as well as handwritten notes and draft passages, many of which did not make it into the typescript. While these materials do not contain solutions to the enigmas of *Engine Summer* (they do help explain where some of these enigmas came from), they are fascinating reading, both in their own right and for what they say about the evolution of *Engine Summer.* Not the least of their fascinations is how "Learning" turns out to be very similar to *Engine Summer,* while in some ways substantially different.

Crowley's remarks on "Learning" gave the impression that the book was a drug-addled, unpublishable "mess."[3] This is far from the case. "Learning" has the same structure as *Engine Summer*; it has basically the same plot, with one crucial exception; and Rush that Speaks, the protagonist, has the same adventures. The framing situation, too, is the same, with Rush's recorded personality telling his story, through a temporary host, to an "angel." In my opinion, "Learning" would have been quite publishable, with minor revisions. Moreover, some of the scenes in "Learning" that were cut in producing the published *Engine Summer* (or at earlier stages) are very well written. Nevertheless, the experience of reading "Learning" is considerably different from that of reading *Engine Summer*. *Engine Summer* is a more focused, but also a narrower, book than its precursor.[4]

Before describing the differences between "Learning" and *Engine Summer*, I should list the similarities. As I said above, the plot and framing situations are essentially the same. Rush, too, is more or less the same character in the two versions, as are most of the people he encounters. Little Belaire is essentially the same in "Learning" as in *Engine Summer*, with its warren, mbabas, gossips, cords, Filing System, truthful speaking, saints, and St. Bea's Bread; and the same is true of the List, with its Service City, "pharmaceutical industry," Letter from St. Boots (as she is known in "Learning"), and "dark and light." The back-story of "Learning" is more or less the same as in *Engine Summer*. In both, the technological wonders of the "angels" eventually lead to the collapse of their society, and the world is remade by the Long League of Women, whose prophet is the transsexual Mother Tom, and which itself eventually dissolves (or transmogrifies) into the List; and in both, we are told of the truthful speakers' exodus from Big Belaire to Little Belaire, and of the League's hostility to the truthful speakers. The current state of the world is the same in both: widely scattered settlements picking over the ruins of the angels' civilization; a few "avvengers" living in the countryside; and, floating in the clouds, the last city of the angels. And in both, the spheres that record personalities play the same role, with the List using theirs to become Boots, and the angels' city using theirs to become first Plunkett and then Rush. With all these similarities, there would hardly seem to be room for any differences between the two versions. And yet these differences are substantial.

Rush's Two Loves

The major difference between the plots of "Learning" and *Engine Summer* concerns Once a Day, the girl whom Rush loves and follows from their native Little Belaire to the mysterious Dr. Boots's List. In *Engine Summer*, Once a Day is so transformed by having repeatedly received the Letter from Dr. Boots that when Rush finally meets her again, she is virtually a different character. In "Learning," this is literally true: Once a Day, whom Rush loves in Little Belaire, and the girl whom Rush follows to the List are two separate characters. The Once a Day of *Engine Summer* is a composite of these two characters.

In "Learning," Once a Day never leaves Little Belaire to join the List. Instead, after Painted Red tells the story of Olive's arrival at Little Belaire (greatly condensed in *Engine Summer*), Once a Day challenges Painted Red, saying that Olive's announcement that the League is dead isn't the end of the story. When she is seemingly at the point of telling her "secrets," though, she runs off. Though Painted Red advises Rush to "Leave her her secrets," he follows her. When he catches up with her, she tells him they have to break up: "we never should have started . . . there are too many things that can never be resolved and it's just too hard to try to go around them always."[5]

Having lost his love, Rush leaves Little Belaire to be a saint, and spends a winter with Blink, as in *Engine Summer*. Unlike *Engine Summer*, Rush then returns to Little Belaire. At this point (when Rush is eighteen, and not nine as in *Engine Summer*), the traders from the List arrive. In "Learning," Once a Day is not present at this scene; instead, Rush catches his first sight of the girl from the

List he falls in love with. He then leaves Little Belaire again, and encounters the travelers from the List, as in *Engine Summer*. From here his relationship with the girl, whose name is A'azheuras[6], follows pretty much the same course as his resumed relationship with Once a Day in *Engine Summer*: they meet by the pool; they are together for about a year; Rush fails to dissuade her from receiving the Letter; in desperation he asks to receive the Letter himself and is permitted to; and she leaves the List and refuses to return until he has left.

Of course, the fact that Once a Day and A'azheuras are separate characters makes a huge difference in how we read Rush's relationship with them. In *Engine Summer* there is the sense that Once a Day's initial flight from Little Belaire was in part a flight from Rush, and that Rush's own departure is a pursuit of her. This is absent from "Learning"; as a result, Rush comes across as less obsessed. And while A'azheuras is characterized similarly to Once a Day when at the List, the fact that she doesn't display the radical personality change that Once a Day does in *Engine Summer* makes her seem less uncanny, and the List seem less sinister.

On matters of detail, too, at times the same incident occurs in both "Learning" and *Engine Summer*, but the merger of Once a Day and A'azheuras gives it an enigmatic character in *Engine Summer* that it lacks in "Learning." The scene where Rush finds Once a Day by the pool begins the same way in "Learning" as it does in *Engine Summer*, with A'azheuras showing no recognition of Rush and reacting with hostility and flight. But since Rush really is a stranger to her, there is nothing bizarre about her behavior, as there is about Once a Day's identical behavior in *Engine Summer*.

Similarly, in *Engine Summer*, Rush, trying to understand the barometer, asks Once a Day at the List why, if the "house on the wall" was about the weather, the figures did not move when a cloud passed over the sun. In response, Once a Day asks mysteriously, "'Then was it about the weather?'"—mysteriously, since she herself had told Rush, in Little Belaire, that the figures moved when the weather changed.[7] In "Learning to Live with It," the same scene occurs and A'azheuras makes the same response to Rush's inquiry; but here there is nothing mysterious about her response, since she has never seen the barometer and knows of it only from Rush.[8]

Rush, A'azheuras and Sex

I said above that Rush's relationship with A'azheuras in "Learning" follows the same course as his relationship with Once a Day at the List in *Engine Summer*. This is true as far as the events go; but the texture of the relationships is different. In *Engine Summer* we don't see Rush and Once a Day do very much at the List aside from hold enigmatic conversations. While these conversations are there in "Learning" (except for the ones which refer to her having come from Little Belaire, of course), the picture of Rush's relationship with A'azheuras is fuller. This is particularly true as regards sex.

For a book originally written in the late Sixties, and set mainly in two societies modeled upon hippie communes,[9] *Engine Summer* is curiously sexless. A few scattered sentences imply, if one is alert, that Rush's relationship with Once a Day is sexual; but, apart from Rush's reference to his futile masturbation, the book is G-rated as far as sex is concerned.[10] Not so "Learning." There, Rush's relationships with both Once a Day and A'azheuras are explicitly sexual. Moreover, Crowley wrote sex scenes involving both girls. The scene with Once a Day, in which, after she shows Rush St. Roy's leg, they masturbate themselves and each other at Once a Day's instigation, apparently did not make it to the typescript version (though some pages are missing from the typescript around this point); but the sex scenes with A'azheuras did.[11]

The first of these comes when Rush finds A'azheuras by the pool. Although the scenes in "Learning" and *Engine Summer* proceed similarly up to the point where Once a Day flees, the two versions diverge thereafter. In "Learning," Rush runs after A'azheuras, and catches up with her in a cave. They pet a bit, and she seemingly invites him to have sex with her, but then runs away again. After a while he finds her again and they do have sex.[12]

The other sex scene follows shortly afterwards, after Rush has been accepted by the List. It is preceded by a lyrical passage in which Rush describes his love for A'azheuras:

> And in all this mostly there was she. In the night near me, in the morning dim and cool with her cup, beside me all day, carrying too and the weight on her back making her breasts stand out; quick and bright, walking and watching—oh, there's no way to say it, there never is; it wasn't her, it was the world, become all rich and thick with my knowledge of her . . . I longed to be alone with her to say See, that day has come we waited for; and she could only nod, and we would be in that day whose night was never. I would walk with these strangers and smile at their odd talk, carry for them and never go home: because I was home, with her, wherever. I have felt that twice: once was with Once a Day. Now it was again. It won't be, I don't think, anymore. That's okay too.[13]

There follow four paragraphs, describing one of the times they make love. The scene ends:

> I started to laugh . . . and she laughed the same, as though we had done something to be really proud of.
> I guess we had.[14]

Nor is Rush's sex play quite confined to Once a Day and A'azheuras. At the end of the chapter in which Rush meets the twin boys Blooming and Budding, where *Engine Summer* says only that "with true Leaf cord politeness, they [Blooming and Budding] let me choose where I would sleep,"[15] "Learning to Live with It" has "with that strange Leaf cord politeness, they let me, their guest, be in the middle for their last game, but then let me be on the outside to sleep, away from the wet spots."[16]

The Dear Diary and Marilyn Monroe

Not only is sex described in "Learning to Live with It," it is a major theme of the book, and points to an important contrast between Little Belaire and the List. It receives its significance largely from two texts surviving from "ancient times" that play important roles in "Learning" but were completely eliminated from *Engine Summer.*

Virtually the only specific detail about "Learning" in Crowley's interview was the tantalizing tidbit that it included "Marilyn Monroe's lost diary." But there is no trace of Marilyn Monroe's diary in the "Learning" materials at Austin, nor any hint that one ever existed; and Crowley has confirmed that he was mistaken.[17] There is, however, an ancient diary which plays a significant role; and Marilyn Monroe's dying thoughts also play a crucial role. Both of these, as it turns out, are largely about sex.

The diary—the "Dear Diary," as Rush calls it, after the salutation of each entry—was written by a man who was fourteen at the time of the collapse of the angel's world, and who lost track of his lover during the collapse; after searching for her for a long time, he decided to write down their year together in the diary. It appears that the diary is mainly about sex: as Rush tells A'azheuras, "They had no one, being so young, to tell them all the things two people can do together, so they just found it out for themselves, and really thought of just about everything anybody else has been able to think of. Even one he couldn't write down. I asked my friend Seven Hands about that, and he said nobody knows whether he could fuck so well or not tell it so well."[18] (Rush in "Learning" uses the f-word matter-of-factly.) In Little Belaire, the Dear Diary has an almost scriptural status. Not only do "we still know the Dear Diary, some of us, all the way through by heart," but the lovers are painted on the dome of Rush's Mbaba's room: Rush describes it as "two people fucking painted on two sides of a pointed dome."[19] Rush himself recites the first four entries of the diary to the angel (these entries do not have any sex in them) and cites it in other places; and one of the three questions he asks Mongolfier is what happened to the girl in the Dear Diary. (There is no reason Mongolfier should know this, of course, but coincidentally he does, because the girl had boarded the City in the Sky before it took off.)

The Dear Diary represents sex as joyful communion between man and woman; its opposite is Marilyn Monroe's dying thoughts, which present sex as the objectification of women by men. In "Learning," Mother Tom, who often hears the voice of Janice (the girl whose genitals were transplanted onto and into Mother Tom) after having sex, one time after "her man had rolled off and lay asleep" has a vision of herself as Marilyn Monroe dying, and hears Marilyn Monroe's voice speak her dying thoughts. "And when she woke up she was All Woman."[20] Mother Tom transmits these words to the Long League of Women. In a handwritten fragment, they served to stiffen the women's resolve when they were pleading with male officials.[21] Now they seem to have a devastating impact when a woman speaks them to a man. When the words are brought to Little Belaire after the League's last meeting, they are "a new power."[22] Talking of Whisper cord's esoteric knowledge, Once a Day tells Rush:

> "There are powerful things."
>
> . . .
>
> "What's so powerful?" [Rush asks]
> "I can't say. It would hurt you too much."[23]

The only thing Once a Day can be referring to here is the words. And in a handwritten fragment not included in the typescript, Rush speaks of "Laugh Aloud's saying [to Blink, here called Thumb] those words that blighted him," referring to the words.[24]

Rush himself finds the words too traumatic to speak. Each time he comes to a point in his story when they are spoken, he withholds them from the listening angel (and us).[25] Finally, when his story is nearly over, the angel asks him to say them, and he refuses again, saying "Those are women's words." The angel replies, "*For*

the story's sake, then, I'll tell them. After all they're mine too."
And we finally read Marilyn Monroe's dying thoughts, which are:
"Even when you get to be Marilyn Monroe, and so the ones who
get to fuck you get to fuck Marilyn Monroe, it still doesn't make
any difference." [26]

The opposition between the Dear Diary and Marilyn Monroe's
dying thoughts is also an opposition between Little Belaire and the
List. Though the words are known to the women of Little Belaire,
Rush says that they "have never been spoken there, that I know
of" [27]; but at the List, they are spoken to Rush himself, as will be
described below. Conversely, while A'azheuras is a willing sexual
partner, the celebration of sexuality manifest in Little Belaire's
reverence for the Dear Diary is absent from the List. Another handwritten fragment not included in the typescript makes this contrast
explicit. A woman who had loved a man from Little Belaire and left
the List tells Rush:

> "There is no power left on earth any longer strong as
> love. The League [which is the ancestor of the List], . . . ,
> they all knew that, and that love could, only love could,
> destroy the League, as the League destroyed the Angels.
>
> "And he loved me. Not the way the List loves who are
> careful and circumspect as St. Boots teaches them, and
> know, oh, a thousand tricks to play to tease the men out
> of invasion into . . . into what there we call love; a gentle
> thing despite its flaring heats and rages, common and
> familiar with all its glooms and fallings-out." [28]

These themes—sex, the contrasting attitudes of Little Belaire
and the List towards sex, and Marilyn Monroe's dying thoughts—
culminate in the crucial scene in which Rush fails to dissuade
A'azheuras from receiving her Letter. This scene serves the same
function in "Learning" as it does in *Engine Summer*, driving Rush
to ask to receive the Letter himself, which leads to A'azheuras's
rejection of him, his leaving the List, and ultimately his finding the

ball and glove. But the scene itself is completely different in "Learning."

In "Learning" Rush does not plead with a determined Once a Day to come away with him; in fact, he does not plead at all. Instead, A'azheuras, about to get the Letter, is slightly apprehensive, and her glance and posture seem to invite Rush to make love to her. He approaches her, but for a reason he is unable to explain, he stops short: "May's thunder went away, and it was silent where I was, and to move to her seemed more fearful than the first time I walked into way-wall—far more, that fear . . . I stopped." Frozen to the spot, he finally speaks, "and said like, I'm afraid; only ask me; only say—You, only say . . . " A'azheuras then speaks Marilyn Monroe's words:

> But not even to me, really, almost by the way, to save her light I think now. To no one in particular. It freed me, in a way: broke what I seemed bound in. It was its power. Probably, yes probably, I had asked her to say it, to spoil it, to free me. I could get up, then, and walk away; in fact it was all I could do.

Rush concludes his account of this scene with the words: "The last riddle was about bodies, you see, and I hadn't solved it." [29]

This scene is not easy to interpret: it is not apparent why Rush was unable to go to A'azheuras, or what he means by his final statement. What is clear is that, in choosing to receive her Letter, A'azheuras is decisively choosing the anti-sexual vision of Marilyn Monroe's words over the sexual communion of the Dear Diary, which Rush has brought her in the past but is unable, for whatever reason, to offer her at the crucial moment.

The World

While the overall background of "Learning" is the same as that of *Engine Summer*, certain themes are explicit in "Learning" which are only implicit, or absent, in *Engine Summer*. One of these is the theme of pollution, and of the angels' abuse of nature. About the angels' "monstrous race between destruction and perfection," where in *Engine Summer* Rush talks about how television turned out to be poisonous, in "Learning" he says "our air grew dark and brown from the angels' waste and the rivers grey with poison till men recoiled from all things and refused to go about."[30] Later Rush tells the angel about "blights," which are places permanently polluted or devastated by the angels: an entire sea has been blighted.[31] The "ancient war of man with the world,"(141) which in *Engine Summer* seems to refer to men's efforts to keep their settlements and works from being overwhelmed by nature, in "Learning" refers to the angels' destruction of nature.

Michael Andre-Driussi has argued that in *Engine Summer*, the population of Little Belaire is decreasing, and Crowley has confirmed that this is the case.[32] But in "Learning" there is no need for argument or asking the author; it is explicitly stated that the population both of Little Belaire and of the surrounding area is decreasing. At the end of Rush's winter with Blink, Blink tells him that by "adding up . . . silly facts and little bits" he has discovered a "secret": that the world is going through a second "tragedy," comparable to the collapse of the angels' world.

> "When my fathers [sic] were young [Blink says] there were towns to the south of Little Belaire. Travellers came. And Little Belaire. It grew, for a while after it was built . . . But that was long ago. Now: it seems to close around itself, like a cat in the cold. It smallifies."

Hearing this, Rush thinks:

> "I knew . . . where we stood. Not on the ground, you know, but in time. Like the angel's clock: I saw then where the bar had come from and where it moved to, and how, though it seemed not to move at all, did, and at that was almost done. Almost come around full circle."[33]

The angel responds by acknowledging that the world "does . . . smal-
lify. It has been," but holding out the hope that "things that . . . keep
getting smaller, can keep getting smaller, almost forever." She uses a
variation of Zeno's paradox as an analogy, but concludes that it is
"only a hope . . . in the end it may be as Blink thought." [34]

Later, Rush meditates on the decline in population and man's
war against the world:

> All our men's things were stained and touched by the
> world and winter . . .
>
> It won't be like that always, I guess. Someday the
> world will be whole again, not seem to encroach upon
> men's things any longer, but otherwise: our things will
> be the last stain upon its wholeness. [35]

Fatherhood

The theme of fatherhood runs beneath the surface of "Learning."
The first indication of this theme is negative: Rush never refers to
Seven Hands as his father. He is "a man in my cord," and later
"my friend." In a variant opening, he is a man "who lived with my
mother." [36] In fact, though Blink (Thumb) refers to "my fathers,"
the social role of father does not appear to exist in Little Belaire. [37]
Nevertheless, we can surmise that Seven Hands is in fact Rush's father. In "Learning," as in *Engine Summer*, Rush has a "knot" with
Seven Hands at the start of the book, but this knot is not described,
and is not Seven Hands' projected trip; I conjecture that the knot
derives from the fact that Seven Hands' paternity of Rush is never
acknowledged.

When Rush visits Painted Red for the first time, it is to untie
his "knot" with Seven Hands, not because he is seven years old
as in *Engine Summer*. The drug Rush is given does not act as a
sort of truth serum, as it seems to in *Engine Summer*. Instead, it
causes Rush to dream that he is trying to go outside Little Belaire,
but though he follows the Path, it keeps turning back inwards. He
notices a room where there is "a young man I seemed to know but

couldn't quite see," who makes some not too friendly remarks; behind him is Rush's mother smoking, who ignores Rush. In the room there is a door leading outside, but Rush doesn't want to enter the room, go by the young man and disturb his mother. Eventually he does step into the room, and wakes up.[38] Painted Red tells Rush to tell Seven Hands his dream and see if he makes a suggestion; if he does, Rush should follow it. The suggestion Seven Hands makes is to go on an excursion with him.

Again, this dream seems to be about fatherhood. The young man Rush "couldn't quite see" represents not so much Rush's father as the role of fatherhood; and the fact that Rush can't get outside Little Belaire without entering the room and going by the young man indicates that Rush must become aware of the role of fatherhood before he can transcend the values of Little Belaire, and so psychologically "leave" it.

Fatherhood comes up once more in "Learning," again in a negative way. In *Engine Summer* Rush witnesses his mother refusing the "medicine's daughter" that will make her fertile for the year. In "Learning" this scene takes place at the List, and it is A'azheuras who declines to have a child with Rush that year, while Rush, it is implied, wants one.[39] A'azheuras's refusal to have a child with Rush, like his ultimate failure to hold her, indicates that he and A'azheuras have not fully attained the true partnership between a man and a woman which is found nowhere in "Learning" or *Engine Summer*, but which is suggested by the Dear Diary. The theme of fatherhood may also connect with an early note written by Crowley, stating that "Truly he has gone through a rite of passage, and emerges a young adult—the only one, really, in the book."[40]

Additions: Once a Day and the Frame-Tale
For the most part, the process of turning the typescript of "Learning to Live with It" into *Engine Summer* was one of cutting, but there were some significant additions too. Some have been mentioned: all the dialogue between Once a Day and Rush at the List

that refers to her having come from Little Belaire, for example. Of the other additions, some of the most significant involve Once a Day in Little Belaire. The scene in which Once a Day and Rush re-enact the story of Olive and St. Roy was added, as was Once a Day telling Rush the List are her cousins, and her leaving with the List. In the papers at Austin there are pages with cut-up pieces of copies of the "Learning" typescript glued to them, with these additions written on in pen.[41] I believe that the scene in which Rush first sees Once a Day playing whose-knee, and the scene in which Once a Day gives Rush Money, were also added, although I did not have time to definitively confirm this (and some of the pages from around this section of the book are missing from the typescript). Another significant addition written in pen is Rush's realization that Seven Hands will never leave Little Belaire.[42]

The other major set of additions involves the narrative frame in the angels' city. As I said at the start, the basic situation is the same. But all the exchanges between "Rush" and the listening angel that indicate that "Rush" feels, or is likely to feel, distress at his status are absent from "Learning"; as is the dialogue at the start of the fourth crystal in which "Rush" asks the angel why she records his story, and whether it has changed from telling to telling. And while Rush's host is the angel's lover in "Learning," the beautiful ending of *Engine Summer*, in which Rush asks to be "freed" and asks the angel to take care of his host when he returns to himself, is missing. Instead we have this flat ending (following the angel's statement "It is all you here now"):

> Why? You have xiled [sic] me here . . . Why? Why is it me, why my story? Why am I here?
>
> *I've answered that. You only ask because you are here. If you weren't, it wouldn't be your story; and you wouldn't ask.*
>
> *Now close your eyes.*[43]

How, precisely, Crowley conceived of "Rush"'s situation and emotions in *Engine Summer* is a difficult question. But whatever his conception, he developed it after writing "Learning."

The Doctor

The typescript I have been discussing is the only nearly complete version of "Learning." But the Crowley Papers at Austin also contain a large number of handwritten fragments, ranging from a single page to fifteen pages in length, with various scenes from "Learning," which sometimes contradict each other as well as the typescript. (There are a few typewritten fragments mixed in with the handwritten material that are also incompatible with the typescript, and presumably predate it.) Most of the material in these fragments which was not incorporated into "Learning" represents "roads not taken" which left no mark upon *Engine Summer*. There is a major exception to this, though: the fragments dealing with the doctor.

One of the strangest scenes in *Engine Summer* is Rush's departure, after taking the "confusion," from the giant head in which he is living, carrying an otherwise unidentified character he calls "the doctor," who turns out to be a hallucination. In *Engine Summer* "the doctor" seems to be Rush's hallucinatory vision of Dr. Boots, whom he does not yet consciously know is a cat. In the typescript of "Learning," the doctor is also a hallucination, although since in "Learning" Boots is St. Boots, it is harder to say where she comes from. But in the handwritten manuscripts of "Learning," the doctor is real. Much of the dialogue in *Engine Summer* between "Rush" and "I" after Rush has left the List comes from conversations between Rush and the doctor in these manuscripts, as do some of the more cryptic utterances in the hallucinatory game of whose-knees. And the doctor speaks more explicitly about A'azheuras and the List than does anyone, including Rush himself, in *Engine Summer*, although her statements still need interpretation.

In the handwritten manuscripts, the doctor appears after Rush leaves the List. Rush fetches the doctor for the cat Brom, who has followed him (as in *Engine Summer*), and is sick or injured. In *Engine Summer*, the hallucinatory doctor has cat's legs; but in the manuscripts the doctor really does have cat's legs. Where these come from is not stated, but in another passage Thumb (Blink) says that the List can grow or graft cat's legs on people.[44] Rush carries the doctor to where Brom is, and she works on him (unsuccessfully; Brom dies, and Teeplee helps Rush bury him); and while she works, she and Rush talk. There is no continuous text of the doctor's conversation(s) with Rush; instead, there are fragments on disconnected pages.

The doctor tells Rush about the List, her own life, and A'azheuras. She can speak with authority about the List, because she was a native of the List. She left it out of love for a man from the List, who would become the character known as Blink in *Engine Summer*, but is Thumb in these fragments. Eventually they broke up—apparently their different backgrounds proved impossible to reconcile—and, according to Zhinsinura, "neither of them healed." [45] It is the doctor who speaks the passage beginning "There is no power left on earth any longer strong as love," quoted above. She also says, of her relationship with Thumb: "that's what the list fears, what the League feared: to be fixed as a man can fix you in his mind. Thumb and I struggled the same way; and I won." [46]

But if Crowley ever wrote the full story of the doctor's relationship with Thumb, it is not in the papers at Austin. Primarily the doctor talks about the List. One passage in particular, while cryptic, states something never explicit in *Engine Summer* about the "dark and light" that so preoccupies Rush. Rush asks the doctor:

> "What is dark and light?"
> "Dark and light is a game. The object of the game is never to discover you're playing it."
> "Why?"
> "Why do you speak truthfully?"
> "Painted Red said: to live many lives in the moment

between birth and dying."

"How many lives has a cat?"

Nine, I was going to say, till I saw the path she was taking. "Many lives. Each is different, and no life remembers any of the others."

"And if a cat remembered, if it knew all its lives like beads strung on a string, then how many lives would it lead?"[47]

To fully understand this passage, we can look at the synopsis Crowley prepared for *Engine Summer* when it was to be called "Many Lives." While the synopsis would have been prepared several years after this passage was written, the idea behind the passage remains in the synopsis, and in the eventual *Engine Summer.* Crowley writes:

> the List . . . has developed a system of forgetting past and future altogether . . . and living completely in the Now. They are attempting to reverse their human consciousness and become conscious only of each moment as it passes: to become like a cat. Of course it can't be done completely; it's a trick—as Zen is a trick—that you try not to let yourself know you're playing on yourself[48]

Thus dark and light is a game "whose object is never to discover you're playing it."

This dialogue in "Learning" is the source for two passages in the hallucinatory game of whose-knees, which in *Engine Summer* are unexplained:

> "How many lives does a cat have?" she [Once a Day] asked.
> "Nine," said Painted Red.
> "Miss," said Houd (189)

And "'The object,' said Houd, "is to never discover you're playing it.'"(190)

Another of the doctor's statements is: "Her [A'azheuras's] only satisfaction can be in death. That is why we fear the dead men. Your only salvation is in eternal life: that is why you remember the saints. . . . The list, like the League before it, is in love with death, and so their lives are long and happy. The Truthful Speakers have been in love with life, and so their lives are searches, short and hard."[49] The List is "in love with death" either because, in constantly forgetting the past, they are in a sense "dying" again and again; or because it is only in death that they can fully forget their human consciousness. Why the Truthful Speakers' lives are described as "searches, short and hard" is less clear. It may have something to do with the fact that in "Learning" the search for a "new thing" is a widespread concern in Little Belaire, not just the province of eccentrics like Seven Hands, as in *Engine Summer*.[50]

This passage continues with dialogue between Rush and the doctor, from which the "dialogue" in *Engine Summer* between "Rush" and "I," just before Rush takes the "confusion," is drawn. In the manuscript this dialogue is less cryptic, though, since we have been given hints as to why A'azheuras wants to be "opaque."(187-188)

An enigmatic note of Crowley's indicates that the doctor was to have some symbolic significance:

> The doctor must be made more symbolic and weighted, so that the fact of her cats legs is not just a wierd [sic] aberration. It should be at that point that the only three people thing comes up [see below]; and of course there is a fourth, a cat. The doctor is all four. And perhaps in her can be resolved the strange generation gap that is in the book.[51]

But in the materials preserved at Austin, the doctor remains a mysterious figure, although her words help to solve other mysteries. And in the typescript of "Learning," as in *Engine Summer*, she was eliminated as a real character altogether, leaving only an even more mysterious hallucination.

Roads Not Taken

As mentioned above, most of the "Learning" materials that did not make it into the typescript left no visible trace in *Engine Summer.* Still, they make fascinating reading, showing alternative ways the book might have developed, and details Crowley imagined for his world but decided to omit.

Some of the fragments suggest a continuation of Rush's story beyond what the book or typescript supply. A note states: "He won't be going back to Belaire in the end; if the world is wide enough to contain The List and the Speakers, what else must it contain? Tomorrow to fresh fields and pastures new." This is followed by a passage of third-person narrative describing Mongolfier releasing "he who would be Great Saint Rush," ending with the final six words above.[52] In another fragment Rush mentions having seen the "blighted" sea.[53] And in a fragment of a (thankfully omitted) scene Painted Red, apparently on her deathbed, tells Rush that he is the "new thing" which they have awaited and which, as the Filing System has revealed to her, has finally arrived.[54]

Several fragments, taken together, sketch out part of a very different version of the encounter with Mongolfier. In this version it is Seven Hands, who here does go on his journey, who encounters Mongolfier and asks him the three questions (which are different here, and include the question about the girl in the Dear Diary). Mongolfier then asks Seven Hands to take him to Little Belaire, where he shows Uncle Plunkett to Seven Hands, Painted Red, and Rush, together in one room.[55] How this version would have resolved is not revealed in the manuscripts at Austin. There is also a cryptic fragment that fits into neither this version of the encounter nor the one in the typescript and *Engine Summer.* In it Mongolfier meets Rush and tells him:

> "We'll need the woman," he said. "And the cat."
> "The cat," I said, "is dead [Brom]. And the woman [the doctor] can't come."[56]

The early manuscripts also provide more detail about the framing situation. One discarded (typed) opening is headed "FIRST CRYSTAL, SERIES 1999" and begins with the words "I haven't been a guide before; the auditors must forgive me if I have marred this Series with . . . well, with the wrong questions, or any incompleteness. I know he can't be touched by anything I say, and yet . . . I'm afraid for him, that he can be hurt . . . "[57] And there are two versions of the ending which show the return to awareness of Rush's host, whose name would have been Zhominka or Jommika (John Michael? John McCall? Alas, Crowley's middle name is William, not Michael). In one of these endings, just before the angel releases Rush, she delivers this peroration: "Rush: in our exile we bless you for this; in our loneliness are comforted in you; in our hunger eat you; in our . . . oh, goodbye, my dear, myself; in our ignorance learn to live through you, in our flight are anchored in you, in our return are released though you are not . . . "[58]

In a cryptic fragment which is different from anything in the typescript or *Engine Summer*, Rush dreams he is, apparently, in the angels' city in the sky, listening to a voice lecture on the four men in the spheres and on the saints. In the dream, he remembers that the first saint was "Great Saint Rush . . . dead for a thousand years." Was this intended to have been the dream of the recorded Rush, who had somehow retained some of his hosts' memories? Did this idea leave a trace in *Engine Summer* in the angel's fleeting suggestion that "Rush" might dream in the sphere?[59]

Rush, who seems almost uncritically fascinated by the angels' world in *Engine Summer*, is somewhat more critical in the typescript (e.g. his description of blights, mentioned above). In the fragments, he is even more so. In one passage, after telling the angel that the women of the angels' world had "every thing they wanted," Rush goes on to say:

> if the Going Off had not come about, partly because of
> the League, every thing we wanted would have turned us

to poor haunted piles of nothing that the slightest puff would have blown away. The League it was that saved us from the Angels and the dead cold planet that was the only thing that would satisfy this angelic hunger.

. . .

. . . We were doomed: but now the last Angel is dead, and we learned to live with it. And we are free at last.[60]

And elsewhere Rush tells the angel that the despair of the angels' city after their discovery of Plunkett is due to their being "bound in glass, here, without the world, here, without the months, with nothing at all but each other[.]"[61]

We get further details about the angels' world. All their cities were surrounded with plastic bubbles and climate-controlled (something *Engine Summer* alludes to briefly), and "people the Angels feared and hated," like the Long League, lived outside the bubbles.[62] There is more detail on the bringing of St. Bea's Bread to earth, including fragments on the ship that brought it back.[63] And there is a fragment describing what happened when the angels realized that there was no reason but fun for them to go into space themselves, rather than sending machines. Some of the angels responded by exploring space with machines; while "those who wanted the fun . . . found places to go that cost nothing," "places your body does not move to." The second group were known as "Extended Rangers," and survived when the machines did not: "Some of those places they found have been thoroughly explored and charted, thanks to their explorations, places like that contained in the fourth of the four pots, and many others." Rush goes on to suggest that:

It may be that it was partly the Extended Rangers that led to the going off: they made one more reason that the machines couldn't do what was needed: because it was soon seen that what was necessary was what they called fun: exploration; and what they called necessary—gath-

141

ering in from the furthest reaches of space information
of the most outlandish kind—was really just fun. [64]

This is the only direct reflection of Sixties drug culture in the
"Learning" materials that was not carried over into *Engine Summer.*

Antagonism between women and men, of course, plays a major role in the "future history" of *Engine Summer*; and there is a hint (the sex-segregated audience for the retelling of the story of the League) that traces of this antagonism persist into the book's present. In the typescript of "Learning," the antagonism is clear, as the reiteration of Marilyn Monroe's words reveals. In the fragments, this antagonism is still more pointed, in both the past and the present. We are told that "In the ancient ancient days when black men were beginning to try to punish their oppressors, their hatred was so fierce that no man not their color—imagine—could be received among them . . . Many centuries later the Long League was the same"; and a League member wanting to know if other women were also members of the League or not "would say, if she thought she could, 'Women are niggers, of course;' and then wait with heart pounding to see if she had guessed right." [65] In the present of the manuscripts (that is, the time when Rush's story takes place), Rush witnesses a conversation between Thumb and Laugh Aloud (the gossip present at Rush's birth; in both the typescript and the manuscripts she has left Little Belaire and visits Thumb/Blink while Rush is there) in which Laugh Aloud says "Women are niggers." [66] And when the women of the List separate from the men to hear the story of the League, Rush remarks: "It's odd when you come from the warren to be separated as we were; such distinctions just aren't made. Of course we feel them in the warren, especially the men . . . " [67]

A couple of miscellaneous items are also of interest. In one type-written fragment Rush provides a different rationale for truthful speaking:

And that's the secret, you see? . . . in order for them to learn the phones, they had to know that they were the same: had to know that there was nothing to hide, to admit that there was nothing shameful, that to allow the truth of your speech to get around the tricks of your mind was to make everything easier, make in fact anything possible: love and good times. What everybody wants.[68]

One very strange idea found in Crowley's notes was that "The two children of the calendar are the two of the barometer. There is in the world only one boy and one girl and one old one: the girl was Once a Day and A [A'azheuras]; the old one Painted Red and Blink, Zhinsinura and Mongolfier"; and in the next paragraph Crowley adds that there is also a cat.[69] Crowley actually did employ this idea in a couple of fragments: in one, Hrzftsrh'aa [Houd in *Engine Summer*] tells Rush: "there are only three people in the world, and of the two that aren't you, one of them will give you pain because she isn't, the other because he's there. Just remember there's a cat—even an eternal one—there too, not shown."[70] But what, if anything, it meant to Crowley seems impossible to say. On the other hand, the memory of this idea may have influenced, consciously or not, his decision to merge Once a Day with A'azheuras in *Engine Summer.*

Conclusion

There are other differences between "Learning" and *Engine Summer* that I have not mentioned, mostly the elimination of details peripheral to the book's main themes. But what I have described is enough for an overall comparison of the two texts. Above all, *Engine Summer* is much more tightly focused upon Rush's quest for knowledge about the past, and in particular his desire to learn the "secrets" Once a Day possesses, than was "Learning," whether this was Crowley's motive in making the changes or not. The material cut from *Engine Summer* was peripheral to, or a distraction from, this theme.

Merging Once a Day and A'azheuras increases Rush's perceived obsession with Once a Day's secrets, since his following her to the List now seems motivated largely by this obsession; and it makes the plot tighter, as well (apparently Crowley's chief consideration[71]). Removing the sex scenes, Marilyn Monroe's dying thoughts, and the Dear Diary, and substituting a new scene for Rush's final scene with A'azheuras, eliminates sexuality as a theme competing with Rush's quest for secrets. The book gains in other ways from these cuts as well. By downplaying the sex in Rush's relationships, his interest in Once a Day appears more motivated by her secrets. Marilyn Monroe's dying thoughts, and their power, was a clumsy device; and Little Belaire's veneration of the Dear Diary's sexuality does not fit well with its otherwise laid-back vibes.

Other changes point in the same direction. The added scenes with Once a Day in Little Belaire add to our understanding of the origins of Rush's obsession. And transferring the scene of A'azheuras declining to have a child to Rush's mother eliminates the picture of Rush as prospective family man, which clashes with Rush as dedicated seeker of knowledge.

But these changes do involve some trade-offs. Compared to A'azheuras, the Once a Day Rush encounters in the List is an insubstantial character, whose sole purpose seems to be to tantalize him with enigmas and then retreat from him. The added scenes with Once a Day in Little Belaire are only partial compensation, especially since they are in much the same vein. Rush's character, in *Engine Summer*, shows some darker sides that were not present in "Learning," although most readers will overlook them in the smoothness and persuasiveness of his narrative voice. In his obsession, he is someone who won't take no for an answer from Once a Day. And his love for Once a Day itself seems abstract, motivated more by her secrets than by Once a Day herself.

Cutting the Dear Diary and Marilyn Monroe's dying thoughts are more obvious gains, but here too there are trade-offs. In *Engine Summer* as in "Learning," both the patriarchies of the angels' world and the avvengers, and the static matriarchies of Little Belaire and the List, embody wrong relationships between the sexes. But in "Learning" the Dear Diary at least suggests a better relationship. In *Engine Summer* this suggestion is missing.

And the elimination of Marilyn Monroe's thoughts has an unfortunate effect upon the reader's perception of Mother Tom. In "Learning," Mother Tom's primary role was to transmit Marilyn Monroe's words to the League. Her having received these words justified her role as the League's prophet. With Marilyn Monroe's words gone from *Engine Summer*, but with Mother Tom retaining her leadership role, Crowley gives the impression of saying that women, even feminists, need a man to tell them what to do.

What can "Learning" tell us about the meaning of *Engine Summer*, as opposed to its evolution? Directly, not much. It does not directly resolve any of the major enigmas of the book. And using an earlier draft of a work to interpret the final version is always problematic when one doesn't know why the changes were made. For instance, in "Learning" Blink tells Rush that the population of Little Belaire is declining, while in *Engine Summer* he doesn't; nor is this stated explicitly elsewhere in *Engine Summer*. But did Crowley omit it because he wanted to leave it implicit rather than explicit, in which case it would still be "true" (as he has since confirmed[72]); or did he omit it because he changed his mind about Little Belaire's population declining? The manuscripts cannot answer this question. Similarly, Rush's desire to learn Once a Day's secrets is more important in *Engine Summer* than it was in "Learning"; but knowing this does not tell us just how important it actually is in *Engine Summer*. Only *Engine Summer* itself can tell us this. These difficulties are particularly acute in the case of a book like *Engine Summer*, in which years separated the first version from the final version, during which Crowley's conception of the book changed in important ways.

Though "Learning" does not directly answer our questions about *Engine Summer*, it does tell us something surprising about the book: that Crowley's cut-and-paste (literally!) technique, which he alluded to the *Locus* interview, affected the composition of the tightly constructed *Engine Summer*.[73] We have seen how Crowley's cutting and pasting is partly responsible for the uncanniness of Once a Day at the List, as well as some of the book's more cryptic lines.

For those who believe that the author's intention determines the meaning of a text, this cut-and-paste technique is worrying. If an author writes a sentence or passage in one context, and later reuses it unchanged in a quite different context, can it be said to have a determinate meaning at all in this new context? However, in the case of *Engine Summer* we do not need to be too concerned with this question. Crowley, after all, did rework A'azheuras's scenes in transferring them to Once a Day. The fact that *Engine Summer* contains no clearly obtrusive sections (unlike "Great Work of Time") shows that Crowley's reworking was successful.

As I have said, the differences between "Learning" and *Engine Summer* are substantial. While there were some losses, the gains outweighed them, though in my opinion "Learning" is not as inferior as Crowley asserts. But the real surprise is how similar the books are. A decade before *Engine Summer* was published, Crowley had conceived the book's basic structure and ideas. And the typescript of "Learning" is already on a higher level of achievement than *The Deep* or *Beasts*. It was in this unpublished typescript, and the manuscript fragments that preceded it, that Crowley's genius first manifested itself.

Coda: The Sky Is Grass

"Learning" does solve one of *Engine Summer*'s enigmas, although as far as I know it's not an enigma anyone has noticed. Why is the "fourth crystal" entitled "The Sky Is Grass"? Of course, this refers to the List's July calendar tile, which shows grass at the top of the picture and the sky below; but how this relates to the fourth crystal is not at all clear.

It turns out that this is a joke of Crowley's. In "Learning," when the angel is describing life in the angel's city to Rush, he describes listening to the angel's music, *"forgotten centuries on earth. . . . louder than thunder"* and quotes from *"the ancient violence of the city's song: The sky is grass, it sings, the sea is brown, and everything is upside down."* [74] This is a slightly altered quotation from the lyrics of the song "Armenia City in the Sky," found on the Who's album *The Who Sell Out* (in the original, the sky is glass, not grass; whether Crowley misheard it or changed it deliberately I don't know). And the name of the angel's city in "Learning" is Arm'nia.

Appendix

After I had finished the first draft of this essay, I received an e-mail from John Crowley answering some questions I had asked him about the revisions that turned "Learning" into *Engine Summer.* His answers, while brief, are revealing of his philosophy of writing at the time of the revisions, and well worth reprinting. To be candid, I did not do a very good job of guessing what his motives were; and Crowley's recollected view of "Learning" is different from mine. For these reasons, and for more convenient reference, I am placing an abridgement of the questions and answers here.

AS: In LTLWI Once a Day, and the girl from the List whom Rush loves and follows to the List, are two separate characters. Why did you combine them into a single character?

JC: The short answer is mere novelistic neatness. The first version was essentially plotless; when I rewrote it I wanted it to be more accessible, more like other books (thus the structure of Crystals and Facets, which weren't in the original). Also, though, it seemed to make the two intertwined cultures of the story more interdependent as well: like the spot of black in the white side of the yin-yang symbol.

AS: In LTLWI Rush's relationships with both Once a Day and the girl from the List are explicitly sexual, and there are a couple of sex scenes. In ES the sex scenes are gone, and Rush's relationship with Once a Day is sexual only by implication. Why the change?

JC: Delicacy. It[75] seemed when I took up the old version after some years that I had been fantasizing a little too openly (and unconvincingly). Now readers who wish to fantasize, or imagine, can do so on their own.

AS: Why did you eliminate MM's dying thoughts and the Dear Diary from ES?

JC: The Dear Diary seemed unnecessary in establishing the collapsed world out of which the new society came; and I felt I had enough leftovers and artifacts charged with antique meaning, and one more might strain credulity. Marilyn Monroe . . . just too extravagant, I guess. Mother Tom had the connection with Janice; a connection with MM seemed too close to the telepathic or magical, and I wanted to avoid all that. (MM had to wait till *Dæmonomania* to return to my books.)

AS: In LTLWI Blink tells Rush his "secret" that the population of Little Belaire, and the surrounding region, is declining, and by implication that humanity is dying out. Why did you eliminate this?

JC: I don't believe I did. It was only left for the reader to gradually intuit. The general method in the rewrite was to make it more readable and like other stories, and to remove what seemed to me to be too specific (and therefore able to be rejected by the reader as unbelievable, unlikely, whatever.)

AS: In ES there is a scene in which Rush's mother refuses the concoction that will make her fertile for the year. In LTLWI this takes place at the List, and it is Rush's lover who declines to have a child with Rush. Why did you transfer this scene?

JC: I think that, as with so many of the changes between the two versions, I was trying to get the book to conform to common reader expectations. You noted that the mother is a vague figure without much to do, and the putative father's relations with her are also vague: I think I transferred this action to her in order first of all to give her more substance as a character and to account, perhaps, a little bit for the distance between her and Seven Hands. I also thought the subject was unlikely to come up between Rush and Once a Day.[76]

My thanks to John Crowley for his cooperation, and to Pat Fox, Cathy Henderson, Tara Wenger and the rest of the staff at the Harry Ransom Humanities Research Center, The University of Texas at Austin, for their assistance.

NOTES

[1] Alice K. Turner, "One Writer's Beginnings: John Crowley's *Engine Summer* as a portrait of the Artist," this collection, p. 60.

[2] John Crowley, "Great Work Takes Time," *Locus* (May 2001), 4-5.

[3] Ibid., p. 5.

[4] I should enter a caveat here. I spent only four days at Austin, and some of this time was spent looking at the rest of the Crowley Papers. So my examination of the manuscripts was necessarily abbreviated, and everything I say here should be regarded as provisional.

[5] Typescript, p. 75, Box 12, Folder 3, John Crowley Papers, Harry Ran-

som Humanities Research Center, The University of Texas at Austin.

[6] One of the less fortunate characteristics of "Learning to Live with It" is Crowley's fondness for apostrophes. Houd, the List's tobacco smoker, is in "Learning" called Hrzftsrh'aa; the phrase "medicine's daughters" is in "Learning" "med'cin's daughters" (and refers to something different); and That River is known as the G'ned'nit (typescript, p. 88, Box 12, Folder 4, John Crowley Papers).

[7] John Crowley, *Engine Summer* (New York: Bantam Books, 1980), pp. 38, 133.

[8] Typescript, p. 212, Box 12, Folder 4, John Crowley Papers.

[9] For Little Belaire and the List as modeled upon communes, see Alice K. Turner, personal communication.

[10] Crowley, *Engine Summer*, pp. 42, 132, 142, 186.

[11] Holograph manuscript, pp. 48-49, Box 12, Folder 1, John Crowley Papers.

[12] Typescript, pp. 178-181, Box 12, Folder 5, John Crowley Papers.

[13] Ibid., p. 185.

[14] Ibid., p. 188.

[15] Crowley, *Engine Summer*, p. 76.

[16] Typescript, p. 87, Box 12, Folder 4, Crowley Papers.

[17] "John Crowley," p. 5; John Crowley, personal communication.

[18] Typescript, pp. 189-90, Box 12, Folder 5, John Crowley Papers.

[19] Ibid., p. 190, John Crowley Papers.

[20] Typescript, pp. 238-39, Box 12, Folder 4, John Crowley Papers; typescript, p. 259, Box 12, Folder 5, John Crowley Papers.

[21] Handwritten manuscript, p. 60, Box 12, Folder 1, John Crowley Papers.

[22] Typescript, p. 69, Box 12, Folder 3, John Crowley Papers; typescript, p. 239, Box 12, Folder 4, John Crowley Papers.

[23] Typescript, p. 63, Box 12, Folder 5, John Crowley Papers.

[24] Handwritten manuscript, p. 59, Box 12, Folder 1, John Crowley Papers.

[25] Typescript, p. 239, Box 12, Folder 4, John Crowley Papers; typescript, p. 247, Box 12, Folder 6, John Crowley Papers.

[26] Typescript, pp. 258-59, Box 12, Folder 5, John Crowley Papers (underlined in original).

[27] Typescript, p. 239, Box 12, Folder 4, John Crowley Papers.

[28] Handwritten manuscript, p. 1, Box 11, Folder 7, John Crowley Papers. Note that the phrase "There's no force on earth left stronger than love" occurs in *Engine Summer* (188).

[29] Typescript, pp. 245-47, Box 12, Folder 6, John Crowley Papers (ellipsis Crowley's).

[30] Crowley, *Engine Summer*, p. 90; typescript, p. 111, Box 12, Folder 4, John Crowley Papers.

[31] Typescript, p. 266, Box 12, Folder 5, John Crowley Papers.

[32] Michael Andre-Driussi, personal communication; below, p. 148.

[33] Typescript, pp. 130-31, Box 12, Folder 4, John Crowley Papers.

[34] Typescript, pp. 131-32, Box 12, Folder 4, John Crowley Papers (underlined in original).

[35] Typescript, pp. 219-20, Box 12, Folder 4, John Crowley Papers.

[36] Typescript, p. 12, Box 12, Folder 5, John Crowley Papers; typescript, p. 189, Box 12, Folder 5, John Crowley Papers; typescript, p. 4, Box 12, Folder 6, John Crowley Papers.

[37] Typescript, p. 130, Box 12, Folder 4, John Crowley Papers.

[38] Typescript, pp. 23-24, Box 12, Folder 4, John Crowley Papers.

[39] Typescript, pp. 219-22, Box 12, Folder 4, John Crowley Papers.

[40] Handwritten notes, Box 11, Folder 6, John Crowley Papers.

[41] Typescript with handwritten additions, n. p., Box 12, Folder 3, John Crowley Papers.

[42] Ibid., p. 29.

[43] Typescript, pp. 302-3, Box 12, Folder 5, John Crowley Papers (underlined in original).

[44] Unfortunately, while I remember this, I did not write it down, and don't remember the location.

[45] Handwritten manuscript, p. 66, Box 11, Folder 7, John Crowley Papers.

[46] Handwritten manuscript, p. 2, Box 11, Folder 7, John Crowley Papers.

[47] Handwritten manuscript, n.p., Box 11, Folder 7, John Crowley Papers.

[48] John Crowley, "Many Lives (Synopsis of a proposed novel)," this col-

lection, p. 116.

[49] Handwritten manuscript, p. 4, Box 11, Folder 7, John Crowley Papers.

[50] In the typescript, Sewn Up tells Rush that when he was a young man, "there was something like a new thing at Little Belaire, and a lot of young men of that time went off, and went to look for a new way of seeing it all and doingit" [sic]. (p. 84, Box 12, Folder 4, John Crowley Papers) For the handwritten manuscripts, see below.

[51] Handwritten notes, Box 11, Folder 6, John Crowley Papers.

[52] Handwritten notes, Box 11, Folder 6, John Crowley Papers.

[53] Handwritten manuscript, p. 80, Box 11, Folder 7, John Crowley Papers.

[54] Handwritten manuscript, p. 16, Box 11, Folder 7, John Crowley Papers.

[55] Handwritten manuscripts, pp. 20-26, Box 11, Folder 7, John Crowley Papers; handwritten manuscript, n. p., Box 12, Folder 1, John Crowley Papers.

[56] Handwritten manuscript, n. p., Box 12, Folder 1, John Crowley Papers

[57] Typewritten manuscript, p. 1, Box 11, Folder 6, John Crowley Papers (underlined in original).

[58] Handwritten notes, Box 11, Folder 6, John Crowley Papers (ellipses Crowley's); handwritten manuscript, p. 27, Box 11, Folder 7, John Crowley Papers; "John Crowley," p. 4.

[59] Handwritten manuscript, pp. 5-7, Box 11, Folder 7, John Crowley Papers; Crowley, *Engine Summer*, p. 208. Another fragment continues this dream and talks about cats (handwritten manuscript, n. p., Box 12,

Folder 1, John Crowley Papers).

[60] Handwritten manuscript, pp. 60-61, Box 12, Folder 1, John Crowley Papers.

[61] Handwritten manuscript, n. p., Box 11, Folder 7, John Crowley Papers.

[62] Handwritten manuscript, n. p., Box 11, Folder 7, John Crowley Papers; Crowley, *Engine Summer*, p. 133.

[63] Handwritten manuscripts, n. p., Box 12, Folder 1, John Crowley Papers.

[64] Handwritten manuscripts, pp. 93-94, Box 12, Folder 1, John Crowley Papers

[65] Handwritten manuscript, p. 57, Box 11, Folder 7, John Crowley Papers.

[66] Handwritten manuscript, n. p., Box 12, Folder 1, John Crowley Papers.

[67] Handwritten manuscript, p. 55, Box 12, Folder 1, John Crowley Papers.

[68] Typewritten manuscript, n. p., Box 11, Folder 6, John Crowley Papers.

[69] Handwritten notes, Box 11, Folder 6, John Crowley Papers.

[70] Handwritten manuscript, n. p., Box 11, Folder 7, John Crowley Papers; see also handwritten manuscript, p. 24, Box 11, Folder 7, John Crowley Papers.

[71] Below, p. 147.

[72] Below, p. 148.

[73] "John Crowley," p. 67.

[74] Typescript, pp. 298-99, Box 12, Folder 5, John Crowley Papers.

[75] Emended from "There."

[76] John Crowley, personal communication.

LITTLE, BIG

BEST AND BIGGEST
Thomas M. Disch

LITTLE, BIG, BY John Crowley, is a novel about fairies, a novel in which trout can speak and a changeling is spirited off from her cradle by an old witch riding a stork (the stork talks too), a novel in which magic can make a person invisible or allow an ancient hero to wake from a sleep of 800 years.

It is also a novel in which four-fifths of the way through the book (which is 538 pages in length) the hero, Auberon Barnable, can ask his father, "Do you believe in fairies?" and that question is still valid and important not just for those two characters but also for readers who've been witnessing all those other extraordinary happenings. This is because it's also a book about ordinary people living completely typical lives—falling in love, getting married, having kids, growing up and growing old, failing, forgetting, and (last but never least) dying. Seen from this angle, all the stuff about fairies is moonshine, imagination, and metaphor.

It's an incredible tightrope act. Too much magic and the realistic side of the story would no longer register as home truth; too little and it would start to sound like soap opera or, worse, like Serious Literature. But Crowley strikes just the right balance, and the result is the best fantasy novel I've ever read. Period.

Best and biggest (which is part of its being best).

Biggest in conception. It spans the entire twentieth century (including the near future) and tells the stories of six generations of the Drinkwater family, including at least a dozen full-length portraits of characters so memorable and (there's no other word) lovable that by the end of the book I looked on them as my own cousins and in-laws. They are the Universal Family.

Biggest, as well, in the scope of the writing. Tolkien's characters cover a lot of territory but it's all like hiking through a national park or taking a hotel room in Disneyland. The difference between Middle Earth and the world of *Little, Big*—even at its most fantastic moments—is the difference between a cartoon and a movie. In the first 200 pages, Crowley creates a panorama of an ideal but very real New England that combines the best qualities of Hawthorne, Grandma Moses, and Andrew Wyeth. Then, having conjured up a world you'd want to live in forever, he switches the scene to a day-after-tomorrow New York just as memorable in the equal and opposite direction of grimness. Yet even Crowley's urban squalor has something magical about it. We're not in New York but in The Big Apple, a semi-mythical city poised on the brink of Apocalypse.

Biggest, finally, in the range and scale of the emotions it connects us to, in the wisdom it brings to bear on the Human Condition, capital H, capital C. In the story that opens his tale of Smoky Barnable's marriage to Alice Drinkwater, Crowley describes their loving but quite peaceful family life with so much verve and excitement that he could give lessons to Tolstoy. And then, a generation later, in the romance between Smoky's and Alice's son, Auberon, and Sylvie, the darling of the *barrio*, Crowley pulls out all the stops and writes about first love and first sex with such magic that if the book had only half as many readers as it deserves the birth rate would be noticeably affected. There's love and lust, and faith and doubt, and heart-wrenching loss and bitter failure, and one stretch of such raw grief that on first encountering it I cried more tears than any book or movie had wrung out of me before.

And all this in a novel about fairies? Those little people with gauzy wings that live inside flowers? Fairies we're never entirely sure are real? I know it sounds unlikely, but there is an explanation of sorts in the first half of the title: *Little, Big.*

It's easy to praise a book for the things that make it big—a sweeping story, characters larger than life, ideas that give the brain growing pains (all of which *Little, Big* has got)—but, as every writer knows, you can't make a Big Success out of a lot of Little failures, Books are written little by little, literally word by word, and so when a writer is praised for his Style something more important is at stake than good manners or high polish. Style is what makes the Big story happen, what heats it up and gives it color and—the final magic—makes it come alive. *Little, Big* works that magic on every page.

Crowley wrote three novels before this one—*The Deep, Beasts,* and *Engine Summer*—each better than the last. But none of them can boast the sweep and depth and power of *Little, Big.* It's fair, therefore, to call the book a masterpiece, since a book is a masterpiece in relation only to the author's earlier works.

"Classic" is another matter. It's readers who make a book a classic by reading it and getting their friends to read it, by treasuring it and making its wisdom part of their own. *Little, Big* deserves to be that kind of classic.

So read it.

ABOUT *LITTLE, BIG*
John Crowley

WRITERS DO NOT like to admit it—any more than parents like to admit they prefer one child over another, or believe one to be smartest or best looking—but most of them have a favorite among their works, and one they consider the best, as well: for after all one must be, and it may well not be the last one, or the next. *Little, Big* is the book in which I discovered the extent of my own powers as a writer; it's so far the one best liked by the majority of my readers, or at least regarded with the most affection. I will have to go far (in my own estimation) to do as well again.

I began thinking about this book (or rather a book which would eventually become this one) in the summer or fall of 1969 (it was completed in 1978). What I originally conceived was a sort of long family chronicle that, rather than beginning in the far past and arriving eventually in the present, would begin more or less in the present and continue on into the far future. Something of this original impulse remains in the book, but it is overshadowed by other concerns that actually came much later in the work of conceiving the book, the idea, for instance, of a fairy religion. Marianne Moore defined poems as "imaginary gardens with real toads in them"; I thought I would try to create an imaginary garden with real fairies at the bottom of it.

I came upon a Persian parable called *The Parliament of the Birds*, which supplied me with a plot remarkably—uncannily—suited to what I had already thought up.

Lastly, I had toyed for some time with the idea of writing a story, or a series of them, about a powerful mage who solves crimes or puzzles like a detective, puzzles which turn out to be cosmogonic or otherwise earthshaking: the reawakening of a sleeping emperor, for instance—something like that.

And so—not entirely by my choice—these various impulses collided and combined; and I tried to tie them together with the string and tape of fictional techniques I was trying out for the first time; and I saw that my book would finally turn neatly and poignantly in upon itself. All that remained was to write it down. Among the very first images I had had of my family was of a man packing his married life in a bag, and setting off on a final journey: and some eight years later I wrote down that scene, close (at last!) to the end of the book, the book you have.

[4/11/90]

LITTLE, BIG GIRL:
THE INFLUENCE OF THE ALICE BOOKS AND OTHER WORKS OF LEWIS CARROLL ON JOHN CROWLEY'S NOVEL *LITTLE, BIG OR, THE FAIRIES' PARLIAMENT*
William H. Ansley

Introduction

JOHN CROWLEY'S NOVEL *Little, Big or, The Fairies' Parliament* contains many references to the works of Lewis Carroll. No one with even a passing familiarity with Carroll's books could miss spotting at least some of them. The commentary on *Little, Big* that I have read mentions these Carroll references in passing, if at all, perhaps considering them merely playful or an embellishment and therefore unworthy of comment or discussion. Crowley has a playful side, no doubt, but the writings of Lewis Carroll have a serious role in *Little, Big*: they are an important influence on details of plot, character, and subject matter.

Carroll's best-known books are *Alice's Adventures in Wonderland* and *Through the Looking-Glass and What Alice Found There*; from now on I will refer to these individually as *Wonderland* and *Looking-Glass* and collectively as the Alice books. *Little, Big* also refers to Carroll's much less well-known work, *Sylvie and*

Bruno and *Sylvie and Bruno Concluded*. (Although published separately, Carroll considered these two books to be a single novel.)

References to the Alice books turn up in Crowley's earlier novel *Engine Summer*, too, but here I think that they really are an embellishment rather than integral. A comparison of the two books will demonstrate that Carroll's role is much larger in shaping *Little, Big*.

Little, Big: A Family Tale

Little, Big is the Tale of the Drinkwater family. That is, they have a special destiny that is being managed by fairies for reasons that aren't completely clear to the Drinkwater clan and may not be entirely clear to the fairies, either. Because of their role in the Tale, the Drinkwaters are Protected, but the fairies are manipulating the Tale to their own ends as well.

The Tale starts (at least the earliest part of it we see) in Victorian England. An American architect named John Drinkwater meets a girl named Violet Bramble and her father, Dr. Theodore Burne Bramble. Violet can see and talk to fairies. Her father cannot but has formed elaborate theories about the relation of the world the fairies inhabit to our own.[1]

He says the fairies' world is a "converse infundibulum," a series of concentric rings that gets larger and larger the farther you go into it. In the outermost circle, which human beings inhabit, the fairies are so small they cannot be seen. There are many "doorways" into the next ring, and if you pass through one into the next, the fairies will appear as tiny creatures a few inches high. The ring inside this one has a smaller perimeter, even though it is much larger inside, and has fewer, smaller doorways by which it can be entered. If you do enter it, the fairies appear as small beings about the size of children, the "Little People." The doorways into the next ring are even fewer and smaller; it is very hard to enter. Within this ring, the fairies appear to be the size of adult human beings. Doorways into the final, innermost ring are so few and so small that it is almost impossible to enter. This ring, the land of Faëry itself, is of infinite (or very, very large) extent and there the fairies appear as heroic figures, larger than human beings.

Dr. Bramble comes to America on a speaking tour and brings Violet with him. John Drinkwater marries Violet and she and her father remain in America. They all live in a peculiar five-sided house called Edgewood that Drinkwater builds especially for Violet, really five different houses somehow packed into the space of one.

Violet is pregnant with a child by another man when John Drinkwater marries her. (The other man is Oliver Hawksquill, father, also, of Ariel Hawksquill.) He adopts the boy, Auberon, as his son. They have three more children: Timothea Wilhelmina (Timmie Willie), Nora Angelica, and August.[2]

Timmie Willie marries Alexander Mouse, the son of Lionel Mouse, her father's partner in the architectural firm of Mouse, Drinkwater, Stone. Her grandson is George Mouse, who plays a considerable part in the present-day Tale. Nora marries Harvey Cloud. August, who makes a deal with the fairies to have power over women, fathers many illegitimate children, one of whom, John Storm Drinkwater, is raised at Edgewood. August later goes back on his deal, is transformed into a fish as punishment and becomes known as Grandfather Trout.

John Storm Drinkwater marries Sophie Dale. They have two daughters: Alice Dale (known as Daily Alice) and Sophie Dale (known as Sophie).

Daily Alice marries Evan S. Barnable[3] (known as Smoky). They have four children: Tacey, Lily,[4] Lucy,[5] and Auberon. Much of the book is devoted to chronicling their life together and the lives of their children, especially Auberon.

Auberon Barnable leaves Edgewood to seek his fortune in the City. There he meets, falls in love with, is loved by, lives with, and loses Sylvie.

Crowley and Carroll

In Crowley's foreword to the Quality Paperback Book Club edition[6] of *Little, Big*, he says:

> What I originally conceived was a sort of long family chronicle that rather than beginning in the far past and arriving eventually in the present, would begin more or less in the present and continue on into the far future. Something of this original impulse remains in the book, but it is overshadowed by other concerns that actually came much later in the work of conceiving the book, the idea, for instance, of a fairy religion.

The fairy religion, specifically, may have been inspired by remarks Lewis Carroll made in his introduction to *Sylvie and Bruno Concluded*, which I will describe in discussing that book and its preceding volume. Indeed, the whole idea of using fairies as one of the major plot engines of *Little, Big* may have come from Crowley's studies of Carroll.

Probably, Crowley read Lewis Carroll's Alice books first, as most people do. The only Carroll references in Crowley's earlier novel *Engine Summer* that I could find were Alice references. These are very cleverly woven into the book, but they could be removed without causing major changes and they seem to be a secondary addition rather than an underlying impetus for any parts of the plot, settings, or characters. Crowley no doubt then went on to read other works by Carroll, especially *Sylvie and Bruno* and *Sylvie and Bruno Concluded,* and to find out more about Carroll himself. There is ample evidence to support this conjecture in *Little, Big*, as well as the inference that Crowley discovered a great deal about fairies as he did so; fairies were very much "in the air" in Lewis Carroll's Victorian England. A major character in *Little, Big*, Auberon Drinkwater, the fairy seeker, is partially based on Lewis Carroll himself.

Alice in *Engine Summer*

I found only five references to the Alice books in *Engine Summer,* though in an earlier version entitled *Learning to Live with It* there were more.[7]

On the very first page of the published novel, a character says, "Begin at the beginning; go on till you reach the end. Then stop."[8] This is almost exactly what the King of Hearts says to the White Rabbit in the trial scene in *Wonderland.*[9]

A group of people in *Engine Summer* called the truthful speakers has a motto: "We really mean what we say and we say what we really mean."[10] Compare this to these lines from the Mad Tea Party in *Wonderland.*[11]

> "Then you should say what you mean," the March Hare went on.
>
> "I do," Alice hastily replied; "at least—at least I mean what I say—that's the same thing you know."

This passage in *Engine Summer*[12]

> We had a shade house we shared for summer, under two maples that grew together on a hill . . .
>
> "Sun's come around," someone said. "Everybody move one place."

echoes another line from the Mad Tea Party.[13]

> "I want a clean cup," interrupted the Hatter: "let's all move one place on."

The following passage refers to hares going mad in March, which might not, by itself, be a *Wonderland* reference, but it also quotes another line from the Mad Tea Party.[14]

> "When the moon is full in March," said Zher, "the hare goes crazy." His eyes grew wide and fierce. "He

stamps his feet." Zher's leg kicked the ground with a thump. "He balls his fists and can't *stand* it, can't *stand* it." He stared around him, his leg twitching to kick again. "When another comes, he shouts out, 'No room, no room!' even if there's plenty."

"No room! No room!" is what the Mad Hatter and the March Hare shout out to Alice as she approaches their tea table, which does indeed have plenty of room.[15]

Finally, towards the end of *Engine Summer*, a character says the following:[16]

> "You say 'gloves,'" he said. "I've seen gloves compared to which these are bare hands."

This remark has the same structure as the ones the Red Queen makes to Alice in *Looking-Glass*:[17]

> "When you say 'hill'", the Queen interrupted, "I could show you hills, in comparison with which you'd call that a valley."

Carroll's Life

The Reverend Charles Lutwidge Dodgson (1832–1898) was a lecturer in mathematics and clergyman at Christ Church College in Oxford. As most people know, Dodgson used the pseudonym Lewis Carroll for his nonsense writings for children.[18]

Lewis Carroll was very fond of children, especially little girls, and spent as much time as he could with them. He was more likely to be able to befriend children when he knew their parents, such as Henry George Liddell, the dean of his college. Dean Liddell's daughter, Alice Pleasance Liddell, was Carroll's favorite child friend. During a rowing excursion on the river Isis, with Alice and two of her sisters, Lorina Charlotte and Edith, Carroll told the story that would eventually become *Alice's Adventures in*

Wonderland. (Isis is the local name for the portion of the Thames that flows through Oxford.) The story featured characters based on Alice and her sisters, and additional characters were based on other family members and friends of the Liddell family. As Martin Gardner put it in his *Annotated Alice*:[19]

> In the case of ALICE we are dealing with a very curious, complicated kind of nonsense, written for British readers of another century, and we need to know a great many things that are not part of the text if we wish to capture its full wit and flavor. It is even worse than that, for some of Carroll's jokes could be understood only by residents of Oxford, and other jokes, still more private, could be understood only by the lovely daughters of Dean Liddell.

Mrs. Henry George Liddell, the dean's wife and Alice's mother, was well known in Oxford for her efforts to find well-born, noble or even royal husbands for her daughters. Her nickname was "the Kingfisher."[20] A fairy that manifests itself as a kingfisher plays an important role in *Little, Big.* One of the ways the fairies manipulate the Drinkwater's Tale is to arrange their marriages, as with that of Daily Alice and Smoky.[21]

Carroll was an early practitioner of photography and became quite good at it. He combined his love of photography and little girls by taking many pictures of them, and soon carried this a step further by taking pictures of little girls in the nude. He did this only if both the child and her parents were comfortable with the idea and he never exhibited these pictures or showed them to anyone but the girl's parents, with a very few exceptions, always with the permission of the parents.[22] The Victorian idea that children, and especially little girls, represented an ideal of purity was quite prevalent during Carroll's lifetime, so that many people found nothing wrong with representing children in the nude, at least up to a few years before puberty.[23] There is absolutely no evidence that Carroll had any kind of sexual relation with any of his child friends. (He had no known sexual relations with adults of either gender.)[24]

In *Little, Big*, Auberon Drinkwater took photographs at first as a hobby, but eventually to get proof that fairies exist. He could not see fairies himself, but other members of the Drinkwater family could and they seemed to attract fairies, as well. When Auberon took pictures of fellow members of the Drinkwater clan, he would sometimes see fairies in the developed photographs that he had not been able to see in the actual scenes they recorded. But the pictures were always ambiguous (with one notable exception)[25] and he kept on trying to get a series of photographs that would offer unmistakable proof. Many of these pictures were of Daily Alice and Sophie Drinkwater, his half-grandnieces. Auberon eventually took some pictures of them in the nude—and then of many other children—and ultimately the nudes became his major focus. Unlike Carroll, Auberon kept his pictures a secret from everyone but the subjects and he convinced them not to tell by presenting it as a game. Like Carroll, he never had any sexual contact with the children he photographed, but he did admit to himself that he got sexual pleasure from the pictures. Auberon was "almost" a virgin,[26] while Carroll, so far as is known, was one.

Lewis Carroll was a prolific writer and inventor, especially of games and puzzles. An invention that deserves special mention with regard to *Little, Big* is his *Memoria Technica*, an aid to remembering information that involved encoding numeric information using letters so that dates and other numbers were associated with significant words.[27] This is very different from Ariel Hawksquill's *Art of Memory*,[28] but the goal of both was to improve memory by artificial means.

Another of Carroll's inventions was the portmanteau word, which he used in some of his books and poems. A portmanteau was a kind of suitcase and a portmanteau word (as Humpty Dumpty explained in *Looking-Glass*)[29] was two words (and meanings) packed into one.

I like to think of Edgewood, five different houses somehow packed into the space of one,[30] as a portmanteau house.

Carroll's Times

England, during the Victorian era, was characterized by a great increase in interest in the supernatural. This resulted in, among other things, the development of spiritualism[31] and a sort of fairy craze.[32] Carroll shared this craze, at least to a degree.[33]

> When thirteen, he revealed in a poem that he had a fairy by his side; later, he called *Alice's Adventures in Wonderland* a fairy-tale. When he asked an eight-year-old niece if she believed in fairies and she replied that she did not know, he said, "Ah, that is because you have never seen one." A good many fairies romp through Charles's [Lewis Carroll's] verse and letters; one of his favorite gift books was William Allingham's *Fairies*; and when he engaged Gertrude Thompson to draw pictures for him, he asked her to draw only fairy pictures.

William Allingham's *Fairies* (or *The Fairies*) must have contained Allingham's most famous poem, "The Fairies," a quote from which is used as a chapter heading in *Little, Big.*[34] Because of its interest to both Crowley and Carroll scholars, "The Fairies" is included in its entirety in Appendix A.

The fairy craze more or less culminated in the episode of the Cottingley fairy photographs.[35]

> The fairies that caused the greatest stir were seen, so it was claimed, in July 1917 by Elsie Wright, aged fifteen and her cousin France Griffiths, aged eleven, at Cottingley in Yorkshire, and they faked photographs of them to support their story. Their cause was taken up by Sir Arthur Conan Doyle . . . then in the grip of spiritualistic fervour, and he described the incident in *The Coming of the Fairies* (1921). At the end of her life Elsie admitted

that the images were faked, saying it was the only way
that their sighting of the fairies would be believed.

Crowley is obviously playing with this incident when he has
Auberon Drinkwater lend his Kodak to his sisters Nora and Timmie Willie to take pictures of each other and they come back with
photographs of fairies.[36]

The Cottingley fairy photographs were satirized by Terry Jones
(of Monty Python fame) in a book he created with Brian Froud,
Lady Cottington's Book of Pressed Fairies. The following paragraph from the preface links Lewis Carroll with the fairy photographs.[37]

> Of course every one is familiar with the famous pho-
> tograph of the small girl surrounded by fairies, which
> caused such a sensation when it was first published in
> *The Regular* magazine in 1907. It inspired many imita-
> tions and was circulated around the world. While some
> skeptics dismissed it as a hoax, it was hailed in many
> quarters as the final, irrefutable proof of the existence of
> fairies. No less an authority on the subject than Sir Ar-
> thur Conan Doyle was fully persuaded of its authentic-
> ity, and spoke to packed audiences about its significance,
> particularly in the Manchester area. J. M. Barrie himself
> was convinced that he recognized at least one of the
> fairies in the photograph and the Rev. Charles Dodgson
> (better known as Lewis Carroll) appeared from beyond
> the grave to clairvoyants up and down the country to
> vouch for the veracity of the photograph.

Of course, this is all nonsense, but it does show how Carroll is
linked to fairies in the mind of at least one well-educated contemporary British man.

The Alice Books
One technique Crowley uses fairly often is to create a relatively

short reference that spans a long passage of Carroll's text, or even two or more non-adjacent passages. Through references to Carroll's Alice books are peppered throughout *Little, Big*, only two seem overt. "The Fool card . . . showed a full-bearded man in armor crossing a brook. Like the White Knight he was in the act of pitching head-first and straight-legged from his brawny horse. His expression was mild . . ."[38] The White Knight is a major character in *Looking-Glass*.[39] Many people think he was meant to represent Carroll himself.[40]

One of the quotations at the head of Book Six, Chapter Five[41] is from *Wonderland*. "'I want a clean cup,' the Hatter interrupted. 'Everyone move one place.'"[42] In *Little, Big* the fairies' universe consists of a series of concentric rings, and just as the Drinkwaters move one ring inward to replace the fairies, who move a ring further inward as well, everyone at the Mad Tea Party moves over to the next place setting.[43]

The most obvious not-quite-overt reference is the name of Daily Alice herself. Crowley came up with it when he saw an advertisement in *The New York Review of Books* for *Dali's Alice* (an edition of *Wonderland* illustrated by Salvador Dali), which he momentarily misread as Daily Alice.[44] The Drinkwater family name may also have *Wonderland* associations; in a famous scene, Alice finds a little bottle labeled "Drink Me."[45] Of course, this bottle turns out not to contain water.

The most extended reference involves the names of Smoky and Daily Alice Barnable's daughters, Tacey, Lily, and Lucy. These names are based on names from *Wonderland*, Elsie, Lacie and Tillie. Tacey and Lily are obviously derived by spoonerism from Lacie and Tillie, which leaves us to get Lucy from Elsie. This seems less easy to follow; Lucy seems closer to Lacie, leaving nothing for Elsie to do. But with a little background information, Elsie leads straight to Lucy.

The names Elsie, Lacie, and Tillie come from a story told by the Dormouse during the Mad Tea Party[46] about three little girls who live in a well. The "three little girls" were the three Liddell girls (Liddell was pronounced to rhyme with fiddle), Alice and two of her sisters, Lorina Charlotte and Edith. Lorina Charlotte was known as L.C., which became Elsie, and Edith's family nickname was Matilda, which became Tillie. Lacie is an anagram of Alice.[47] It seems just as easy to derive Lucy from L.C. as it does Elsie, or nearly so. Other Alice references are tied up in one of these names: Lily is also the name of a white pawn in *Looking-Glass*[48] and one of the talking flowers later in the same book is a Tiger-lily.[49] Crowley gives the game away when George Mouse says to Auberon Barnable, newly arrived at Old Law Farm, "How's Elsie, Lacy, and Tilly, whatever their names are?"[50] Crowley didn't spell two of them quite right, but there can be little doubt that these names are from *Wonderland*.

The second major reference to the Alice books is for me the most extraordinary. There is an extended passage[51] in *Little, Big* that parallels in structure and phrasing a poem from *Looking-Glass*, except that it turns the structure back to front in a looking-glass reversal. Here is the end of the passage from *Little, Big*, elided for brevity and relevance:

> [George Mouse] hadn't heard what Smoky had said, though he had heard Smoky talking. He said, "But what's the story? What's the real story?"
>
> "Well, we're Protected you know," Smoky said vaguely, digging the black ground with his stick . . . .
>
> But George had been thinking of a plan to represent the basic notions of Act Theory (that he had read of in a popular magazine and which seemed to him just then to make sense, a lot of sense) by means of a *display of fireworks* . . . The notion faded in sparks. He shook Smoky's shoulder and said, "But how goes it? How are you getting on?"
>
> "Jesus, George," Smoky said standing. "I've told you all I can . . . . "

And here is the beginning of the poem from *Looking-Glass*:[52]

> 'I'll tell thee everything I can;
>   There's little to relate.
> I saw an aged aged man,
>   A-sitting on a gate.
> "Who are you, aged man?" I said,
>   "And how is it you live?"
> And his answer trickled through my head
>   Like water through a sieve.
>
> He said, "I look for butterflies
>   That sleep among the wheat:
> I make them into mutton-pies,
>   And sell them in the street.
> I sell them unto men," he said,
>   "Who sail on stormy seas;
> And that's the way I get my bread—
>   A trifle, if you please."
>
> But I was thinking of a plan
>   To dye one's whiskers green,
> And always use so large a fan
>   That they could not be seen.
> So, having no reply to give
>   To what the old man said,
> I cried, "Come, tell me how you live!"
>   And thumped him on the head.

There is considerably more both to the passage from *Little, Big* and the poem from *Looking-Glass*, each of which continues along the same lines.

Another reference: Grandfather Trout has a bad dream.[53] "[A] colored engraving, was projected before him on the water: a be-wigged fish in a high-collared coat, a huge letter under his arm, his mouth gaping open. In air." This is certainly a description of an illustration of the Fish-Footman.[54] But exactly which illustration is problematic. *The Illustrators of Alice in Wonderland and Through the Looking-Glass* states, "Well over a hundred artists have illustrated Lewis Carroll's *Alice's Adventures in Wonderland* and *Through the Looking-Glass and What Alice Found There* since they were first published in 1865 and 1871."[55] This was written in 1979; the number of illustrated editions of *Alice* may well have pushed past 200 by now. The most famous illustrations for the Alice books are the originals by John Tenniel, in black and white in the original *Wonderland*, but colored in some later editions.[56] But Tenniel's Fish-Footman does not have the letter under his arm, he is handing it to the Frog-Footman. However, a picture that perfectly matches the description in Grandfather Trout's dream can be found in an edition published in 1907 and illustrated by Bessie Pease Guttman.[57] It is the only illustration of the Fish-Footman I can recall in which he has a fish's tail rather than legs.

When Violet Bramble sees Edgewood for the first time, her exclamation echoes Alice's most famous phrase, spoken when she is opening up like a telescope in *Wonderland*.[58] "'Curious,' she said out loud when she had rounded the corner. 'How very curious.'"[59]

Later, George Mouse quotes Alice exactly. "'Curiouser and curiouser,' George said."[60]

Auberon Barnable echoes Humpty Dumpty from *Looking-Glass* very closely. "Auberon had a name for all this: Glory. If it wasn't what was meant by Glory, he didn't care. His plot—who was to be master, that's all—didn't really much interest him . . ."[61]

Humpty Dumpty has the following conversation with Alice.[62]

> " . . . There's glory for you!"
>
> "I don't know what you mean by 'glory,'" Alice said.
>
> Humpty Dumpty smiled contemptuously. "Of course you don't—till I tell you. I meant 'there's a nice knock-down argument for you!'"
>
> "But 'glory' doesn't mean 'a nice knock-down argument,'" Alice objected.
>
> "When I use a word," Humpty Dumpty said, in a

rather scornful tone, "it means just what I choose it to mean—neither more nor less."

"The question is," said Alice, "whether you can make words mean so any different things."

"The question is," said Humpty Dumpty, "which is to be master—that's all."

During his conversation with August Drinkwater,[63] the fairy kingfisher displays the mannerisms of the Red Queen from *Looking-Glass* and hints of the bad temper of the Queen of Hearts from *Wonderland*.

"If I had to live on fish," [August] said, "I'd grow a beak."

"You shouldn't speak," said the kingfisher, "until you're spoken to. There are manners, you know."

"Sorry."

"First *I* speak," said the kingfisher, "and you wonder who it is that's spoken to you. Then you realize it's me; then you look at your thumb and your fish, and see that it was the fish's blood you tasted, that allowed you to understand the voices of creatures; *then* we converse."

"I didn't mean . . ."

"We'll assume it was done that way." The kingfisher spoke in the choleric, impatient tone August would have expected from his upshot head-feathers, his thick neck, his fierce, annoyed eyes and beak: a kingfisher's voice. Halcyon bird indeed!

"Now you address me," the kingfisher said. "'O Bird!' you say, and make your request."

Early in *Looking-Glass*, Alice and the Red Queen have the following exchange.[64]

"But you make no remark?"

"I—I didn't know I had to make one—just then," Alice faltered out.

"You *should* have said," the Queen went on in a tone
of grave reproof, "'It's extremely kind of you to tell me
all this'—however, we'll suppose it said . . ."

Later, the Red Queen says to Alice,[65] "'Speak when you're spoken to!'" and, half a page later, "'We gave you the opportunity
of doing it, but I daresay you've not had many lessons in manners
yet.'"[66]

"O Bird!" echoes the mode of address Alice used to the mouse
in the pool of tears in *Wonderland*, "O Mouse!"[67]

Later in their conversation, the kingfisher says to August, "'But
let's discuss payment first, reward after.'"[68] This recalls the Queen
of Hearts' remark during the trial of the Knave of Hearts in *Wonderland*, "'Sentence first—verdict afterwards.'"[69]

Two passages call to mind the wood where things have no names
in *Looking-Glass*.[70] In the first[71], George Mouse is in a forest with
Auberon Barnable and Fred Savage trying to get to the Fairies' Parliament; he lags behind the other two and forgets who he is, where
he is, and what he is doing.[72]

Later Auberon, on the same journey, catches sight of Sylvie, but
cannot remember her name.[73]

> He would have called to her, if he hadn't been unable
> to remember her name. He had sorted through the alpha-
> bet to jog his memory, but it had turned to wet leaves, to
> staghorn, snails' shells, fauns' feet; it all seemed to spell
> her, but gave him no name . . .
>
> . . .
>
> . . . Laurel, cobweb, something like that; bramble, or
> something that began with a bee, or a sea.

This resembles a specific passage in *Looking-Glass*, just after
Alice has walked into the wood where things have no names.[74] She
finds she can't remember the names of things such as a tree or the
wood itself.

She stood silent for a moment thinking: then she suddenly began again. "Then it really *has* happened, after all! And now, who am I? I *will* remember, if I can! I'm determined to do it!" But being determined didn't help her much, and all she could say, after a great deal of puzzling, was "L, I *know* it begins with L!"

Sophie Drinkwater tries to count the remaining fairies towards the end of *Little, Big* and she ends up matching them against cards in her tarot deck. This deck has 52 cards in four suits (wands or sticks, cups, swords, and coins) as well as nonstandard trumps called the Least Trumps. She matches the non-trump cards against the fairies and decides there are probably 52 left, but she is not quite sure of this conclusion.[75] Later, her daughter Lilac confirms the number. "'Fifty-two,' Lilac said. 'Counting them all.'"[76]

As she tries to tally the remaining fairies, Sophie names them by their functions. One such function is "one to go messages, no, two to go messages, one to go and one to come back again."[77] This recalls the White King's messengers in *Looking-Glass*, which the King describes this way, "'I must have two you know—to come and go. One to come and one to go.'"[78] The phrase "going messages" is used by Alice when she is sent on an errand by the White Rabbit in *Wonderland*:[79]

> "How queer it seems," Alice said to herself, "to be going messages for a rabbit! . . ."

"Going messages" is a British idiom for what is called "running errands" in the United States.[80]

The exact number of fairies and the fact that they are being matched against a pack of cards calls to mind the Queen of Hearts and her entourage in *Wonderland*. The royal family and members of the court number 52 by necessity because they are a pack of British playing cards (with a knave where American packs would have a jack). Aside from the King and Queen, the knave of hearts is the King's page, the lesser hearts are the Royal Children. (When Sophie is counting her cards, she thinks, "Queen of Coins and King of Coins and ten low cards for their children . . . ").[81] The diamonds are the courtiers, the clubs are the soldiers and the spades are the gardeners. The other court cards or face cards are members of the court or royal guests.[82, 83]

A banquet ends both *Little, Big* and *Looking-Glass*. The number of guests at each is uncertain, but it may be fifty-two, and the guest lists have similarities. At the dinner party for Queen Alice in *Looking-Glass*, Alice observes "that there were about fifty guests, of all kinds: some were animals, some birds, and there were even a few flowers among them."[84] In *Little, Big*, Sophie is looking out over the people who are to come to the banquet (although they don't know it yet): "She looked around at them all, Drinkwaters and Barnables, Birds, Stones, Flowers, Weeds, and Wolfs . . . "[85] Later, at the banquet, Sophie tries to count the guests. "She'd count them, but they moved around so, . . . anyway, she didn't need to count in order to know how many were here."[86] The reason Sophie doesn't need to count is that she knows that the number of guests must equal the number of fairies being replaced by them: fifty-two.

John Storm Drinkwater writes stories for children. In one of them, "Brother North-wind's Secret," a dog named Fury is mentioned by a mouse.[87] A dog named Fury is featured in the figured poem in *Wonderland* known as the Mouse's Tale.[88]

In the City, a small park features a plaque on a pillar by the gate that says "Mouse Drinkwater Stone 1900." When Smoky is carrying on a courtship by correspondence with Daily Alice he describes it to her in a letter:[89]

> It has a little pavilion of the Seasons, and statues, and all the walks curve so that you can't walk straight into the middle. You walk and walk and find yourself coming back out.

Later, Ariel Hawksquill is in the same park with Auberon Barnable:[90]

> . . . she walked with him along the curiously curving paths that seemed always about to lead them deeper within the park but in fact always contrived to direct them back to its perimeters. She knew the secret of these—which was, of course, to take those paths that seemed to be heading outward, and you would go in . . .

In the looking-glass world, when Alice tries to get somewhere by walking toward a place, she ends up heading back into the door of the looking-glass house where she started out instead. She finally follows the advice of a taking flower and walks in the opposite direction of the way she wants to go. This succeeds beautifully.[91]

Sylvie reenacts Alice's fall down the rabbit hole, after a fashion.[92] She goes "down, down, down" a flight of stairs and finds a "small door," which "opened on a narrow, low-ceilinged corridor." At the end of the corridor she finds a door "even smaller than the one she'd come in by." When this door opens a "strange, outdoor, summer-gold light seemed to come through it."

Although the sequence of events is not identical, the similarities (Alice falling "down, down, down" the rabbit hole, ending up in a "long, low hall" and eventually finding a tiny door that opens into a lovely garden[93]) are not likely to be accidental.

There are several other possible references in *Little, Big* to the Alice books, but they begin to become vague and possibly wholly imaginary. I will mention a few of the more definite. The table on the porch of Edgewood that Nora Cloud uses for her tarot readings is referred to as a glass-topped table the first time it is mentioned[94] but as a glass table later on.[95] There is, of course, a famous glass table in *Wonderland*.[96]

John Drinkwater first encounters Violet and Dr. Bramble in a vicarage in Cheshire.[97] The Cheshire Cat is a major character in *Wonderland*.[98]

Daily Alice Drinkwater and George Mouse meet unexpectedly, after they have both begun their journeys to the Fairies' Parliament. "They walked together through dark woods, talking of many things."[99] Compare this to the following lines from "The Walrus and the Carpenter" from *Looking-Glass*.[100]

> The Walrus and the Carpenter
> Were walking close at hand:

And[101]

> 'The time has come,' the Walrus said,
> 'To talk of many things:[']

Shifts in size or changes in scale are very important elements of both *Little, Big* and *Wonderland*. Dr. Bramble gives a lecture in which he describes the different sizes fairies can take on: tiny ("no bigger than a large insect, or a hummingbird"), small ("a foot to three feet in height"), normal ("fairy maidens . . . the size of human maidens") and large ("huge, larger by far than men").[102] These correspond roughly with the different sizes Alice takes on in *Wonderland*.

Daily Alice is often described as changing size and, while it is mostly or wholly metaphorical, this brings to mind Alice in Wonderland again. Look at the following passage from *Little, Big*:[103]

> Astonishing, astonishing that there could be no end
> to growing bigger, she thought years ago that she had
> grown so huge that she could grow no more, and yet she
> hadn't even begun.

And compare it to this one from *Wonderland*. Alice is in the White Rabbit's cottage and has just drunk something that has made her grow so large she nearly fills the room she's in:[104]

["]There ought to be a book written about me, that there ought! And when I grow up, I'll write one—but I'm grown up now," she added in a sorrowful tone: "at least there's no room to grow up any more *here*."

In a scene where Lilac is approaching Edgewood, riding on the back of a stork with Mrs. Underhill, the following passage occurs.[105]

It grew smaller as they grew closer. It shrank, as though running away. If that goes on, Lilac thought, by the time we're close enough to look in its windows, one of my eyes only will be able to see in at a time, and won't they be surprised inside as we go by, darkening the windows like a stormcloud!

This brings to mind the moment in *Wonderland* when Alice finds she is much too large to fit through a tiny door into a beautiful garden. "It was as much as she could do, lying down on one side, to look through into the garden with one eye . . ."[106] Portmanteau-fashion, Crowley packs in another Alice reference, this one to the monstrous crow in *Looking-Glass*.[107]

It was getting dark so suddenly that Alice thought there must be a thunderstorm coming on. "What a thick black cloud that is!" she said. "And how fast it comes! Why, I do believe it's got wings!"

Given the number of references, resemblances and resonances between *Little, Big* and the Alice books, the temptation to set up a one-to-one correspondence between the characters of the former and the latter becomes very great. Below is one such scheme (provided by Adam Stephanides):[108]

Daily Alice	Alice
Sophie	Alice's sister
Cronos	White King
Eigenblick	Red King
Mrs. Underwood	White Queen
Ariel Hawksquill	Red Queen
George Mouse	White Knight

John Crowley described this as "an amazing scheme! I wouldn't have thought it would work out so neatly." But Crowley went on to say, "Alice would not be Alice. It would be Smoky, obviously, who is Alice . . . Well, of course it couldn't be Smoky, because he doesn't make it to the other side of the mirror."[109] I think this rather nicely illustrates the difficulty of setting up such a correspondence. A second difficulty is that the characters in *Little, Big* often have characteristics of more than one *Wonderland* or *Looking-Glass* character. For example, George Mouse could be named for the mouse (from the pool of tears)[110] but he smokes like the Caterpillar.[111] Sophie's ability to sleep at the drop of a hat (before she loses it) recalls the Dormouse from the Mad Tea Party.[112]

Sylvie and Bruno

Sylvie and Bruno is all about fairies. It is a book Carroll wrote towards the end of his life, long after the Alice books. (*Sylvie and Bruno* was published in 1889 and *Sylvie and Bruno Concluded* in 1893.) In it he tries to make amends for not putting a serious, morally uplifting and religiously instructive message into the Alice books by piling on moral and religious instruction by the cartload, in addition to an enormous weight of Victorian sentimentality. The result is almost unreadable, though Crowley clearly read it. It was an important source of inspiration for *Little, Big*, especially concerning the idea for a fairy religion.

In the introduction to *Sylvie and Bruno Concluded*, Carroll shares with his readers some background information about the book.[113]

It may interest some of my Readers to know the theory on which this story is constructed. It is an attempt to show what might possibly happen, supposing that Fairies really existed; and that they were sometimes visible to us, and we to them; and that they were sometimes able to assume human form: and supposing, also, that human beings might sometimes become conscious of what goes on in the Fairy-world—by actual transference of their immaterial essence, such as we meet with in 'Esoteric Buddhism.'

Carroll goes on at some length about the various mental states in which people can see and interact with fairies and vice versa. He also postulates that, in the proper mental state, people can travel to the "Fairy-world" and that fairies can also visit the human world, taking on human form at will.

In *Sylvie and Bruno*, Oberon[114] and Titania[115] are mentioned as the king and queen of the fairies. Of course this tradition predates Carroll's books by many, many years.

A passage in *Sylvie and Bruno Concluded* that seems to apply to *Little, Big* as a whole is one in which the idea of races of men of various sizes is discussed.[116] The passage is a conversation between characters whose identity isn't important.

"The other alternative . . . would be a *diminuendo* series of repetitions of the same type . . . Begin with the race of men . . . Well, then we'll have a second race of men half-a-yard high . . . a third race of men, five inches high; a fourth race, an inch high . . ."

. . .

"Don't you think we ought to have a *crescendo* series, as well? . . . Only fancy being a hundred yards high! . . ."

Sylvie and Bruno appear the size of human children in most of *Sylvie and Bruno* but occasionally as fairy children only a few inches high.[117]

One of the many oddities in *Little, Big* is a statement both by a member of the Noisy Bridge Rod and Gun Club[118] and by Grand-father Trout[119] to the effect that there is no force on earth stronger than love. This may be may be at least partly explained as a reference to *Sylvie and Bruno*. While the phrase doesn't occur anywhere in the book, it serves very well as a summary of the theme of *Sylvie and Bruno*. See Appendix B for the complete lyrics of the "love song" that Sylvie and Bruno sing to get an idea of the central role Love plays in the *Sylvie and Bruno* scheme of things, as well as a taste of Victorian sentimentality at its most cloying.

The section of *Little, Big* entitled "Sophie's Dream" contains the following passage:[120]

> "I dreamt that I had learned a way of saving time I didn't want to spend, and having it to spend when I need-ed it. Like the time you spend waiting in a doctor's office, or coming back from someplace you didn't enjoy going to, or waiting for a bus—all the little useless spaces."

Compare this with *Sylvie and Bruno Concluded*.[121]

> " . . . For example, suppose you have a long tedious evening before you: nobody to talk to: nothing you care to do: and yet hours too soon to go to bed . . . By a short and simple process—which I cannot explain to you—they store up the useless hours: and, on some other occasion, when they happen to need extra time, they get them out again."

The most obvious references are the names Sylvie and Bruno themselves. In Carroll, Sylvie and Bruno are, as well as being fairy children, a brother and sister. In *Little, Big*, Sylvie and Bruno are also brother and sister and there is also another Bruno, who is Syl-vie's nephew and the first Bruno's son. A section title in *Little, Big* is "Sylvie & Bruno Concluded."[122] In *Little, Big*, the younger Bruno is described as a "child of almost visionary beauty."[123] Carroll's fairy children, Sylvie and Bruno, are both beings of great beauty.

In *Little, Big*, Sylvie is thinking about her feelings for Auberon Barnable.[124]

> Love, she said again to herself; and yes, there was the feeling, the word was like a swallow of rum. For George Mouse, her buddy for life, no matter what, who had taken her in when she had no place else, she felt deep gratitude and a complex of other feelings, mostly good; but not this heat, like a flame with a jewel held at its heart. The jewel was a word: love.

This calls to mind an episode from *Sylvie and Bruno*. Sylvie is given a magic locket by her father. In fact, her father has her choose from two lockets. Both are shaped like hearts and carved from solid jewels. One is blue and has the phrase "All will love Sylvie." The other is red and is inscribed "Sylvie will love all."[125] Sylvie chooses the red locket, which is the "right choice," but in the end it turned out that they were just two sides of the same locket all along.[126]

Conclusion

My favorite Lewis Carroll poem is *The Hunting of the Snark*, but Crowley didn't seem to have *Snark* in mind when he wrote *Little, Big*. However, the ultimate fate of the Drinkwater clan as it must have looked to the outside world gives me my opportunity. The Drinkwaters "softly and suddenly vanished away and never were met with again."[127]

I don't think I have tracked down every single Lewis Carroll reference in *Little, Big*, nor do I think it is important to do so (assuming it is even possible). I do hope that my attempt to list a good many of these references and to explain the influence they may have had on Crowley is helpful in explicating certain aspects of *Little, Big* or is at least entertaining.

APPENDIX A

The Fairies
by William Allingham

Up the airy mountain,
  Down the rushy glen,
We daren't go a-hunting
  For fear of little men;
Wee folk, good folk,
  Trooping all together;
Green jacket, red cap,
  And white owl's feather!

Down along the rocky shore
  Some make their home,
They live on crispy pancakes
  Of yellow tide-foam;
Some in the reeds
  Of the black mountain lake,
With frogs for their watch-dogs,
  All night awake.

High on the hill-top
  The old King sits;
He is now so old and gray
  He's nigh lost his wits.
With a bridge of white mist
  Columbkill he crosses,
On his stately journeys
  From Slieveleague to Rosses;
Or going up with music
  On cold starry nights
To sup with the Queen
  Of the gay Northern Lights.

They stole little Bridget
  For seven years long;
When she came down again
  Her friends were all gone.
They took her lightly back,
  Between the night and morrow,
They thought that she was fast asleep,
  But she was dead with sorrow.
They have kept her ever since
  Deep within the lake,
On a bed of flag-leaves,
  Watching till she wake.

By the craggy hill-side,
  Through the mosses bare,
They have planted thorn-trees
  For pleasure here and there.
If any man so daring
  As dig them up in spite,
He shall find their sharpest thorns
  In his bed at night.

Up the airy mountain,
  Down the rushy glen,
We daren't go a-hunting
  For fear of little men;
Wee folk, good folk,
  Trooping all together;
Green jacket, red cap,
  And white owl's feather!

APPENDIX B

From *Sylvie and Bruno Concluded*
(Chapter XIX: A Fairy-Duet, pp. 779-781)

Say, what is the spell, when her fledglings are cheeping,
    That lures the bird home to her nest?
Or wakes the tired mother whose infant is weeping,
    To cuddle and croon it to rest?
What's the magic that charms the glad babe in her arms,
    Till it coos with the voice of the dove?

'Tis a secret, and so let us whisper it low—
    And the name of the secret is Love!
      For I think it is Love,
      For I feel it is Love,
    For I'm sure it is nothing but Love!

Say, whence is the voice that, when anger is burning,
    Bids the whirl of the tempest to cease?
That stirs the vexed soul with an aching—a yearning
    For the brotherly hand-grip of peace?
Whence the music that fills all our being—that thrills
    Around us, beneath and above?

'Tis a secret: none knows how it comes, how it goes:
    But the name of the secret is Love!
      For I think it is Love,
      For I feel it is Love,
    For I'm sure it is nothing but Love!

Say, whose is the skill that paints valley and hill,
    Like a picture so fair to the sight?
That flecks the green meadow with sunshine and shadow,
    Till the little lambs leap with delight?

'Tis a secret untold to hearts cruel and cold,
  Though 'tis sung, by the angels above,
In notes that ring clear for the ears that can hear—
  And the name of the secret is Love!

    For I think it is Love,
    For I feel it is Love,
  For I'm sure it is nothing but Love!

ANNOTATED BIBLIOGRAPHY

Carroll, Lewis. *Alice's Adventures in Wonderland: The Ultimate Illustrated Edition*. Compiled and arranged by Cooper Edens. New York: Bantam Books, 1989.

Carroll, Lewis. *The Annotated Alice*. With an introduction and notes by Martin Gardner. New York: Bramhall House, 1960.

Carroll, Lewis. *The Complete Illustrated Works of Lewis Carroll*. Edited and with an introduction by Edward Guiliano. New York: Avenel Books, 1982.

Cohen, Morton N. *Lewis Carroll: A Biography*. New York: Alfred A. Knopf, 1995.

Crowley, John. *Beasts/Engine Summer/Little, Big*. New York: Book of the Month Club, 1991.

Jones, Terry. *Lady Cottington's Pressed Fairy Book*. Illustrated by Brian Froud. Atlanta: Turner Publishing, 1994.

Martineau, Jane, ed. *Victorian Fairy Painting*. London: Merrell Holberton, 1997.

Ovenden, Graham and John Davis. *The Illustrators of Alice in Wonderland and Through the Looking-Glass*. New York: St. Martin's Press,

1979.

Quiller-Couch, Arthur Thomas, Sir, ed. *The Oxford Book of English Verse*. Oxford: Clarendon, 1919.

Stoffel, Stephanie Lovett. *Lewis Carroll in Wonderland: The Life and Times of Alice and Her Creator*. New York: Harry N. Abrams, 1997.

Yates, Frances A. *The Art of Memory*. London: Pimlico, 1966.

All references to the works of Lewis Carroll are from *The Complete Illustrated Works of Lewis Carroll*. I have given chapter numbers and titles along with the page numbers because there are so many different editions of Lewis Carroll's works in so many different formats that I wanted to make it as easy as possible to find the references in editions other than the one I used. *Wonderland* starts on page 3 in this edition, *Looking-Glass* on page 81, *Sylvie and Bruno* on page 491 and *Sylvie and Bruno Concluded* on page 655.

All of my information about Charles Dodgson's life comes from *Lewis Carroll: A Biography* by Morton N. Cohen.

For references to *Little, Big* and *Engine Summer* I have used page numbers from the Quality Paperback Book Club Beasts/*Engine Summer*/*Little, Big* omnibus edition. I have also included book and chapter numbers and section titles (where they exist) to make it easier to find the relevant passages in other editions of these books.

NOTES

[1] *Little, Big*, Book One: Edgewood, Chapter Three, "Call Them Doors," pp. 50–51.

[2] *Little, Big*, Book One: Edgewood, Chapter Three, "All Questions Answered," p. 65.

[3] *Little, Big*, Book Two: Brother North-wind's Secret, Chapter Four, "Letters to Santa," p. 193.

[4] *Little, Big*, Book Two: Brother North-wind's Secret, Chapter Three, p. 171 (Tacey and Lily).

[5] *Little, Big*, Book Two: Brother North-wind's Secret, Chapter Three, "Cocoa and a Bun," p. 177 (Lucy).

[6] This is an omnibus edition that also includes *Beasts* and *Engine Summer*.

[7] Adam Stephanides, personal communication.

[8] *Engine Summer*, The First Crystal: Many Lives, First Facet, p. 3.

[9] *Alice's Adventures in Wonderland*, Chapter XII: Alice's Evidence, p. 76.

[10] *Engine Summer*, The First Crystal: Many Lives, Fourth Facet, p. 27.

[11] *Wonderland*, Chapter VII: A Mad Tea-Party, p. 44.

[12] *Engine Summer*, The Third Crystal: A Letter from Dr. Boots, Second Facet, p. 115.

[13] *Wonderland*, Chapter VII: A Mad Tea-Party, p. 47.

[14] *Engine Summer*, The Third Crystal: A Letter from Dr. Boots, Third

Facet, p. 130.

[15] *Wonderland*, Chapter VII: A Mad Tea-Party, p. 43.

[16] *Engine Summer*, The Fourth Crystal: The Sky Is Grass, Second Facet, p. 161.

[17] *Through the Looking-Glass and What Alice Found There*, Chapter II: The Garden of Live Flowers, p. 102.

[18] The information that follows is complied from several of the sources given in my bibliography but primarily from *Lewis Carroll: A Biography* by Morton N. Cohen.

[19] *The Annotated Alice*, p. 7, Introduction.

[20] *Lewis Carroll in Wonderland*, p. 82.

[21] *Little, Big*, Book One: Edgewood, Chapter One, "Life is Short, or Long," p. 21.

[22] *Lewis Carroll: A Biography*, pp. 165–71.

[23] *Lewis Carroll in Wonderland*, p. 46.

[24] *Lewis Carroll: A Biography*, pp.226–31.

[25] *Little, Big*, Book One: Edgewood, Chapter Two, "Houses & Histories," p. 37.

[26] *Little, Big*, Book One: Edgewood, Chapter Five, "These Few Windows" and "To See What He Could See," pp. 95-99.

[27] *Lewis Carroll: A Biography*, pp. 393-94.

[28] *Little, Big*, Book Three: Old Law Farm, Chapter Four, "The Art of Memory," pp. 288-89.

[29] *Looking-Glass*, Chapter VI: Humpty Dumpty, p. 137.

[30] *Little, Big*, Book One: Edgewood, Chapter Two, "Houses & Histories," p. 37.

[31] Jeremy Maas, "Victorian Fairy Painting," *Victorian Fairy Painting*, pp. 13–14.

[32] Charlotte Gere, "In Fairyland," *Victorian Fairy Painting*, p. 63.

[33] *Lewis Carroll: A Biography*, p. 369.

[34] *Little, Big*, Book Six: The Fairies' Parliament, Chapter One, p. 499.

[35] Charlotte Gere, "In Fairyland," Victorian Fairy Painting, p. 70.

[36] *Little, Big*, Book One: Edgewood, Chapter Five, "Can You Find the Faces," pp. 91-95.

[37] Terry Jones and Brian Froud, *Lady Cottington's Book of Pressed Fairies*, p. 1.

[38] *Little, Big*, Book Three: Old Law Farm, Chapter Four, "A Geography," p. 295.

[39] *Looking-Glass*, Chapter VIII: "It's My Own Invention," p. 149, ff.

[40] *The Annotated Alice*, p. 296, Note 4.

[41] *Little, Big*, Book Five: The Art of Memory, Chapter Five, p. 595.

[42] *Wonderland*, Chapter VII: A Mad Tea-Party, p. 47.

[43] This was verified by John Crowley, in an interview with Alice Turner, personal communication.

[44] John Crowley, in an interview with Alice Turner, personal communication.

[45] *Wonderland*, Chapter I: Down the Rabbit-hole, p. 8.

[46] *Wonderland*, Chapter VII: A Mad Tea-Party, pp. 46-48.

[47] *The Annotated Alice*, p. 100, Note 9.

[48] *Looking-Glass*, Chapter I: Looking-Glass House, p. 92.

[49] *Looking-Glass*, Chapter II: The Garden of Live Flowers, p. 98 ff.

[50] *Little, Big*, Book Three: Old Law Farm, Chapter One, "News from Home," p. 219.

[51] *Little, Big*, Book Two: Brother North-wind's Secret, Chapter Three, "Up on the Hill," pp. 174–76.

[52] *Looking-Glass*, Chapter VIII: "It's My Own Invention," pp. 157-59.

[53] *Little, Big*, Book One: Edgewood, Chapter Four, "Suppose One Were a Fish," p. 84.

[54] *Wonderland*, Chapter VI: Pig and Pepper, p. 35.

[55] *The Illustrators of Alice*, p. 5.

[56] *Lewis Carroll in Wonderland*, p. 167, List of Illustrations, Number 11.

[57] *Alice's Adventures in Wonderland: The Ultimate Illustrated Edition*, p. 88. This illustration by Bessie Pease Guttman was originally in an edition of *Alice's Adventures in Wonderland* published by J. Coker and Co., Ltd.: New York, 1907.

[58] Wonderland, Chapter II: The Pool of Tears, p. 10.

[59] *Little, Big*, Book One: Edgewood, Chapter Three, "A Turn Around the House," p. 58.

[60] *Little, Big*, Book Five: The Art of Memory, Chapter Four, "Three Lilacs," p. 484.

[61] *Little, Big*, Book Four: The Wild Wood, Chapter One, "Glory," p. 331.

[62] *Looking-Glass*, Chapter VI: Humpty Dumpty, p. 136.

[63] *Little, Big*, Book Two: Brother North-wind's Secret, Chapter One, "What You Most Want," p. 127.

[64] *Looking-Glass*, Chapter II: The Garden of Live Flowers, p. 105.

[65] *Looking-Glass*, Chapter IX: Queen Alice, p. 161.

[66] *Looking-Glass*, Chapter IX: Queen Alice, p. 162.

[67] *Wonderland*, Chapter II: The Pool of Tears, pp. 13-14.

[68] *Little, Big*, Book Two: Brother North-wind's Secret, Chapter One, "What You Most Want," p. 128.

[69] *Wonderland*, Chapter XII: Alice's Evidence, p. 78.

[70] Looking-Glass, Chapter III: Looking-Glass Insects, pp. 111-12.

[71] I owe this reference to Michael Andre-Driussi, personal communication.

[72] *Little, Big*, Book Six: The Fairies' Parliament, Chapter Four, "A Watch and a Pipe," p. 580.

[73] *Little, Big*, Book Six: The Fairies' Parliament, Chapter Five, "Only the Brave," p. 604.

[74] *Looking-Glass*, Chapter III: Looking-Glass Insects, p. 111.

[75] *Little, Big*, Book Six: The Fairies' Parliament, Chapter One, "Fifty-

Two," p. 503.

[76] *Little, Big*, Book Six: The Fairies' Parliament, Chapter Two, "A Parliament," p. 534.

[77] *Little, Big*, Book Six: The Fairies' Parliament, Chapter One, "Fifty-Two," p. 503.

[78] *Looking-Glass*, Chapter VII: The Lion and the Unicorn, p. 143.

[79] *Wonderland*, Chapter IV, The Rabbit Sends in a Little Bill, p. 21.

[80] *The Annotated Alice*, p. 56, Note 2.

[81] *Little, Big*, Book Six: The Fairies' Parliament, Chapter One, "Fifty-Two," p. 503.

[82] *Wonderland*, Chapter VIII: The Queen's Croquet Ground, p. 50.

[83] *The Annotated Alice*, p. 107, Note 1.

[84] *Looking-Glass*, Chapter IX: Queen Alice, p. 167.

[85] *Little, Big*, Book Six: The Fairies' Parliament, Chapter Three, "Is It Far?" p. 553.

[86] *Little, Big*, Book Six: The Fairies' Parliament, Chapter Five, "She's Here, She's Near," p. 624.

[87] *Little, Big*, Book Two: Brother North-wind's Secret, Chapter Two, "Brother North-wind's Secret," p. 153.

[88] *Wonderland*, Chapter III: A Caucus-Race and a Long Tale, p. 19.

[89] *Little, Big*, Book One: Edgewood, Chapter One, "Correspondence," p. 15.

[90] *Little, Big*, Book Five: The Art of Memory, Chapter One, "A Secret

Sorrow," p. 408.

[91] *Looking-Glass*, Chapter II: The Garden of Live Flowers, pp. 98–101

[92] *Little, Big*, Book Four: The Wild Wood, Chapter Four, "Lost for Sure," p. 386.

[93] *Wonderland*, Chapter I: Down the Rabbit-hole, pp. 6–7.

[94] *Little, Big*, Book One: Edgewood, Chapter Two, "Led Astray," p. 30.

[95] *Little, Big*, Book One: Edgewood, Chapter Five, "In the Woods," p. 107.

[96] *Wonderland*, Chapter I: Down the Rabbit-Hole, p. 7.

[97] *Little, Big*, Book One: Edgewood, Chapter Three, p. 44.

[98] *Wonderland*, Chapter VI: Pig and Pepper, pp. 37, 39-42 ff.

[99] *Little, Big*, Book Six: The Fairies' Parliament, Chapter Five, "Her Blessing," p. 595.

[100] *Looking-Glass*, Chapter IV: Tweededum and Tweedledee, p. 116.

[101] *Looking-Glass*, Chapter IV: Tweededum and Tweedledee, p. 117.

[102] *Little, Big*, Book One: Edgewood, Chapter Three, "Call Them Doors," p. 50.

[103] *Little, Big*, Book Four: The Wild Wood, Chapter One, "Not Yet," p. 333

[104] *Wonderland*, Chapter IV: The Rabbit Sends in a Little Bill, pp. 22-23.

[105] *Little, Big*, Book Four: The Wild Wood, Chapter One, "Rainy-day Wonder," p. 314.

[106] *Wonderland*, Chapter II: The Pool of Tears, p. 11.

[107] *Looking-Glass*, Chapter IV: Tweededum and Tweedledee, p. 123.

[108] Adam Stephanides, personal communication.

[109] John Crowley, in an interview with Alice Turner, personal communication.

[110] *Wonderland*, Chapter II: The Pool of Tears, p. 13 ff.

[111] *Wonderland*, Chapter IV: The Rabbit Sends in a Little Bill, p. 27 ff.

[112] *Wonderland*, Chapter VII: A Mad Tea-Party, p. 42 ff.

[113] *Sylvie and Bruno Concluded*, Introduction, p. 661.

[114] *Sylvie and Bruno*, Chapter XV: Bruno's Revenge, p. 586.

[115] *Sylvie and Bruno*, Chapter XXIV: The Frog's Birthday-Treat, p. 641.

[116] *Sylvie and Bruno*, Chapter XX: Light Come, Light Go, pp. 619-20.

[117] *Sylvie and Bruno*, Chapter XIV: Fairy-Sylvie, p. 586 [Sylvie] and p. 580 [Bruno].

[118] *Little, Big*, Book Three: Old Law Farm, Chapter One, "The Club Meets," p. 234.

[119] *Little, Big*, Book Four: The Wild Wood, Chapter Three, "Let Him Follow Love," p. 37.

[120] *Little, Big*, Book One: Edgewood, Chapter Two, "Sophie's Dream," p. 28.

[121] *Sylvie and Bruno Concluded*, Chapter VII: Mein Herr, p. 706.

[122] *Little, Big*, Book Five: The Art of Memory, Chapter Two, p. 435.

[123] *Little, Big*, Book Three: Old Law Farm, Chapter Two, "The Bee or the Sea," p. 240.

[124] *Little, Big*, Book Three: Old Law Farm, Chapter Four, "Princess," p. 303.

[125] *Sylvie and Bruno*, Chapter VI: The Magic Locket, p. 530-31.

[126] *Sylvie and Bruno Concluded*, Chapter XXV: Life Out of Death, p. 823.

[127] *The Hunting of the Snark*, Fit the Third: The Baker's Tale, p. 191 (paraphrased slightly).

LITTLE, BIG FOR LITTLE FOLK
Alice K. Turner

"I never had a childhood . . . not like you had. In a way I never was a child. I mean I was a kid, but not a child . . . "

"Well," she said; "you can have mine then. If you want it."

"Thank you," he said, and he did want it, all of it, no second left ungarnered. "Thank you."

Little, Big, Bantam, p 80

TOWARD THE END of the first section of John Crowley's *Little, Big*, on the day after the great picnic at which Smoky Barnable marries Daily Alice Drinkwater, the newlyweds don rucksacks to go on a hiking honeymoon. By noon of the next day, they have reached the edge of an old-growth forest, and it has begun to rain; they plan to take shelter with Alice's cousins, the Woods. Alice finds what she thinks is a shortcut through the brush, but it is dark, and the two become separated. Smoky blunders along till he comes to a glade in which stands a miniature cottage, five-sided like

THORNTON W. BURGESS

The animal stories of Dr. John Strong Drinkwater, father of Daily Alice and Sophie, are based so directly on those of Thornton W. Burgess, writer and amateur naturalist, as to amount to—well, more than an homage, let's say an *appropriation*.

Burgess was an amateur naturalist, an active wildlife conservationist and an extraordinarily prolific writer for children. He was a lifelong resident of Massachusetts, born in Sandwich in 1874, brought up on Cape Cod and dying in Hampden in 1965.

From 1912 to 1960, without missing a weekday, Burgess wrote a syndicated daily newspaper column titled "Bedtime Stories." These chronicled the adventures of the likes of Danny Meadow Mouse, Reddy Fox, Jimmy Skunk, Grandfather Frog, and many other denizens of wood and wetland, often as told to Old Mother West Wind by her Merry Little Breezes. Crowley's (or his editor's) minimalist evasion of outright copy-catting in *Little, Big* is to leave off the first names of Dr. Drinkwater's animals (thus *the* Meadow Mouse, rather than Danny), the "Old" from Mother West Wind and the "Merry" from the Little Breezes. I noticed a slip-up: one "Merry" survives in the Bantam paperback. It doesn't matter: Burgess might well have been delighted by the appreciation and tickled by the notion that his beasties spoke to him directly.

In all, Burgess wrote 171 books, most of them compilations of more than 15,000 columns, and these hold up remarkably well as amusing, lightly moralizing, stories for pre-schoolers and other youngsters. Little, Brown, the original publisher for a great deal of his work, keeps some of them in print, and as others fall into public domain they are being reprinted,

Edgewood, the grand, eccentric house where the Drinkwaters live (and now Smoky, too), "but all colored, with a bright red tile roof and white walls encumbered with decoration. Not an inch of it hadn't been curled or carved or colored or blazoned in some way. It looked, odder still, brand new." He approaches and "[t]he little round [green] door, knockered and peepholed and brass-hinged, was flung open as he came close, and a sharp small face appeared around its edge."

"Is this the Woods'?" Smoky asks tentatively, and he is warmly welcomed by name by his host, who is wearing a striped nightcap and presents "the longest, flattest, knobbiest hand Smoky had ever seen."

The inside of the cottage seems larger than the outside ("the further in you go, the bigger it gets"), and the room contains "a grandfather clock with a cunning expression, a bureau on which pewter candlesticks and mugs stood, a high fluffy bedstead with a patchwork quilt," also a table with a splinted leg and "a domineering wardrobe." And three more people: "a pretty woman busy at a squat stove, a baby in a wooden cradle who cooed like a mechanical toy whenever the woman gave the cradle a push, and an old, old lady, all nose and chin and spectacles, who rocked in a corner and knitted quickly on a long striped scarf." This last is introduced as Mrs. Underhill.

Now at this point the kind of reader who takes up *Little, Big* to start with must surely be feeling some sort of, well, perhaps not a shock but surely a nudge of recognition. We've been here before. We know this place, these people. And not just generically, either, in some cases specifically. That cottage, yes, certainly a fairy tale cottage, but isn't it perhaps one of those bright, cheerfully askew cottages that John R. Neill drew so charmingly for L. Frank Baum's Oz books? And surely that is Bilbo Baggins's door! And the affable Mr. Woods, doesn't he also go by the name of Mole? Or is he perhaps Mr. Badger, another formidable digger? Is the nightcap pinched from Lewis Carroll's Red King, or is it too from *The Wind in the Willows*? The rather Dickensian baby, hmmm, a better-tempered baby than the one belonging to Alice's Duchess, and not likely to turn into a pig. But a Sheep was last seen knitting that scarf on the other side of the looking glass.

Mrs. Underhill, whose name also recalls J.R.R. Tolkien's Bilbo[1], suggests several powerful old ladies from Victorian children's literature (I'm thinking specifically of the books of Charles Kingsley and George MacDonald), but we learn later she is Mother Goose herself, and a great deal more than that.

As for the furnishings, perhaps a sharper memory than mine will recall the exact table with the splinted leg or the blue-flowered plates. (I'd love them to belong to Wendy's kitchen in *Peter Pan*, as I can't find any other reference to Barrie—but maybe they were in Mrs. Tiggie-Winkle's kitchen.) The cunning clock—hickory, dickory, I ought to know that, but there are almost too many grandfather clocks in British children's books. The bedstead with the patchwork quilt—

with the original illustrations by Harrison Cady (and others, but Cady was predominant), by Dover, at rock-bottom prices. And it's easy to find second-hand copies of books that are no longer in print. Particularly recommended for older children are the nature books, with good, accurate wildlife illustrations in color (not by Cady: he was strictly for fiction) and excellent information for young naturalists: *The Burgess Bird Book for Children*, *The Burgess Flower Book for Children*, *The Burgess Seashore Book for Children*, *The Burgess Animal Book for Children*.

Vacationers can visit the Thornton W. Burgess Museum in Sandwich, which houses a collection of memorabilia in a pretty Cape Cod salt-box adjacent to a pond (the property belonged to a cousin, not to Burgess himself), and features a wildflower garden and extensive nature trails through a large preservation area. The Burgess Society, which operates it, has for twenty-five years been active in preservation and environmental education. The Society presents lots of free or inexpensive activities for local children, and for adults too.

LITTLE ENOSH IN DREAM-LAND

Little Nemo in Slumberland was the extraordinary Sunday newspaper comic strip drawn and written by Winsor McCay (c.1867-1934), starting in 1905 for the New York *Herald*, then from 1911-1914 for the Hearst papers, for which it was retitled *In the Land of Wonderful Dreams*. It was revived in the *Herald* 1925-1927 and after McCay's death his son Robert made a couple of attempts to resurrect it again without much success. It has often been collected in book form, most recently in a multivolume hardcover set (Fantagraphic Books 1989-1993). It has also been made into a musical play (1908) and a movie (1993), graced a postage stamp (1995), and McCay was even given an exhibit at New York's Metropolitan Museum of Art in 1966—rare acclaim for a cartoonist.

Nemo (the name is Latin for "nobody") is a little boy who in his dreams explores a fantastic (and beautifully drawn) surreal kingdom of many mishaps. In the last panel of each Sunday strip he wakes up safely in his own little bed—or tumbled on the floor beside it.

Here is the reference to the strip in *Little, Big*, in a letter from Daily Alice to Smoky, when he is still in New York: "There were these comic strips about a boy who dreams. The comic strip is all his dream, his Dreamland. Dreamland is beautiful, palaces and processions are always fold-

well, it's not an exact fit, but I'm thinking of A. A. Milne and the counterpane on which so many adventures happened.

But the wardrobe! That's almost too blatant a clue. We all know what's on the other side of that. A lamppost! It's the portal to the magical land of Narnia.

When a mortal goes to the Other World, conventional wisdom has it that he must not eat or drink a single thing—remember Persephone, let alone Tam Lin, this tradition goes all the way back to Sumeria—but the rules are different in Children's-Book Land. Just about the first thing a mortal always does there is to sit down to a nice tea. With buns (actually, C. S. Lewis's Mr. Tumnus served soft-boiled eggs with sardines and toast, toast with butter and honey, and a sugar-topped cake). Of course, crafty Crowley may have it both ways. Smoky eats a delicious bun iced with a five-pointed star, that star referring to the pentacle of five towns of which Edgewater is the exact center. And that, perhaps, is what seals his fate, for Smoky will never leave that pentacle again, not ever.

In response to their query, Smoky tells the Woods and Mrs. Underhill that Alice has given him her childhood for a wedding gift but he can't see how to use it, as he doesn't believe in the fairies that the Drinkwaters seem to take for granted. Mr. Woods approves of this gift, however. He tells Smoky that he must have a bag to put it in. First, though, he produces a necklace of gold and drapes it twice around Smoky's neck. Next, "a red hat, high-crowned and soft, belted with a plaited belt in which a white owl's feather nodded." And finally, "a faded and mouse-chewed Gladstone carpetbag."

The first of these gifts is a little generic. Gold figures in any number of fairytales, and fairy gold is tricky, always. The hat is quite specific—"green jacket, red cap and white owl's feather" (you can find the whole poem on p. 190 of this volume). Both are extraordinarily heavy. But that bag must have been separated from its former owner a long time for any rash mouse to dare to chew it. And what a bag it is! Certainly it can hold a childhood; that bag has been known to hold whole universes. That Gladstone bag was last seen firmly attached to the capable hand of Mary Poppins!

Fairy food consumed, fairy gifts bestowed, Alice's childhood reading graphically displayed, Smoky is sent on his way, through the back of the wardrobe, of course. Politely, he pauses to thank his host.

"*Forget it,*" says Mr. Woods.

And Smoky does, immediately. Nothing but a creeper is twined around his neck when he catches up to Daily Alice, dead leaves festoon his hair and he carries a long-dead hornet's nest with a bright ladybug who flies away home.

"What on earth," she says.

And he says, "I've been in the Woods'."

"I guess you have," says Alice.

ing up and shrinking away, or growing huge and out of hand, or when you look closely turn out to be something else—you know—just like real dreams, only always pretty."(15) An architect named Stone drew the strip in this novel, partner to Alice's great-grandfather and George Mouse's in the firm of Mouse, Drinkwater, Stone.

Neither the boy nor the strip has a name in *Little, Big*. But they (or their cousins) turn up again in *Love & Sleep*, the second volume of the Ægypt series (Chapter 1.13).

Young Pierce Moffett, each year that he lives in Kentucky, gets a Christmas present, a year-end compilation, in book form, of the newspaper comic strip he has missed by being away from the city: "Little Enosh: Lost Among the Worlds. On the book Enosh's little minnow-like spaceship circled the letters of the title, emitting puffs of smoke." (136) The bad guys are the Uthras, their queen Rutha, proprietor of the Inn of Worlds. Enosh's mother and frequent rescuer is Amanda D'Haye, who lives in the Realm of Light.

Crowley seems to have conflated Nemo's adventures with those of another remarkable dreamer. Enoch (Gen. 5.18-24), who "walked with God" and was one of two men (the other was Elijah) to be bodily transported, without dying—not to heaven, because heaven's gates were not opened till after the crucifixion, but to "the bosom of Abraham." Because of this supernatural status, all kinds of Jewish visionary and prophetic writings were attributed to him; these began to be collected around the second century BCE (and over the next several hundred years) into what we now call The Book of Enoch (Enoch 1) and The Book of the Secrets of Enoch (Enoch 2); they are books of the apocryphal Bible. In them, the dreamer, accompanied by the angel Raguel, has visions of the heavens, hell, "the place where no flesh walks," "the mountains of the darkness of winter," "the four winds that bear the earth and the firmament of heaven" and many other marvels, including what modern fantasies of this sort tend to call The Rapture.[2]

This material was extremely popular among early Christians, and why wouldn't it be? They thought the End Time was right around the corner (as some of the Rapturous today do), and it certainly sounded exciting. Enoch spawned a whole genre of supposedly true accounts of the Jewish, then Christian (Muslim too, eventually) otherworld that has come to be known as "vision literature." These visions, perhaps the medieval equivalent of "I was abducted by aliens" stories, were experienced by ordinary people, written down by the literate clergy and accumulated steadily until they finally fell out of favor in the fourteenth century (just as Dante's huge—and clearly fictional—best-seller began to be distributed)[3].

Just to confuse things, there is also a briefly mentioned Enosh in

There are many other references to children's books throughout *Little, Big*. Grandfather Trout's plight recalls stories from all over the world of humans metamorphosed into animals, but also the medieval creatures of Crowley's earlier novel, *Beasts*, the folktales of magical fish that grant three doubtful wishes, Grandfather Frog from the animal stories of Thornton W. Burgess, and, rather specifically, Kingsley's *The Water Babies*. Book Four is titled "The Wild Wood," also the title of a famous chapter in *The Wind in the Willows*. Dr. Drinkwater publishes his stories "under the name of Saunders," a reference to Rabbit's house in Milne's *Winnie the Pooh*. Hans Christian Andersen's storks also turn up. (Crowley has a nice knack for gentle parodies of his elder authors; he does it with Kingsley in some of the trout sections, Andersen in the stork sections, and, of course, with Burgess—see the sidebar. He's not trying to rival James Joyce; it's done with a whisper-light touch.)

Lewis Carroll is present throughout, and credited. His immortal Alice is invoked in Daily Alice, as are Sylvie and Bruno from the (far from immortal) pair of Carroll's books bearing their names. Considerable homage is paid to Shakespeare's *Midsummer Night's Dream*, which could be called a play for children of all ages. Classical myth gets a nod, with Charon the ferryman, the Gate of Horn beside which the changeling child, Lilac, dreams, and with Fred, the unlikely dryad. Comics get a nod, via *Little Nemo in Slumberland*, probably the only strip really appropriate to *Little, Big*'s curious world—see the other sidebar. Victorian fairy paintings and the illustrations of Arthur Rackham and Edmund Dulac shade the landscape. Even Santa Claus, that jolly old elf, makes an appearance.

I should say a word, too, about Russell Eigenblick, a.k.a. the Emperor Frederick Barbarossa, in a subplot that reads as though it had slouched in from *Beasts* (I wish it had stayed there). It refers back to a kind of turn-of the-century boy's adventure book, now more commonly a book for grown boys, as manufactured by Ian Fleming, Robert Ludlum et al. (many al, even Stephen King). In it, the heroes, boys or men, thwart a Dire and Malevolent Plot to Take Over the World. Here, supernatural complications on both sides thicken that plot; the dénouement is, technically, deplorable, a literal *deus ex machina*.

But it is the set-piece that I admire most, the deceptively homely visit *chez* Woods that Smoky will never recall (and wouldn't believe if he did), but that loads on him the burden of family life with the Drinkwater clan that he so obediently, and indeed gladly shoulders. Crowley is good at set-pieces, and this is one of his best. A world of reading is invoked in just a few pages, a homage to the past, to the writers who shaped our imaginations as well as his own.

the Bible, the son of Seth, Adam's son (Gen. 4.26). And both Enoch and Enosh show up in I Chronicles 1.1 as ancestors of Noah. But it is Enoch the apocryphal dreamer who counts here.

For the Ægypt series, Crowley has made the strip overtly Gnostic, specifically Mandaean. In that mythology, Anosh or Enosh is "man" temporarily exiled in the world of darkness. Manda d'Hayye, "knowledge of life," is the central divine savior figure, called down from the Realm of Light to the lower world. There dwell the Uthras, spirits who can be angels or demons, and Ruha ("spirit") is the chief female demon, mother of the seven Planets and keeper of the Inn of Worlds. All of these figures can be found in Hans Jonas's *The Gnostic Religion*[4] in its survey of Mandaeanism.

Other spirits are introduced in *Love & Sleep*. In Chapter 2.8, in Blackbury Jambs, Val, the local astrologer, and Pierce are both (separately) enduring a sleepless night. She is reading about little Eros (287), whose father was (usually) Hermes, in a book that Pierce had encountered in graduate school ("Little Eros in his chariot, pulled by naked girls . . . Love." 242). Simultaneously, Pierce is reading the 1952 volume of *Little Enosh*, the year that introduced the Robot, Rutha's servant, who talks with Enosh about Higher Things (291).

And a night or two later, little Eros, under the name of Robbie (perhaps the most famous of fictional robots, from the movie

Forbidden Planet), whose father is (sometimes) Pierce, comes to visit dad. Their discourse is not about Higher Things.

In *Dæmonomania*, the strip is directly predictive. Pierce, baby-sitting for five-year-old Sam, reads to her, from the same 1952 volume, the episode in which Enosh tries to rescue Snoopie Sophie, the Kurious Kid, from the Inn of Worlds where Rutha and the Uthras have shackled her. Sophie is his own sister, though Enosh does not know that and their mother has "sort of forgotten"(337). In the central myth of Valentinian Gnosticism[5] (also surveyed in *The Gnostic Religion*), Sophia ("wisdom") is brought down from the Realm of Light by her own curiosity and undergoes much suffering, leading indirectly to the forma-tion of our world and its woes. In Crowley's tale, only pages later, Pierce, the Enosh of the Ægypt series, must himself set out to rescue Sam, this novel's Sophia, from the Powerhouse, a Raptur-ous bunch of latter-day Uthras.

Readers can learn more about this rescue in the interview with Crowley in this collection, though it must be said that the structure of the novel is far from obvious. Here, in the same scene in *Dæ-monomania*, is perhaps Crowley's apologia for indirection:

"Pierce had forgotten how much of the story was always left out, intentions and an-nouncements often standing for deeds, which in the next day's panels have already been done,

Addendum: In the above essay, first written in 1999, I made many errors of assumption, which the author has amiably pointed out to me. He is un-familiar with John R. Neill's eccentric Oz cottages. He had not read Kenneth Grahame's *The Wind in the Willows* when he wrote this scene, and the ap-pearance of the knobby-handed Mr. Woods was inspired not by Rackham's Mole or Badger (in my edition of *The Wind in the Willows*) but by the knob-by gnomes that Arthur Rackham made real for us in his more specific fairytale illustrations. (Not that they're so very different.) Dulac and Rackham were great influences on *Little, Big* from the very beginning, he told me. Amazingly, he had not read C. S. Lewis's Narnia series at that time either—I was certain I'd got that wardrobe right! And I was even more stupefied by his unfamiliar-ity with the uncanny Gladstone bag that P. L. Travers gave to her militant Mary Poppins.

Still, modern criticism allows the reader to bring some baggage (even Gladstone baggage) to a book as well, and I am certain that this scene in this book is meant to be read in exactly the way that I read it—with consid-erable nostalgic feeling—so while I acknowledge them, I'm not correcting these mistakes. With pleasure, instead,

I join my tall namesake in presenting Smoky with my own childhood to stow in that bag. Dear Smoky, please accept your wedding gift with my love.

NOTES

[1] From the Book 1, Ch. 3 heading

There was an old woman
Who lived under the hill
And if she's not gone
She lives there still.

or forgotten. Here was Enosh awake, going down the circular stair of the Inn of the Worlds toward the deepmost Lockup for panel after panel (his little bun feet never actually touching them though, their shadows are clearly visible upon the treads; the most moving thing about Enosh is that he can suffer and be brave and at the same time never actually be touched at all; Pierce beside Sam thought this thought for the first time)"(337).

NOTES

[2] Enoch quotes are from *The Other Bible*, edited by Willis Barnstone, Harper & Row, 1984.

[3] Some of the best of these odd tales are collected in *Visions of Heaven and Hell before Dante*, edited by Eileen Gardiner, Italics Press, 1989.

[4] Hans Jonas, *The Gnostic Religion*, Beacon, 1963.

[5] Valentinius [c.135-160], at first a Christian, introduced the Valentinian Gnostic heresy. Note Val's name.

SHORTER WORKS
AND OVERVIEWS

THE *NOVELTY* OF ÆGYPT
Michael Andre-Driussi

HOW TO BEGIN? That's the danger of handling this material—it is highly infectious. John Crowley's *Novelty* is a virus that comes in through your eyes, rolls around from brain to heart to spleen before finally dribbling out your pen in wooly, stuttering spurts. Not unlike some of the characters in the book: "I sort of go in spurts" (222). Crowley makes it look so easy. *Novelty* examines "Novelty versus Security" from four different-yet-similar perspectives along an evolving continuum: "The Nightingale Sings at Night" (a revisionist fantasy); "Great Work of Time" (a time travel story); "In Blue" (a science fiction dystopia story); and "Novelty" (a story about inspiration and writer's block—a mimetic story). The last one was first published in *Interzone* (1985); the others were previously unpublished. The word going around is that the story "Novelty" was a blueprint for *Ægypt*. Well, this is absolutely and obviously true. I want to go out on a limb and boldly assert that all of *Novelty* is a blueprint for the as-yet-incomplete Ægypt series.

Novelty has a narrative structure, starting in the Garden of Eden where Boy and Girl are together; next comes the abortive Boy's world, or "History"; then the dystopian Girl's world, or "Herstory"; and finally the bitter end of irreconcilability that might also serve as the "Genesis" for Ægypt. Throughout these stories and modes, "novelty" always wins in the struggle between novelty and security: the security of Eden is warped by novel thought and then left behind; the "sea of perpetual peace" endpoint in "Great Work" is so repugnant that the Cape-to-Cairo timeline is erased; the security of the Revolution's heterarchy in "In Blue" is so stifling that Girl escapes and Hare goes insane; the security of marriage is abandoned for the novelty of being lonely in middle age.

"Nightingale" offers the promise of old-made-new through revisionist/gnostic fantasy. Yet this bubble is burst when the end result, expulsion from Eden, is the same; and even the promise becomes tarnished as it becomes clear that the end is actually worse—men and women have gone separate ways.

"Great Work of Time" is likewise the hope and death of science fiction, especially that early brand of youthful, optimistic, technophilic, "can-do" sort of sf. The boyish dream of making a better present by altering history via time machine has spawned a large subgenre, and this particular example also features a multi-ethnic crew of men and woman, the sort of retrofit to the boy's dream that we associate with the genre's "progress," "maturity," etc. That this is a boy fiction is made abundantly clear: "that remark of George Santayana . . . about the British Empire . . . 'Never since the Athenians has the world been ruled by such sweet, just, boyish masters'" (57). Again, in the end it all comes crashing down in a silent implosion, and this time collateral damage spreads out into genre, since Crowley built his demolition palace out of timbers named Philip K. Dick, Keith Laumer, and H. G. Wells. But don't get too incensed; Crowley turns a savage criticism against himself.

Welcome to Crowley Country.
Everything in this book links back into another Crowley work—that "Novelty" is the blueprint for Ægypt is only the most blindingly obvious, but in addition, that story is set in "the Seventh Saint Bar & Grill" which ties it to the place of that name in *Little, Big* (book 4, ch. 2, section 3). Even Victor the bartender is from

Little, Big, where he plays the exact same sort of role of "victor" (Auberon knows that Victor went to Florida and believes he took with him Auberon's girlfriend Sylvie). The capital-b Blue, symbol of the Party throughout the story "In Blue," bears strong echoes of *Beasts*, where the politicals wear the same sort of blue uniforms ("Sten in Blue, playing with other boys" [ch. 3]), and the wilderness utopians of Candy's Mountain surround themselves with blue in their giant anthill. The science of "In Blue," "act-field theory and social calculus," the philosophical basis of and for the Revolution, first appeared in *Beasts* as "social erg-quotients and a holocompetent act-field" (ch. 4), a tool of USE, the frightening "Jesuits of Empire"; and the motif "Jesuits of Empire" itself appears again in "Great Work of Time" with regard to the Otherhood (86).

There's also the Gnosticism. Crowley has always written about Gnosticism, but he used to be so cryptic about it that it still gives me a thrill when he names it directly in "Great Work" and "Novelty."

But then there's that self-severed penis.

Adonis Lies Bleeding.

This is a central image to Crowley's work, yet one he usually approaches obliquely. The recurring hero is Adonis, the beautiful lover who is genitally mutilated either by the cruel goddess whom he loves or by a jealous warrior god.

The hero of *The Deep* is a sexless android sent to be a warlord, but a bullet wound to its head turned it into an accidental emissary of love and gnosis; it leaves the world and does not see how the world has been changed by its actions.

The hero of *Engine Summer* is an Orpheus type who follows after his cruel girlfriend; she wounds him again and again (at one point he says his penis has become useless); he dies offstage and does not see how the world has been changed by his life story.

One hero of *Little, Big* is a human used for reproduction by his fairy wife and her family; he is abandoned in the mundane world and locked out of the world he made possible.

Denys Winterset of "Great Work," while he avoids love and women and (therefore?) genital mutilation, still is locked out of the better world he destroyed, and if we read his name as "denies Winter," we detect the same endless Summer god evoked by title and text of *Engine Summer*. So here he is again, and for "In Blue" his name is Hare. Why "Hare"? As an animal name, this ties back into *Beasts* where all the main characters have animal associations. The hare features in the phrase "Mad as a March hare" because March is the rutting month of hares, a time when they are in an excited state. (Can't forget the March Hare of *Alice in Wonderland*—Lewis Carroll is an important influence on Crowley.) And our Hare suffers a breakdown when his estranged wife leaves him to go into the wilderness with another man (a reproductive wounding; a post-conception discarding). (Note from John Crowley: "Also, a reference to Samuel Butler's line about running with the hares or running with the hounds [*Way of All Flesh*].")

I said before that "In Blue" is "herstory." This is twofold: first in the sense that the society rejects history; second in that the society is dominated by women. Crowley never explicitly says this, but still: The only male characters are Hare, Willy, and Boy; all the others—friends, strangers, people in power, people riding on the truck—all are women. All the sexual relationships are homosexual (female-female) and/or non-monogamous (Willy boasts of his numerous lovers, male and female), with the exception of Hare and Eva. (Contrast with the "multi-ethnic" mix in "Great Work.")

Hare copies a Latin phrase from a ruinous monument in the unnamed city: IAM REDIT ET VIRGO REDEUNT SATURNIA REGNA. This is from Virgil's fourth Eclogue, or ode to the countryside: "Now the Virgin returns; now Saturn is king again." This signals that Hare is living in a golden age (as the reign of Saturn is said to have been), but in a nod to Robert Graves, the gold is that of a beehive. (The "Virgin" might be seen as all the nonreproducing women that rule—Girl Power!) When Crowley painted the human insect society in *Beasts*, Candy's Mountain emerged as a flawed-but-not-unpleasant utopia: call it suburbia. But this time through there is no mistaking the dystopian nature.

As such, Hare is a drone of the hive, and suffers the wounding of a drone; he is the Saturn of the Latin phrase, and suffers the wounding of Saturn. We can follow this chain to an even more depressing conclusion: Eva, rather than "escaping" (which seems to offer some hope for somebody, at least), might be really just going afield to start up her own hive. "Ave Eva" means "Hail Eve" and "Goodbye Eve."

"I love you, Big Sister"; or the auto-da-fé of John Crowley.

When Hare re-embraces the Revolution we cannot help seeing broken Winston Smith at the end of his re-education. But in fact there is much more to it than that, because Hare's self-criticism sets the dominos tumbling back to "Great Work," and we realize with a start that "Great Work" is a savage critique of *Little, Big*: the creation of an anglophilic world of faerie (i.e., the world of both CC 2015 and *Little, Big*) is a curse which must be erased. "Faerie" is the product of Empire, the offspring of aggressive, unending Colonialism.

In the same way, "In Blue" explodes the soft and pastoral *Engine Summer* by showing a post-apocalyptic nontechnological society that is so far from "pastoral" that the inclusion of allusion to Virgil's odes to the countryside is a cruel irony.

John Crowley's little dark hart.

When people talk of Crowley's fiction they typically characterize it as warm, sentimental, lyrical, sometimes bittersweet, often dancing at the edge of twee yet never falling. All of which is generally true. But there are eruptions of a different voice, which I call "Dark John"—partly in allusion to the light and dark emotions in *Engine Summer*. To paraphrase: "When John was dark he was very very dark, and when he was light he was lighter than air."

"Dark John" is the co-author of *The Deep*, author of *Beasts* and *Novelty* and a few short stories like "Exogamy."

> The American writer William Seabrook has a story of how [Aleister] Crowley demonstrated his magical power on Fifth Avenue. On a deserted stretch of pavement, Crowley fell into step behind a man and imitated his walk. Then, suddenly, Crowley buckled at the knees and squatted for a moment on his haunches; the man collapsed on to the pavement. As they helped him to his feet, he looked around in a puzzled manner for the banana skin.
>
> This is clearly not hypnosis, but it sounds like some curious form of telepathy—of the establishment of a "sympathy" between Crowley and his victim (Wilson 15).

The magic that John Crowley works is another form of sympathetic magic—the more you read, the more you come to identify with the characters. So a person reading *Novelty* as a first exposure to Crowley would be passed over by the dark assassin: but lo, he who has read every other bit of Crowley first (I am speaking of myself here) will be surprised to see Dark John plunge a dagger into his own breast as an act of suicide—and marvel as the reader's blood gushes forth.

Dark John says (in *Beasts*, *Engine Summer*, etc.) that most women are incapable of love (among men, the "Adonis" is a slave of love; the "Warlord" is not). The rare woman warrior, tough, independent, resourceful, is less capable of love than her sisters, until she meets the Warlord who crushes her: and then she becomes his personal slave, and through slavery she finds love.

Men searching for Love; Women destroying Men.
For instance, take Rush of *Engine Summer*—his mother is nearly absent from the text, she is emotionally cool and physically distant. (She is a working woman: her "9 to 5" job is beekeeping—surely

that is a joke, but is it savage satire aimed at all working moms?) His girlfriend is full of wild romance and mystery, but then she suddenly goes away and he follows. Well, good thing—otherwise no story! Likewise the hero in "Exogamy" (collected in *Antiquities*), searching for Love and finding a harpy. And Hare, of course. Smoky of *Little, Big* is the lucky one—he found her, and loved her, for the rest of his life.

Battle of the sexes as Total War.

Often in the background, sometimes in the foreground. The apocalypse which made the world of *Engine Summer* had a few movements, but the most coherent one is a war between the revolutionary Long League of Women and the technophilic "Avvengers" (a blend of "scavengers" and "avengers"). We don't know how the apocalypse came prior to "In Blue," but the cadre seems rather like the Long League. In the Ægypt books, men as werewolves fight women as witches.

"In shape more like a bullet or a bomb."

If the nightingale sings at night in the first section, then the last section might be subtitled "The Crow weeps bitter in the afternoon." Yes, Adonis lies bleeding, once again, and he is getting pretty angry about it. He is making grim resolutions.

The story "Novelty" is about writer's block, a domino that falls back against the writer's block Hare suffered through "In Blue," which falls back on the writer's struggle and surrender in "Great Work of Time." "Nightingale" ends like Pandora's story, with a silver lining of Hope, but then Hope takes a beating through the subsequent stories, so that "Novelty" might be called "Hope is dead."

The story "Novelty" is so full of allusions to Crowley-as-writer that it seems starkly autobiographical—David Wingrove writes of its viewpoint character as "a novelist who could quite readily stand in as a persona for Crowley in his attitudes." The reader, especially the habitual Crowley reader, is sucked into believing that this mask is real: and thus, that Crowley is talking about, or confessing to, a debilitating writer's block, perhaps related to the six-year gap between *Little, Big* and the first volume of Ægypt. The minority view contends that Crowley is not blocked, pointing out that Crowley has always taken several years to write a book.

The situation in "Novelty" is mildly depressing by itself, but this extratextual angle makes it crushing: the writer assures himself that all he has to do is write a page a day and after a year or so he will have a novel; yet the reader knows that many years have gone by without a new novel from Crowley.

But no, it is just Dark John messing with you again. Unless you really believe that Crowley is the sort of Ted Kaczynski-style vengeance seeker that the writer in "Novelty" seems to be, seeing his pen as a bullet or a bomb.

Trapped in a flawed world of his own creation.
Man in his post-Eden world; Denys in his C2 timeline; Hare in his herstory; and the writer who is trapped in the world of *Little, Big*, looking for the doorway out . . . into the world of Ægypt.

Ægypt.
Crowley is in love with Tarot. That's a fact. And Tarot is linked to gypsies; gypsies are so called because they were once thought to have come from Egypt—but it wasn't that Egypt, it was another one, call it "Ægypt." Right, except behind that story is the one saying they came from India. So maybe, just maybe, "Ægypt" is Crowley-code for "Indiana."

First Outward, then Inward, now Backward.
My theory, take it or leave it, is that Crowley thematically explored the seven celestial spheres of the ancients in *Beasts*, saving the modern discoveries "Neptune" and "Uranus" for *The Deep*, and "Pluto" for *Engine Summer*. Then he turned inward with *Little,*

Big, which posits worlds within worlds. And now in the Ægypt series he is going backward to unravel a secret history.

"When we grow older, we realize that life has shapes."
So said Crowley in Michael Swanwick's micro-interview (*The New York Review of Science Fiction* No. 129). The "shape of life" in Ægypt is the seven year cycle of up years and down years (seven being a number tied to the ancient celestial bodies, which is made explicit in the text).

The Ægypt series is projected to have four volumes. A handy number, suggesting the seasons, and the cycle of seasons is close to Crowley's heart. Also the number of stories in Novelty: and what do you know! "Nightingale" is Spring, "Great Work" is Summer, "In Blue" is Autumn, and "Novelty" is Winter.

Does this mean that "Nightingale" matches up to Ægypt and "Great Work" matches up to *Love & Sleep*? No, I don't think so. (Then again, *Love & Sleep* does involve rewriting history . . .)

Each Crowley book seems to have its own central number: The Deep is "52" (for weeks of the year and cards of the deck—not counting the Seven Trumps, which are links to planets again); Beasts is "7"; *Little, Big* is "5" . . . which brings us back to "In Blue" and that curious toy that Willy gave Hare for Boy:

> a nesting set of the five regular geometric solids, all in-
> side a sphere. They could be taken apart, and with some
> trouble, put back together again. (178)

As Boy opens the sphere and withdraws the first shape, the tetrahedron (four-sided pyramid), Eva drops her emotional bomb on Hare and the universe changes (as it nearly always does in Crowley's fiction).

The five regular geometric solids are very important to Pythagorean and Neo-Platonist thought: the cube represents the element earth; the tetrahedron represents fire; the octahedron represents air; the icosahedron (twenty sides) represents water; and the dodecahedron (twelve sides) represents aether or spirit.

So what Crowley has done is to put these all within a sphere, which we might take to represent the physical universe. And he has put them in a certain order, the first element inward is Fire, and the final element at the heart of it all is probably Spirit.

Do you see it yet?

Here: In *Little, Big* we learn all about worlds (plural) within worlds. The 52 member family at Edgewood makes the translation from the mundane world to the next; the 52 denizens of the next world simultaneously translate to the one beyond that; and so on.

In "In Blue," Hare is locked out of the world of Fire that Eva is going to—she flatly excludes him. In *Little, Big*, Smoky Barnable (hmm, that's fire related, no?) is locked out of the next world. Well . . . he dies on the threshold.

Statements.

Novelty is a collection of four unrelated stories.

Novelty is all about writer's block: In the beginning, creation is child's play, but then it becomes hopelessly tangled and convoluted until the writer is mutilated, and then he can only watch, bitter and sad, as the muse gives flowers to others.

Novelty contains several Crowley touchstones: "Adonis Lies Bleeding"; "Gender War"; "White Goddess Triangle"; "Gnosticism"; "A Christ Who Didn't Die on the Cross." Novelty is all outtakes from Ægypt, in the same way that *Engine Summer* might have been an outtake from *Little, Big*. If it reflects Ægypt, it is distortedly, through omissions. At the same time, it reflects Crowley's four previous novels as well.

Novelty is just a book, I'm really talking about myself. For years I've been blocked in my attempts to write a story of seven—imagine my surprise when I was coaxed into rereading *Beasts*! Certain images (even quirky phrases!) had already worked their way into my unpublished fiction—and I don't even like *Beasts*.

I would like to thank Gordon Brain, Matthew Freestone, Nigel Price, and Peter Nagle for their assistance in locating the Arch in London and interpreting the Latin phrases of "In Blue."

WORKS CITED

Crowley, John.
Novelty. Bantam: New York. 1989.

Wilson, Colin.
Aleister Crowley: the Nature of the Beast. The Aquarian Press, Thorsons Publishing Group: Northamptonshire, England. 1987.

Wingrove, David.
"The Wounded King" (an introduction to John Crowley's *Beasts*). *The SF Alternative* (reprint series), John Goodchild Publishers: UK. 1984.

TIMELINES FOR *GREAT WORK OF TIME*

YEAR	ORIGINAL SITUATION	CAPE-TO-CAIRO	CC2
1856	One stamp.	Two stamps.	
1893	Rhodes lives.	Rhodes assassinated by Denys, wills fortune to foundation of the Otherhood.	Rhodes lives, Denys CC (age 33) visits Denys CC (age 23), Denys CC (age 23) stranded in CC2.
1899	Boer War begins.	(no Boer War).	Denys working on railroad (1896-1902)
1902	Rhodes dies.		Rhodes dies.
1914	WWI begins.	WWI begins.	
1915		The 1915 Peace.	
1918	WWI ends.		
1930	R101 crashes.		
1933		R101 flies, Denys born (1933).	Denys CC2 born.
1935			R101 crashes (1935)
1939	WWII begins.	(No WWII [1939]).	War (1939).
1956		Denys on R101, recruited by Otherhood (1956).	British Empire crumbles, Denys CC (age 86) meets Denys CC2 (age 23) in Central Africa (1956).
1960s			Denys CC dies in London (1960s).
1983	Caspar Last invents technique, travels through time to 1856 to get second stamp, returns to sell stamp for high price to proto-Otherhood.	Denys (on behalf of Otherhood) buys technique and stamp for low price from Caspar Last, destroys stamp (1983).	Denys CC2 as ultimate narrator; March 8, 10, the sale of the single known stamp for far less, bought from proto-Otherhood, second stamp destroyed.
1990s	Last leaks secret, proto-Otherhood gets technique.	Denys (33 years old?) goes to future.	
2015		Fairyworld, Denys tells tale of Cape-to-Cairo.	
Endpoint		Sea of perpetual peace.	

NOTES:
OS: historically, R101 crashed in France on its proving flight to India in 1930.
CC: the 1915 Peace (p. 91)
CC2: 1933, Denys born (p. 119)
CC2: R101 crashes after 1933 (p. 119)
CC2: War (1939) children sent to countryside when Denys was six (p. 120)
Secret Insight: while this table matches the text, it apparently does not match John Crowley's intent: in correspondence responding to this information he has indicated that he intended what is labeled here as "CC2" be literally (rather than virtually) "Original Situation"; that is, the alternate timeline is erased and all returns to normal (rather than a third state which only approximates "normal"). It all flows from the date of R101's crash (OS 1930 versus CC2 1933+), and it is difficult to see how this error can be repaired: if Denys's year of birth is simply moved back five years, then he will be perhaps too old (career-wise, as well as mentally and physically) for recruitment in the critical year of CC1956. To fix the crash of R101 to 1930 would mean that Denys's father cannot be crying from first hearing the news after 1933 (p. 119); then again, he could be weeping on the fifth anniversary in 1935.

TIME'S GREAT WORK
AND STRANGE TURNINGS
Brian Attebery

THROUGHOUT JOHN CROWLEY'S fiction, characters are caught up in time's movement (as are we all, of course). They peer anxiously into the future, sift through remnants of the past trying to recapture its wholeness, trap themselves in small loops and eddies of time, run like delayed passengers to catch the next significant historical shift. What they do not do is live placidly from day to day in a continuous untroubled present.

Very little of Crowley's work takes place in the present. His early novels take readers into a disintegrating near-future (*Beasts*), a further distant post-disaster America (*Engine Summer*), and an alien environment that might be a far future but has the atmosphere of the early renaissance (*The Deep*). His breakthrough work, *Little, Big*, begins in what looks like contemporary New York, but his protagonist's first act is to walk away from that present day into a pocket of magical time, and the rest of the novel shifts from there to the Victorian past and a near-future apocalypse. In his four-volume Ægypt sequence, the present is likewise a jumping-off point into various realms of memory and imagination, especially into the memories of protagonist Pierce Moffett and the historical reconstructions of another character named Fellowes Kraft. In addition, the long gaps between novels in the sequence mean that the first book's present has already become part of history before the fourth book is even published, a fact acknowledged and explored in the later volumes. One of the themes emerging in the sequence is the way moments of great change are already over before we notice them.

There is no word for the kind of time Crowley invokes. It isn't circular, like mythic cycles. It certainly isn't linear. The past does not lead right up to the present, with the future unfolding straight ahead. Instead, Crowley's kind of time involves sudden swerves, ninety-degree turns. The past is not behind us but around a corner. There is no future before us but rather a host of possible futures, depending on which way we turn. Actually, Crowley has given us a name for this view of time. It is what characters in "Great Work of Time" call "orthogonal logic," the logic of right angles. In that story such logic makes time travel possible, or rather it makes possible something that looks like time travel but is really wandering among possibilities.

Here is how the story's narrator describes orthogonal logic:

> The universe proceeds out of what it has been and into what it will be, inexorably, unstoppably, at the rate of one second per second, one year per year, forever. At right angles to its forward progress lie the past and the future. The future, that is to say, does not lie "ahead" of the present in the stream of time, but at a right angle to it: the future of any present moment can be projected as far as you like outward from it, infinitely in fact, but when the universe has proceeded further, and a new present moment has succeeded this one, the future of this one retreats with it into the what-has-been, forever outdated. It is similar but more complicated with the past. (63)

This difficult geometrical parable is actually a key to Crowley's work. It conveys something of his characters' sense of always being caught up in something they neither understand nor control: not just change but changefulness, mutagenesis, the universe's incessant drive to remake itself. All the while, his characters try to go on just as they were, imposing continuity, hanging thin strands of memory and narrative across the historical gulfs. Time's great work is to change us, he suggests; ours is to resist that change by treating past and future as if they were here at hand.

The quoted passage also suggests a major difference between past and future. Our relation to the former is more complicated. The past isn't here with us, but its left luggage is all around. Whatever past we reconstruct in imagination must cope with all those trunks and boxes and scattered wrappers. The future is emptier. It exists in the present only as a diagram, a set of dots to be turned into boxes and claimed with an initial.

Crowley's fictions of the future all have a little of that schematic quality. Two examples can be found in the collection appropriately titled *Novelty*. "Great Work of Time" describes a set of futures, each spinning off from the actions of a time-traveling cadre called the Otherhood. Members of this group are dispatched to moments of crisis to avert historical disasters of various sorts. They attempt to make the world safer, saner, and (because they are British) tidier. Each time they act, a new future is generated, a new corner turned. The more they interfere, the more improbable those futures grow; and the more improbable they become, the thinner their texture. In eliminating upheavals, the Otherhood's initiates have also eliminated the free play of history, the richness of the past. In the end, the stability they have aimed for will be merely stasis:

> "The sea is still and the forest is thick; it grows upward from the black bottom, and its topmost branches reach into the sunlight, which penetrates a little into the warm upper waters. That's all. There is nothing else anywhere forever. Your wishes have come true: the Empire is quiet. There is not, nor will there be, change anymore; never will one thing be confused again with another, higher

for lower, better for lesser, master for servant. Perpetual Peace." (116-17)

A similarly bleak uniformity marks the future described in "In Blue," a story about planning. Like the Otherhood, the blue-uniformed planners of this society have developed a mathematical model that allows them to intervene in the course of history. In this case, it is not orthogonal time travel but social calculus, turning human behavior into probabilities. Musing on his discipline, the protagonist Hare compares human actions to snowflakes, each once believed to be unique but now known to vary only to an extent that is statistically insignificant. No wonder the world created by these planners is drab and dystopian, full of boxlike buildings and masklike faces. Hare himself is emotionally vacant. He cannot interact with the non-planning caste, those who are not in blue, because "he had no stories himself that he could tell" (158).

Hare finds a way out of the trap of predictability. It is the past. Studying the architectural remains of a bygone age, he reinvents history, which his society has tried to erase. He learns to see around the corner into the past by studying the corners of buildings:

> The past thought in geometry: in circles, sections of circles, right triangles, squares, sections of squares. The building before him was nothing but an agglomerate of regular geometrical figures, cut in stone and overlaid with these striving figures continually trying, but never succeeding, in bursting them apart. (164)

The more he studies the geometry of the past, the closer he comes to breaking out of the social calculus of the future. The intricacy of one counters the sterility of the other.

The cadres of both "In Blue" and "Great Work of Time" have only the best intentions. Their crime, in both cases, is that they try to treat the past as they treat the future. Futures can be orderly because they have not yet happened. They will always tend toward reduction and rigidity because of the process by which they are created, the angle at which they are thrown off from the present. But pasts must be chaotic and creative. They should not be reduced. Early in "In Blue," storyless Hare speculates on snowflakes and human behavior. He does not realize that he has been constructing a story about the past, about what was once thought and believed, or that the act of composing such a story could be his salvation. Even the unacknowledged possibility makes him afraid, and so "He pressed a key on the composer and held it down, and letter by letter his story about the snowflakes was removed from the screen" (152).

It is probably not by coincidence that another Crowley story concerns memory, change, snowflakes, and viewscreens. The main character in "Snow" is a man whose wife, Georgie, has just died. The couple had inherited from Georgie's wealthy first husband a new device, an unobtrusive electronic "Wasp" that could follow them around and record their moments together. After her death, the protagonist/narrator discovers that he can go to the mortuary to view the recordings: "through the miracle of modern information storage and retrieval systems you could access her: her alive, her as she was in every way, never changing or growing any older: fresher (as the Park's brochure said) than in memory–ever green" (592).

But the viewer has no choice of moments to relive–access is random. And randomness invites entropy. At first, the scenes called up on the screen are a mix of happy moments and sad, summer and winter. The more often the widower comes to the Park, though, the less he sees of the good times with Georgie.

"You might start getting some snow," says the Park attendant, when he tries accessing the Wasp's recordings (600). Interference, he thinks, like a bad television picture. But it is not interference he sees, but real snow. The more he watches--the more compulsively he tries to live in the past--the less rewarding the experience becomes. The picture quality does disintegrate, but more importantly, the random access more and more frequently directs his attention to moments of darkness and cold, not to the sunny life he remembers.

When he complains, the attendant compares the Wasp's recordings to an archive where he once worked. Among "miles of film cans" in the archive, "we had everything, every kind of scene, but you know what the hardest thing to find was? Just ordinary scenes of daily life. I mean people just doing things and living their lives" (602). Like most historical records, the film archive was skewed, slanted toward political speeches and staged events and away from "people long ago, in the summer; having fun, eating ice cream. Swimming in bathing suits. Riding in convertibles" (603). The longer ago, the less fair-weather fun: "The farther back I went, the more I saw these pinched faces, black cars, black streets of stone. Snow. There isn't any summer there" (603).

The protagonist finally decides that there are two sorts of memory. One disintegrates, degrades, turns to ice. The other is "the sleepwalking kind, the kind you stumble into as into rooms with secret doors to suddenly find yourself sitting not on your front porch but in a classroom, you can't at first think where or when, and a bearded smiling man is turning in his hand a glass paperweight inside which a little cottage stands in a swirl of snow" (603). This is the living sort of memory. Without any act of will or planning, a window opens onto a past that is not fixed and frozen but swirling and unexpected. This is the sort of memory that will keep Georgie alive, rather than embalmed in frost. So the narrator leaves the Park and goes back to the present, where there are still summers and where at least occasionally "a memory of that kind will visit me, vivid and startling, like a hypnotist's snap of fingers, or like that funny experience you sometimes have, on the point of sleep, of hearing your name called softly and distinctly by someone who is not there" (604).

Memory plays a major role in Crowley's fiction, from the memory crystals of *Engine Summer* to the Renaissance Art of Memory in *Little, Big* and throughout the Ægypt novels. But I am looking here, not at memory *per se*, but at pasts and futures, history and utopian prophecy. One of Crowley's particular strengths is his ability to convey the personal side of historical change: the sudden sense of solid ground giving way beneath one's feet, the pang of nostalgia for a future that never came into being, the oddness of coming across forgotten relics from one's own earlier existence. He has honed this skill not only by writing stories about historical pasts and science fictional futures, but also by working, like the Park attendant, in film archives. John Crowley's other career is as a writer of documentaries such as the 1985 film *The World of Tomorrow*, about the 1939 New York World's Fair.

The script for this film, just like Crowley's fiction, presents us with both a fluid, unsettled past and a static and curiously archaic future. It shows how both are mediated for us by fantasy. These are the same themes that run through "Snow," "In Blue," "Great Work of Time," and the recent novels. I suspect that his experience as a researcher into and reconstructor of the past has profoundly influenced his fiction.

The World of Tomorrow is framed by a first-person narration, the memories of an imaginary fair-goer looking back on his own past. The narration, spoken with singular conviction by Jason Robards (many viewers think he is simply describing his own experience), is combined with historical footage of an equally fictional family of visitors to the Fair, taken from a short promotional film. Robards's character becomes the older self of the boy in the promotional film–pretty slippery stuff for a documentary, but it works because of the documentary filmmakers' careful research and because of Crowley's desire to show how history really works. History isn't simply there to be grasped, any more than "Snow"'s narrator can grasp his life with Georgie. It has to be reconstructed, narrated, fictionalized. Historical truth is something we can approach only by making things up.

The narrator begins, "The past is black and white. The first decades of this century are black and white. My own childhood is black and white. I look again and again at pictures, snapshots, movies like these, and my earliest memories seem to lose the color they contain and to become like these images." He then describes the building of the amazing Fair, contrasting the sleek futurism of its exhibits with the Depression-era drabness outside. A key moment in the narrative is newsreel footage of the filling of a time capsule for the Westinghouse pavilion.

Any time capsule turns the present into an imagined future's past. Filling one is like posing for posterity: you put on your good clothes and your most rehearsed expression in hopes that someone looking at it later will take the artifice for truth. Yes, that's just like him; I remember that year. Anything left out of the picture is out of the past as well, so we try to select carefully, not knowing that whatever we select will look strange and silly to posterity.

The Westinghouse capsule's inventory is a ridiculous hodgepodge: scientific texts, a pack of Camels, a message from Einstein, a restaurant menu, a golf tee, a Lily Daché hat, a dollar in change. Actually, though, this is no weirder than the sort of inventory, Time's flotsam, from which we construct our own pasts. What sort of world can historians—or documentary film makers—put together from the fragments and odd lots that have washed up on the shores of the present?

Talking about the surviving artifacts from Puritan New England, historian John Demos points out what a weird experience it is to try to put them together into a living model of the past:

> The objects are all right there before you, solid, tangible, real; but gradually they begin to dance before your eyes. Some of them, you feel, *must* have been placed here or there and used in this or that way; functional considerations seem obvious and decisive. But for others the picture is much less clear. Alternative possibilities begin to suggest themselves: chairs move, dinnerware disappears, pots change places, lamps and heddles and buckets hang uncertainly in midair. (20-21)

This is witchcraft. I think Demos must have been influenced by the fact that he was writing about Salem. Most historians are not so candid about their uncertainties or about the degree to which their reconstructions are subject to unexpected transformations every time new evidence or interpretive frameworks emerge.

Crowley invokes the same sort of witchcraft when he writes about the early 20th century shifting from black and white to color, in this film, or about medieval magic suddenly being replaced by science, in *Ægypt* and its sequel *Love & Sleep*, or the threat of the reverse in the third volume, *Dæmonomania*. It's no wonder his pasts are so fluid, so open-ended. He has good evidence that they are. In the documentary, we see a newsreel in which an ordinary event takes place: a politician makes an announcement to the press, cracks a joke, everyone chuckles. Then we see the same event take place all over again, slightly differently. It was a second take. Which was the real event?

At the Fair and in the promotional film about the Fair, we see American society presenting itself in terms of Hollywood-style, all-white, middle-class life, as if Andy Hardy movies were reality. We see a scale model of the country, part of the General Motors exhibit, that is a simulated "plane ride over an America from which the past–my present–had vanished, seemingly without a trace." It is only a small step from this vanishing, this rewriting of the past, to "Great Work of Time," with its corps of time-travelling historical revisionists.

In the Ægypt quartet, various pasts are invoked: Pierce's rural childhood, his would-be decadent youth, Elizabethan England, Renaissance Bohemia. Each is fuller of detail, more ripe with possibility, than the narrative present. That is partly because they are storytellers' pasts. Many of the scenes, such as those concerning the wizard John Dee, come out of historical writings by Fellowes Kraft, a novelist and a bit of a magician himself. The combination of fantasy with the haphazard, junkshop richness that forms the historical record makes the 17th century more vital than the late 20th.

If Crowley's pasts are always in flux and full of possibility, his futures, as noted above, are regimented and somehow passé. From the artificial flat earth of *The Deep* to the engineered dystopia of "In Blue," futures in Crowley's work share a sense of something missing, of lost opportunities and frozen patterns. This too is part of the picture presented in *The World of Tomorrow*. Not only is there the diorama with the past wiped out, but the entire vision of the future evoked at the World's Fair is of "A color-coded city: bright, rational, completely planned." The narrator explains that "City planners and functionalist architects believed they knew what the future had to be like, and what ordinary Americans had to learn to live successfully in it." What they had to learn, it is implied, is to cease being ordinary and to become equally bright, rational, and color-coded–perhaps "in blue."

Utopias almost always have this sort of thinness and rigidity, but Crowley's vision goes beyond the defects of planned societies to suggest that the act of projecting forward inevitably serves to fix the imagined future in one form. Hence, by orthogonal logic the projection is always instantly out of date, since the moment it was projected from is already over. Futures are empty because they have not had time to deposit layer on layer of improbable details like golf tees and Lily Daché hats. It is no wonder that when members of the Otherhood tinker with the past in order to produce their vision of the future, the end result is not only stasis, but a state reminiscent of the distant past, of early Devonian fern trees and slime and silence.

The narrator of "Great Work of Time" tries to explain why the "nexus of possibilities" opened up by time travel has instead closed off all futures. It is because "they were like a man standing at the north pole, whose only view, wherever he looks, is south: they looked out upon a single encompassing reality, which is their opportunity–no, their duty, as they saw it–to make as happy as possible, as free from the calamities they knew of as they could make it" (139).

By contrast, the narrator of *The World of Tomorrow*, standing on a similar nexus sees (in hindsight) the Fair's planned future giving way to unseen forces in the (remembered) present. The result is chaos and tragedy but not stasis. Perhaps the last words spoken by Jason Robards give us some glimpse of the direction Crowley will take in the final volume of his quartet and in works to come:

> I think that there are moments when you can see the world turning from what it is into what it will be. For me the New York World's Fair is such a moment. It is a compass rose pointing in all directions, toward imaginary future and real past, false future and immutable present, a World of Tomorrow contained in a lost American yesterday.

WORKS CITED

Crowley, John.
Ægypt. New York: Bantam, 1987.
Beasts. Garden City, NY: Doubleday, 1976.
Dæmonomania. New York: Bantam, 2000.
The Deep. Garden City, NY: Doubleday, 1975.
Engine Summer. Garden City, NY: Doubleday, 1979.
"Great Work of Time." *Novelty*. New York: Doubleday, 1989. 37-141.
"In Blue." *Novelty*. New York: Doubleday, 1989. 143-202.
Little, Big. New York: Bantam, 1981.
Love & Sleep. New York: Bantam, 1984.
"Snow." *Omni* November 1985; rpt in *The Norton Book of Science Fiction*. Ed. Ursula K. Le Guin and Brian Attebery. New York: Norton, 1993. 591-604.

Demos, John.
A Little Commonwealth: Family Life in Plymouth Colony. New York: Oxford UP, 1970.

The World of Tomorrow. Dir. Lance Bird and Tom Johnson. Script by John Crowley. Direct Cinema, 1984.

MEMORY AND THE WORLD OF JOHN CROWLEY:
TECHNOLOGY AND THE ART OF MEMORY

Jennifer K. Stevenson

I. Introduction

JOHN CROWLEY'S FICTIONS often concern memory, sometimes in the context of Renaissance mnemotechnics, sometimes
using science-fictional devices. Crowley uses organically-based
memory models like the Art of Memory, or fictional variations on
it, to illustrate the beneficent, expansive, even healing aspects of
memory. His mechanical memory devices serve to point up memory's limitations—the painful and tragic limitations of human memory, counterpointed by the limitations of mechanical memory.

Those of Crowley's works that deal most with memory are *Little, Big*, "In Blue," "Snow," *Ægypt* and portions of *Love & Sleep*,
and, most of all, *Engine Summer*, in which natural and mechanical
memory devices work on the characters in the clearest contrasts. A
short summary of those texts follows:

Engine Summer is a very densely memory-oriented pastoral
about a boy growing up in a post-holocaustal America who wants
to become a saint. The surprise ending to this novel is central to my
analysis, for the narrator, Rush that Speaks, is revealed to be not really Rush but someone who has become a temporary host to Rush's

memories, who tells Rush's story as if he were Rush.

The story "In Blue" describes the mental breakdown of Hare, a mathematician whose work falls apart after his lover leaves him. He has been working on the world-making, history-breaking Act-Field Theory, a social application of statistics and chaos theory that has revolutionized this post-collapse world.

"Snow" is a near-future story about a gigolo remembering his dead wife with and without the aid of a spy-bug called the Wasp, whose massed recordings of her life can be accessed only randomly in a kind of posh underground cemetery.

Little, Big, Ægypt, and *Love & Sleep* deal directly with the Art of Memory. *Little, Big* is about a war or conspiracy or Tale involving the fairies and humans; *Ægypt* and *Love & Sleep* treat a theory of history and parallel worlds, and focus on the fascination with magic of two eras: the Renaissance and the New Age.

II. The Art of Memory

The Art of Memory has been central to Crowley's writings from his earliest published work, and versions of the Art can be found throughout.[1] For a brief description of the basics of the Greek or architectural version of this natural memory system, Ariel Hawksquill's explanation in *Little, Big* is perfectly accurate. Hawksquill says:

> The ancients agreed that vivid pictures in a strict order were the most easily remembered. Therefore, in order to construct an Artificial Memory of great power, the first step . . . is to choose a Place . . . any place that has parts which occur in a regular order. This Place is committed to memory carefully and well, so well that the rememberer can scurry around it backwards, forwards, any which way at will. The next step is to create vivid symbols or images for the things one wishes to remember—the more shocking and highly-colored the better, according to the experts[.]
>
> "Architecture, in fact [. . .] is frozen memory."[2]

Hawksquill teaches Auberon Barnable the rudiments of the Art, even using Quintilian's famous law case as example. The most useful thing about the Art, she tells him, is that "out of the proper arrangement of what you *do* know, what you *don't* know may arise spontaneously."[3]

The Art of Memory appears in *Little, Big, Ægypt, Love & Sleep*, and fragmentarily in *The Deep*. It functions benevolently. Hawksquill orders her knowledge with it, solves problems with it, even uses it to talk with the gods. Auberon Barnable uses the Art as a tool for healing: with it he is able to stop searching for Sylvie, give up drink and destitution, and live at Old Law Farm. A television writer for the wildly successful "A World Elsewhere," he is still crippled by his broken heart but also functional, even joyous at times. And later, Auberon returns to the locus in his memory where he placed Sylvia and conjures her, travelling back in time and following her at last into the infundibular world.[4] Crowley's fictional Giordano Bruno stores memory with the Art in much the same way in *Ægypt*[5] and, in *Love & Sleep*, divines with it. Even Pierce Moffett (of the *Ægypt* series) uses a version of it in his system for memorizing history by assigning colors to digits, whole palettes of color to historical dates, and date-colored imaginary tableaux to historical events.[6]

The essential parts of Art of Memory are "Persons, Places, Notions and Things."[7] This set of four words appears regularly in Crowley's work, and signals that Crowley is writing about a memory system descended from the Art of Memory.

III. Crowley's Memory Systems

Crowley's memory systems can be classed in three general types: one, the "natural" or organic, like the Art of Memory; two, the mechanical, like the Wasp system of the story "Snow"; and, three, in-between systems, part mechanical and part human participation. The natural memory systems illustrate the beneficent aspects of memory, offering hope for human happiness via transparent truths, copious detail, and healing integration. The mechanical devices distort, invade or limit memory, and show how distorted, limiting and painful human memory can be. The in-between systems seem to throw their emphasis in one or the other direction, depending upon the degree of mechanical imposition upon human memory.

The mother lode of Crowleyan memory notions is *Engine Summer*, where benevolent natural memory systems work side by side with the more problematical mechanical memory tools of preholocaustal man, whom the main character Rush that Speaks calls angels. The angels created the dreadful technological miracle of the ball, the glove, and the sphere, which are the parts of a mechanical system for copying and preserving a person's memory. The glove controls the mechanism, turning the system on or off. Together with the ball, the glove commands the system to begin recording or to empty itself. The sphere contains the memory. With the glove, the human host retrieves the sphere's memory much as Cicero described the placing of images in their memory houses, by impressing the ensphered memory onto the host's mind, as if pressing a seal into wax.[8] In a sense the sphere-personality possesses or inhabits the human host, temporarily setting aside the host's identity. The ball, glove and sphere bestow all of Rush on the angel who is hosting Rush. Then the angel tells as much of Rush as he can to another angel who records the telling.

Three minds are preserved in the spheres in *Engine Summer*: Boots, who is a cat and whose sphere is owned and used by Dr. Boots's List; Daniel Plunkett, his sphere owned and used by the angels and erased by the angel Mongolfier near the end of the book; and Rush that Speaks himself, who is recorded by Mongolfier[9] into Plunkett's empty sphere. All three are overlaid on human hosts, like transparencies lit up by the hosts' living minds, or pressed into them like seals into wax. The human mind is not wax, however, and the memories of Daniel Plunkett and of Rush that Speaks cause great pain to their human hosts. Only Dr. Boots can bestow peace on her host, and that is by bestowing forgetfulness.

Truthful speaking is another transparent device in *Engine Summer*, a natural system with mind-enhancing powers reminiscent of some aspects of Art of Memory. Truthful speakers "really mean what they say, and [they] say what they really mean." This is the only real fantasy device in the book: the notion that with care and practice one can learn to speak in such a way that one is never misunderstood. Truthful speaking's most noble proponents are the saints, whose stories cannot be forgotten or misunderstood. Rush's people use the saints' stories as teaching tools, exemplary lives; Truthful speaking is the filter through which the lives of the saints become transparent. The saints' stories are *copious*, in that every listener adds them to his own story, layering them palimpsest-wise and enriching both.[10]

Compare also the ball, glove, and sphere mechanism with the Filing System of *Engine Summer*, originally called the Condensed Filing System for Wasser-Dozier Multiparametric Parasocietal Personality Inventories, Ninth Edition, and which the gossips of Rush's Warren have appropriated for a way of studying their society. Each Person is represented by a record, a translucent slide; all the slides for all the Persons in a cord, or clan, make the record of that cord, and certain groups of slides packed together make Places, Things, and Notions:

> "Fourth Finder . . . [and] Little First Slot . . . make Little Knot . . . Little Knot and Hands make Little Knot Unraveled . . . Little Knot Unraveled and the two Stair slides make Great Knot . . . Great Knot and First Trap make Little Trap. Little Trap and the Expedition make Little Second Gate, or Great Trap Unlocked in Leaf Cord. Little Second Gate and the Ball Court make Gate.
>
> . . . It's thought . . . that Gate and the Second and Great Slot slides, together with the Broken Heart and the Shaken Fragment slides, all make Great Knot Unraveled. But no one can read that much[.]"[11]

This system, sister to the Least Trumps of *Little, Big*, is generous, yielding more information every time it is consulted, offering hope and possibility. The Filing System, like the Saints' stories, is copious, like a readable palimpsest.

IV. Copiousness

Let's look at copiousness and its sister notions, infundibularity and "the way meaning arises . . . in folktales and legendary narratives," as Crowley, in the person of Frank Walker Barr, the historian from *Ægypt*, describes it.[12] These three engines drive much of Crowley's work and relate closely to the Art of Memory.

Copiousness was considered a virtue by the medieval scholastics who practiced the Art of Memory; it meant fullness; the business of packing into memory as many texts on a single subject as possible. Copiousness also referred to the benefit of considering as many texts as possible in one's own work, and of inspiring commentaries to one's own work as a way of validating it, thus making it part of the canon. The presence of an audience was crucial to copiousness. Mary Carruthers, in her excellent work *The Book of Memory*, says that for the medieval memory practitioners, "Ethical truths are expressed not singly but copiously."[13]

Copiousness has a family resemblance to Crowley's "infundibularity." In *Little, Big*, Dr. Theodore Bramble lectures on the worlds inhabited by the little people. Dr. Bramble says:

> "It is [. . .] a peculiar geography I can only describe as *infundibular.* [. . . It] is composed of a series of concentric rings, which as one penetrates deeper into the other world, grow larger. The further in you go, the bigger it gets. Each perimeter of this series of concentricities encloses a larger world within, until, at the center point, it is infinite. Or at least very very large . . . We men, you see, inhabit what is in fact the vastest outermost circle of the converse infundibulum which is the other world."[14]

This notion is lifted from the neo-Platonic cosmology featuring concentric spheres of creation.[15] (In her book, *The Rosicrucian Enlightenment*, Yates reproduces an illustration of the hierarchy of celestial spheres from J. Publicius, *Oratoriae artis epitome*, published originally in 1482 (fig. 1). Yates' Figure 2 shows a similar illustration from J. Romberch, *Congestosum artificiose memore*, an edition from 1533. Beau Brachman, in *Ægypt*, takes an out-of-body astral journey through these spheres.)

In turn, through copiousness, infundibularity is related to the Art of Memory; it recurs in different forms in Crowley's work, most clearly in *Ægypt* in Frank Walker Barr's seminar on the History of History. Barr says:

> "It seems to me that what grants meaning in folktales and legendary narratives . . . is not logical development so much as thematic repetition, the same ideas or events or even the same objects recurring in different circumstances, or different objects contained in similar circumstances."
>
> [. . .] "A hero sets out . . . [t]o find a treasure, or to free his beloved, or to capture a castle or find a garden. Every incident, every adventure that befalls him as he searches, *is* the treasure or the beloved, the castle or the garden, repeated in different forms, like a set of nesting boxes—each of them however just as large, or no smaller, than all the others. The interpolated stories he is made to listen to only tell him his own story in another form. The pattern continues until a kind of certainty arises, a satisfaction that the story has been told often enough to seem at last to have been really told."[16]

Notice the resemblance of this model to the Filing System, whose parts, each having discrete meaning of their own, may be added to one another to multiply and consolidate meaning. Like Dr. Bramble's concentric worlds, the Filing System is infundibular, copious, "a set of nesting boxes—each of them . . . just as large, or no smaller, than all the others."

The Filing System; the ball, glove, and sphere; and truthful speaking are all copious memory systems. Within *Engine Summer*, which of these teaches that remembering more is happier than remembering less? Which offers hope in the replication of life stories, and which shows that memory can be painful?

Compare the replicated lives of the saints and of the spheres. Both the floating city of angels and Dr. Boots' List use their spheres much as Rush's people use the stories of their saints—as teaching tools, exemplary lives. The ball, glove and sphere are an angel way of canonizing certain lives.

The angels canonize Daniel Plunkett first. Plunkett overlays and colors their society, like a single dominant Saint. But "Learning Plunkett, living in Plunkett," whose terrible letter is Remember, agonizes the angels so much that they send Mongolfier to find the mechanism that will erase Plunkett's sphere. Mongolfier records Rush in Plunkett's empty sphere, and we are led to presume that the angels find Rush an improvement on Plunkett. For example, we learn that Rush has taught truthful speaking to the angels who play host to his memory-sphere; they in turn teach truthful speaking to the rest of the angels.[17] Also through Rush, the angels learn that the earth has survived man, overturning Plunkett's certainty to the contrary, which had caused them centuries of guilt and pain.

Yet the nameless angel who talks with the narrator tells him that Rush's sphere has been hosted only "three hundred times in twice as many years."[18] Hosting Rush is clearly no picnic. Why? It's a secret. Take the example of Boots, the cat in the sphere.

If Rush gives the angels truthful speaking, perhaps he can also give them Boots, who gifts Dr. Boots's List with her talent for being in the present, her cat-calm, and her forgetfulness. But if Boots can be bestowed on the angels through Rush, it will be at fourth hand. Boots the cat was the real Boots; that's first hand. She was recorded into her sphere, second hand; then her sphere bestowed her on Rush, that's third hand already. At fourth hand the host for

Rush may meet Boots, may even be Boots for a time, as Rush was: this will be a copy of Rush's memory of the copy of Boots.

But the angel listening to Rush's story will only hear about Boots. The truth about her experience will be just too distant to possess. What is truth? the angels ask the spheres. And the spheres answer, Painfully far away, hard to speak of. Painted Red, the gossip, speaking of Whisper cord, says that "for them a secret isn't something they won't tell. For them a secret is something that can't be told."[19]

It becomes clear as *Engine Summer* progresses that the persons remembered inside the spheres do know secrets that can't be told. One of these secrets is another transparent device, the plastic cube with a fly in its center, who "thinks he's in the air . . . and can't see anything that holds him back. But still he can't move." The fly stands for Rush in his sphere: not the real Rush, as we come to realize only at the very end of the novel, but the Rush who awaits a host, unaware of the horror of his own lifeless, deathless waiting, "Like the meaning of a word waiting for the word to be the meaning of . . . like a letter." This copy of Rush becomes aware of the horror anew, every time he is impressed on the wax of a human host, *for he realizes that he is an unfinished story.*[20]

Like the stories of lives of the Saints, the sphere system can make a palimpsest of the two persons, the living host and the stored, long-dead quasi-person. Copiousness is achieved by both systems, but we don't feel pain in the knowledge that the Saints are mostly gone. We are accustomed to accepting the death of heroes. Acceptance of their death is built into the stories we tell about heroes, and even might be said to be necessitated by their heroism. This is a function of closure.

But Rush's interrupted story lacks closure. It hurts. This pain is central to Crowley's work with mechanical memory devices. Maybe it hurts *because* the hiatus is mechanical. If this story had been told by the people of the warren, they would have found a way to bring closure to it, smoothing the hacked-off edge to a shape that meets human needs.

The human mind is elastic, Crowley seems to say about memory, but machines never lie, and in their harsh mechanical way they are like truthful speakers: they "really mean what they say, and [they] say what they really mean." Except that machines really *mean* nothing; only people can supply meanings for them.

V. Divination, Determination, & Hope

I'll look now at the forces of divination in these memory works. How does memory interact or interfere with divination? We know that divination is, as Crowley tells us, one function of the Art of Memory: out of the proper arrangement of what you *do* know, what you *don't* know may arise spontaneously.

Divination is a mediator between the need for hope and the need to know, that is, determinism. The knife-edge between the determinist past and the hopeful future is the present. By whatever method used, divination is a problematical business, even when it is successful. This is the personal dilemma of divination: is it better to hope or to know?

Two examples from Crowley are the Least Trumps from *Little, Big*, and Act-Field Theory from "In Blue," one a deck of cards, the other a computerized statistical model founded on chaos science. The Least Trumps are plainly divinatory. Their Persons, Places, Things, and Notions prove them sisters to the magical memory systems of the Renaissance: the Tarot, the cabala, and the enormous houses of the old heavens. There is no limit to what the Least Trumps might discover.

The central conceit of "In Blue" has a similar ambition: the computers of the Revolution use act-field theory to create a virtual model of the whole world, which is composed of vast probabilistic analyses of the gross motions of the numberless lives that make up the act-field, the world. The real act-field is governed according to this virtual act-field, which knows everything that is going to happen. It is impossible for the theory to predict the behavior of any single mote or person in the act-field. Yet the theory can *account for* any individual event after the fact, write it into its software, and *discount* it. No individual has meaning in the theory. "Every . . . turn of events . . . [is] accounted for." Even "riots slacken in force, go unnoticed, are aberrations that have been accounted for even before they occur . . . there are no longer shake-ups and purges, none at least beyond those that have been accounted for." In effect, meaning has been leached from event by statistical probability modeling. This is not a new idea to that branch of Ludditism that abhors statistics, but Crowley explicates it so much better, as usual, than everybody else.

Unlike act-field theory, the Least Trumps can predict the behavior of individual motes. Through the cards, Sophie learns that Smoky's angina will worsen, that Lily's baby will be a boy, and she learns too little, or too much, about the fate of Lilac, her lost daughter.[21] These predictions are often unhappy. Yet Sophie doesn't fault this tendency of the Trumps to give bad news, or to tell all without explaining all, nor does she fault herself for misreading them. By contrast, the mathematician Hare blames act-field theory and then himself for the theory's failure to explain his romantic tragedy, and his ensuing mental breakdown.

Sophie accepts with patience the need to pack copious falls of the cards into her head, to see through them all at once to the enormous answer to her question. But Hare cannot use act-field theory in the same way. The facts and trends charted by act-field theory are too many to put into one person's head. They will fit only into a machine, which cannot mean anything—they need a human mind to give them meaning. The theory defeats its own copiousness. The very rationality of its scientific approach mandates at best a bleak assurance that certainty and meaning on an individual basis are impossible.[22] This is the same answer that Sophie gets to her questions about her lost daughter: that is, no answer. Why does it hurt more? The key lies in or near to memory.

Act-field theory, for all its powers, has no memory. It allows the computers of the Revolution to create a virtual act-field by compiling enormous quantities of information about the present, yet the theory's calculations can "never calculate the magnitude of coincidences that ha[ve] already occurred." Hare says, "Knowing everything is not different from knowing nothing."[23] Knowledge is not the same as meaning. The theory is a machine. Machines can't mean anything.

But the Least Trumps are magic, and magic in Crowley's work is a business so compact of meaning, so organically integrated with the human mind that it can never attain the objectivity or dissociation of science. The Least Trumps are a gift from the fairies, whose chief schemer is Mrs. Underhill. Mrs. Underhill somehow embodies her world, much as the virtual act-field represents the real act-field. Mrs. Underhill can "remember" the future clearly but must resort to divination to think about the past.[24] Like her, act-field theory "c[an] never work backward" to understand the past; the theory is solely "abstracting and predictive." It has no memory.[25]

Yet Mrs. Underhill, unlike act-field theory, can give just that touch of personal attention that makes the world seem to be done right, all for the best. The good advice offered by the cards is aimed personally at Sophie and her family; it offers them hope, to keep them going on with the Tale. Grandfather Trout spills the beans to Auberon about the "ghosts [and] phantoms" of Sylvie he keeps seeing: "Those phantoms. Those are their work. . . . just to keep you sharp set; lures."[26] Auberon's first revealing photograph of Violet Bramble, John Drinkwater, Elf, "a goad, a promise, to keep him searching . . . "[27] By contrast, Hare tells his skeptical lover Eva, tells himself, and is told repeatedly that the theory proves that everything is all for the best, but he never believes it.

The mechanical memory/divining system, in short, offers no hope, and the natural, magical system does. Act-field theory can't remember, but Sophie, who is integral to the operation of the Least Trumps system, *can* remember. Integrity is the final measure of a Crowleyan memory system.

VI. Integrity and Invasiveness: the Self vs. the Data

The greatest difference between Crowley's use of natural and mechanical memory systems is in their effect on the integrity of the user. Here we find the key to the uneven distribution of pain and hope coloring Crowley's memory systems. It lies in what information management practice calls "data integrity," or, in psychological terms, the integrity of the house of the self.

A natural memory system like Art of Memory inextricably integrates the self with the system and with the data to be remembered. The user supplies the memory house and the memorial images from his own imagination; in this way the user internalizes the data. The data become part of him. By contrast, the mechanical system may impose itself invasively on the personality of its user, but it can never be fully integrated; there is always friction between the human memory and the memory of the machine that invades him.

Here are two of Crowley's mechanical systems: the Wasp from "Snow," and ball, sphere, and glove from *Engine Summer.* The Wasp, a mobile recording device, follows the narrator's wife for over 8,000 hours, recording everything that happens to her that it can see and hear. After her death these recordings become available only in random snippets, viewed like "ordinary . . . home movies," grainy, wobbly, and badly shot.[28]

Compared to the Wasp, the sphere of *Engine Summer* remembers more perfectly: not just visual and auditory memory but sensation, emotion, and meaning. It allows for copiousness through the overlay of the "transparent" ensphered person on the host. However, the sphere is far more invasive than the Wasp. The imposition of Dr. Boots on the host, and (we are led to infer) also that of Plunkett and of Rush, is so complete that the stored person temporarily obliterates the host's memory, and can be shaken off only to the degree that the invasion can be forgotten. Boots has no memory, but Rush and Plunkett have.[29] Contact with them makes long-term changes in the host's self.

The Wasp's system is terribly limited but, perhaps because of its limitations, it does not swallow the viewer alive. The inherent randomness of access to the Wasp's recordings prevents the viewer from losing himself in the Wasp's memory. The access system's random partitioning of experience, its graininess, its dimness, its tunnel vision always focused on one person, the deterioration of sound and visual quality, the Wasp's plain stupidity—all these conspire to protect the viewer from invasion, even while data integrity fails, and perhaps even because it fails.

Worst of the Wasp's failings is its meaningless randomness. Charlie, the narrator from "Snow," finds that the Wasp seems "no better and no worse" at remembering than Charlie's own eye: its powers are the same as his own for sifting the wheat of memory from its chaff.[30] By contrast, the spheres of *Engine Summer* never forget, however truncated they may be. Nor do they confuse valuable memories with trivia, because the *meaning* of the ensphered memories is preserved.

Here are two kinds of problems in data integrity. One is incompleteness of the data. The second problem has to do with the integrity of the *user* of the system. By this second measure, Charlie of "Snow" is inviolate, even benefited by the Wasp system in a small way, in that he learns to give up the machine and rely on his own chancy but vivid memory.

Invasion and breach of integrity for the human hosts of Rush, Boots and Plunkett is severe. The first angel to host Plunkett never spoke again.[31] When Rush takes on the sphere inhabited by Boots, "Boots rose . . . Out of her house deep within me she spoke and said: *Forget.* Forget you were ever other than the perfect house you are forever building." Dr. Boots invades Rush's personal architecture; Boots betrays Rush. While he is under Boots's influence, Rush hears the news of his beloved's departure without comprehending it, thereby losing his last chance to talk to her and, perhaps, to achieve the closure that hangs unclosed like a horrid wound for the rest of the story.[32] The narrator, who is the ensphered memory of Rush impressed on an angel host, begs his auditor to "be gentle with [the One who I am]" "[I am] afraid for him."[33]

Compare such user integrity issues with those for characters who practice one of the natural memory systems—*Little, Big*'s Nora Cloud, Sophie, Hawksquill, Auberon Barnable, and *Ægypt*'s Pierce Moffett. All these characters feel literally inhabited by their memories. Another star-crossed lover, Auberon Barnable is invaded by Sylvie, as surely as Rush is "bot" [bought] by his beloved, yet his use of the Art of Memory heals Auberon by giving him a way to contain Sylvie in a discrete place in the house of his self. Hawksquill works and plays in her memory mansions. Pierce experiences an "old closed door [in himself] . . . blown open in the winds that were rising, and there were other doors beyond it, door after door, opening backward endlessly into the colored centuries."[34]

This architectural metaphor is one of Crowley's signatures. For users of the Art of Memory, the architectural metaphor becomes a permanent feature of their self-image.[35] Rush that Speaks, when he hosts Dr. Boots, finds himself full of doors, an endless path full of "walls and snake's-hands . . . countless steps and twists and false ways and rooms," an endless series of houses each built, demolished and rebuilt by the Now. Even the narrator of Crowley's "Novelty" may be said to possess a mnemonical place, or landscape, in that he "plant[s] the banner" of his notion "amid his memories and imaginings" and the "primitive clans" he needs to write come "clamoring to be marshaled into troops by the captains of his art.[36]"

All these characters are changed by memory systems, but it must be observed that users of the Art of Memory own their systems; they are not owned by them. The mind's house is not, it must be emphasized, a separate thing like the computer or the sphere or the Wasp; it is the very infrastructure of the self. The whole person employs the Art; the Art always works in the context of its whole user.

Memory is not removable from the self, Crowley seems to say. It should be interior, not exterior. Mechanical memory is exterior, an imposition; human memory is interior, a generosity from the wellspring of the self.

VII. Summation

It is difficult to analyze any aspect of a body of work whose circumference is nowhere and whose center is everywhere. What this study concludes is that Crowley's general stance on memory favors the capacity of human memory over the limitations of mechanical memory; that he illustrates the painful aspects of human memory by comparing it with mechanical memory and by manipulating human memory with mechanical paradigms and devices; that his measures of memory's adequacy are transparency, copiousness, and self-integrity; and that out there, incompletely charted as yet, is a map of Memory as Crowley uses it in all his work, wholly faithful to itself, whose parts interlock from book to story to book without a gap.

WORKS CITED

Carruthers, Mary.
The Book of Memory, Cambridge: Cambridge University Press, 1990.

Crowley, John.
Ægypt. New York: Bantam Books, 1989.
Antiquities. Seattle: Incunabula, 1993.
Beasts. New York: Bantam Books, 1994.
The Deep. New York: Bantam Books, 1994.
Engine Summer. New York: Bantam Books, 1983.
Little, Big. New York: Bantam Books, 1994.
Love & Sleep. New York: Bantam Books, 1994.
Novelty. New York: Bantam Books, 1989.

Yates, Frances A.
The Art of Memory. Chicago: University of Chicago Press, 1966.

OTHER SOURCES

Caudill, Harry M.
Night Comes to the Cumberlands: A Biography of a Depressed Area.
Boston: Little, Brown, 1963.

Couliano, Ioan P.
Eros and Magic in the Renaissance. Translated by Margaret Cook. Chicago: University of Chicago Press, 1990.

Ginzburg, Carlo.
Night Battles: Witchcraft & Agrarian Cults in the Sixteenth and Seventeenth Centuries. New York: Penguin Books, 1985.

Shumaker, Wayne.
The Occult Sciences in the Renaissance. Berkeley: University of California Press, 1979.

Yates, Frances A.
Giordano Bruno and the Hermetic Tradition. Chicago: University of Chicago Press, 1979.
The Rosicrucian Enlightenment. London: Routledge & Kegan Paul, 1972.
The Theatre of the World. London: Routledge & Kegan Paul, 1969.

NOTES

[1] In *Ægypt*, Crowley mentions many of his primary and secondary sources for the history of magic and the Art of Memory: Albertus Magnus, St. Thomas Aquinas, Marsilio Ficino, Dee's *Monas Hieroglyphica*, and Apuleius (*Ægypt*, 97, 292-94, 317, 321-24). In *Little, Big*, the magician Ariel Hawksquill also mentions the author's sources on the Art, and on Renaissance thought in general: Quintilian, Giordano Bruno, the Rosicrucian texts attributed to Johann Valentin Andreae and his circle, and Dante (*Little, Big*, 247-49, 307), but she fails to mention two of Crowley's most important secondary sources on it: Frances Yates, and Ioan Culianu. Yates' work on the Art of Memory informs so much of Crowley's work; he says that her book *The Rosicrucian Enlightenment* is a founda-

tion for the final volume of the series. Culianu's book *Eros and Magic in the Renaissance* also has an enormous influence on *Ægypt*. In the context of memory alone, it sheds light on aspects of the Art that Yates frankly admitted were beyond her, that is, the magical *ars memoria* of Lull and Bruno. The importance for Crowley of these two sources cannot be overstated. I would also recommend a book called *The Book of Memory*, by Professor Mary Carruthers, from Cambridge University Press, which will prove useful to readers in Crowley and the Art of Memory.

[2] *Little, Big*, 247, 353.

[3] Ibid., 342, 354.

[4] Ibid., 434-437. Also 520-21.

[5] *Ægypt*, 314-17.

[6] Ibid., 67-8.

[7] Yates, *Art of Memory*, 2 quoting Cicero; ibid., 22 quoting Quintilian.

[8] "As Richard Sorabji notes, for Plato, too, recollection involved 'the seeing of internal pictures' which are imprinted upon the memory as if with signet rings." Carruthers, 16-32.

[9] *Engine Summer*, 207.

[10] Ibid., 29-31.

[11] Ibid., 67-68.

[12] *Ægypt*, 360.

[13] Carruthers, 26-27, 181.

[14] *Little, Big*, 43.

[15] Yates, *Art of Memory*, 111 and 258-60.

[16] *Ægypt*, 360-61.

[17] *Engine Summer*, 205-6.

[18] Ibid., 208.

[19] Ibid., 46.

[20] Ibid., 75, 201.

[21] *Little, Big*, 431, 254-55.

[22] "In Blue," 172.

[23] Ibid., 169, 197. Also, 180: "He knew so much. He knew nothing."

[24] *Little, Big*, 323.

[25] "In Blue," 169.

[26] *Little, Big*, 410.

[27] Ibid., 79.

[28] "Snow," 75.

[29] *Engine Summer*, 207.

[30] "Snow," 83.

[31] *Engine Summer*, 205.

[32] Ibid., 164-65, 169. And: "I felt myself building a house for it to live in." 165.

[33] Ibid., 208-9.

[34] *Ægypt*, 88.

[35] *Engine Summer*, 164-65.

[36] "Novelty," 216.

ANTIQUITIES AND FOUR MORE TALES
Alice K. Turner

A FREQUENT ASSIGNMENT in American writing-school pro-
grams and workshops directs students to retell a well-known story,
usually a fairy-tale. The exercise is attributed to John Gardner, the
famed teacher who died in a motorcycle accident in 1982 (though it
may predate him), and it has been taken up by many other teachers
as a way to demonstrate such manipulable techniques of the writer's trade as point of view, building tension or suspense, allowing or
withholding information, use of dialog and plot—in short, to point
out that that there is more than one way to swing a cat. Cinderella's
adventures differ from the standard version, necessarily, when the
narrator is a self-preoccupied Rat Coachman.

Genre readers have encountered the form in a successful series
of anthologies edited by Ellen Datlow and Teri Windling, who
between them have tapped nearly all the professional English-lan-
guage writers of fantasy, horror, and science fiction, adding some
writers from the mainstream, to perform this identical task. The B-
level results in these volumes do read rather like class assignments,
but the gimmick has built-in virtues and, in a respectable number
of cases, a thoughtful writer has spun gold from musty straw.

John Crowley's contribution to *Black Swan, White Raven*
(Avon, 1995), the fourth of the series, is "Lost and Abandoned,"

a contemporary meditation on "Hansel and Gretel." (Those re-sourceful children had a bumper year in '95: they turned up in three of the anthology's offerings.) The story seems a good starting point for examination of Crowley's infrequent shorter fiction: of the eleven stories considered here (seven of them in the small-press collection *Antiquities*, four at present "independent"), three are based on old legends or ballads while three more touch on Greek mythology. "Lost and Abandoned" is the most sophisticated of these six. Moreover, in it he explains his method in tackling this kind of material—or at least *a* method, since he uses it in only one other story.

The narrator, a divorced father with custody of two just pre-adolescent children, teaches writing as part of an "enrichment" program at a community college. Following Gardner, he assigns his class to retell "Hansel and Gretel," using their own words and experiences. (In this class of blue-collar young people—not one of whom grew up with a father in the house—a fair number are unfamiliar with the story.) The students challenge him to complete the assignment as well, and he agrees. Their task, "in three pages max," is to tell the story "from beginning to end, not leaving any-thing important out." The trick is to decide what's important. Our narrator will tell "a story with a beginning, a middle and no end. No breadcrumbs, no candy, no woods, no oven, no treasure. No who, what, where, when. And it will all be there."

It's there. "Lost and Abandoned"—the whole of it, not just the story within the story—delivers a melancholy view of divorce; the physical and emotional separation, the disillusioned, withdrawn resentment of abandoned children; and the nearly impossible task of the stepmother (there is no actual stepmother in the story)—and of the rootlessness so common to American life, and the moment, known to all parents, when children begin moving from the relative safety of childhood out into the territories of adolescence. Death, the final abandonment, is examined. Deep stuff for a school (or anthology) assignment. And in only three pages.

The first story in *Antiquities*, "The Green Child," also about abandoned children, could not be more differently told. It is an unadorned account of a West Sussex legend of the 12th century, first written down by contemporary chroniclers Ralph of Coggeshall and William of Mowbridge. I'd read it before: Two pale green children, a girl and a younger boy, appear, lost and trembling, at the entrance to a Welsh coal pit. A kindly, childless woman takes them in and the girl slowly begins to learn human ways. The boy will eat nothing but beans ("the fairy food"), he weeps constantly and soon dies. The girl, who tells the villagers that she and her brother have come from St. Martin's Land, a twilight country, grows up, becomes less green, eventually marries. Crowley recounts this tale without embellishment—it could easily have been written for a guidebook to the area—and with no writerly speculation other than wondering what happened to those alien genes as they passed down through the green girl's eventual progeny. It's a very simple piece of writing and seems a somewhat curious start to a collection, especially one so slim (only 100 pages). But perhaps Crowley is up to something.

The second story in the collection is "Missolonghi 1824," which tells us who, where and when right away, if not what. The narrator is Lord Byron, who tells a story to Loukas Chalandritsanos, the devoted Greek boy who, tradition has it, rejected Byron's physical advances, and for whom "On This Day I Complete My Thirty-Sixth Year," his last poem, was written. Byron tells Loukas of an encounter he had some time ago in Arkady in which he encountered and set free a creature of the woods, a creature out of myth. This is not a very original premise. The genre magazines (the story first appeared in *Asimov's*) seem to feature one like it in every other issue—it's amazing how many people, past and present, run into unicorns, dragons, pixies, undines and the like. Even the end-gimmick seems a little pat—the creature gave Byron (he does not tell this to Loukas) something ineffable but important to the Byron legend in return for its freedom. But the charm for me in this story is that Crowley may have written it for Harold Bloom, and maybe for Tom Disch too. It is the perfect gift for them, lovers of poetry who would long for—be ravished by!—the truth of the encounter. What if Byron really *did* meet a satyr? How marvelously appropriate, and wouldn't it be pretty to think so!

Next is the title story, with a complete change of pace. Here is a tone-perfect P. G. Wodehouse story of improbable events, with the Travellers' Club standing in for the Drones', or perhaps Arthur Clarke's White Hart. (Looking over this, John Crowley mentions Lord Dunsany's Joseph Jorkens, teller of tall-tales.) The plot has to do with mummified cats, agriculture, succubi (miscalled incubi in this edition) and the Egyptian cat-goddess Bastet. It is written as an entertainment, and it succeeds in its mission.

An Earthly Mother Sits and Sings, published as a chapbook (see bibliography), is another plain tale based on a world-wide legend, that of the creature from the Other World who mates with a human. Most often, the otherworldly being is female (Swan Lake, the selkie wives of Scotland, the fox wives of Japan, and, of course, the girl in "The Green Child"), but here it is a man from the sea, a merman or sea-godling who half-rapes (she consents) and impregnates Ineen ("girl") Fitzgerald while her sick father lies in the next room and her lover, down on the beach, vainly tries to prevent his fellow Irish villagers from murdering the Spanish sailors cast ashore as the ships of the Armada crash on the rocks. What will come of this mating? Ineen wonders later, just as Crowley himself earlier wondered at the green girl's genetic heritage.

(Crowley watchers will take note of the storm in this story, the storm that conquered the Armada, the great wind conjured by Dr. John Dee that plays an important role in the Ægypt series. A wind like this one opens fissures in the mundane world, according to Crowley, and here we have a demonstration of just what can happen.)

"The Reason for the Visit," the fourth story in the collection, brings Virginia Woolf to the narrator's unprepared apartment.

All he can find to offer her is instant tea, with lemon juice from a plastic lemon, and mayonnaise sandwiches made with Pepperidge Farm bread. He has read little of her work and has no titles on display—"I was a friend of hers, not a fan"—though, with perfect tact, she hides her disappointment. Toward the end of this *petit jeu d'esprit*, the narration switches to Woolf in *Mrs. Dalloway* mode, but I confess that I never did quite grasp her reason for the visit. The story was written for an anthology called *Interfaces*, which presumably featured other encounters of this sort, and perhaps that was reason enough.

It is followed by "Her Bounty to the Dead," a more complex ghost story that uses one of Crowley's favorite tricks, the Mobius strip, in which time and space twist and repeat themselves. An elderly woman who, several decades earlier, sold the family house to an appreciative young man now takes her nephew, another appreciative young man, on a trip toward that house that seems to double into the past and conflate the two men.

Of these eleven stories, two are out-and-out science fiction, with futuristic "inventions": "Snow," in the collection, and "Gone," published in September, 1996, in *The Magazine of Fantasy & Science Fiction*. In "Snow," the gadget is a Wasp, a surveillance device that, once installed, tracks its owner till death. This Wasp was installed by the rich first husband of a fashionable woman, but after her death it is the second husband, the narrator, who applies to view the more than eight thousand recorded hours of her life, only to find deep flaws in the retrieval system. In "Gone," the artifact is an "elmer," one of an unexplained army of aliens who, like the hoboes of the 1930s Depression, offer temporary yard-work services—mowing the lawn, taking out the trash, shoveling the snow, washing the windows—though with no clear recompense in mind other than the signing of a Good Will Ticket that may have strange future consequences. Pat Poynton's elmer fails to retrieve the children that her ex-husband has kidnapped, but in some curious psychological way the creature appears to have opened a door for the rancorous relationship: perhaps she and the ex can work custody out like reasonable people, with an effort, in fact, toward Good Will.

This leaves "The War Between the Objects and the Subjects," another even more *petit jeu* to appear in an anthology based on images by the artist J. K. Potter; it discourses, playfully, on grammar. And then there is the last very short story in *Antiquities*, "Exogamy." This is my favorite of these short pieces, together with "Lost and Abandoned" (another reader might prefer the more neatly honed conventional tales, perhaps the two mentioned above, but I like genre-benders: there's no reason either of my chosen stories could not have appeared in, say, *The New Yorker*). Here, in an alien setting, perhaps on an alien planet, a man is rescued from drowning by a huge female bird that "smelled like a mildewed sofa": the allusion is to Sinbad the Sailor and the giant roc from *The Arabian Nights*. She shelters him with her feathers, scavenges sometimes repulsive gobbets of meat for him. She sickens, and in a turnabout he cares for her. Somehow, together, they reach a green land where, in a castle, the object of his quest, the queen of the tower, must surely be waiting for him. He abandons his roc—she will just have to understand—and strides forward confidently. Up the endless stairs of the tower he climbs, and, passing through the last door, he steps onto the topmost parapet "littered with bones, fetid with pale guano. A vast shabby nest of sticks and nameless stuff." His bird alights. "Did you guess? she asks." No, and he is so heartsick he considers jumping over the side. She would catch him, of course. What is next? "Another direction entirely."

And this strange little tale, with its echo of Browning's "Childe Roland to the Dark Tower Came," becomes, all at once, a potent, surprising, and even hopeful, metaphor for marriage. It is like a wonderful cartoon, an amalgam of James Thurber (his fiercely predatory females) and Saul Steinberg (his uncanny ability to metamorphose). This is Crowley, the alchemist, at work. If loss and abandonment are his potions, and they are, through many of these stories as in many of his longer works, the objects (and subjects) can gleam like fairy gold, but with human substance. The sophistication of this last story perhaps explains the positioning of "The Green Child," too. The little collection moves from simplicity to intense complexity with plenty of variation in between. Short stories may not be Crowley's metier—he really does seem more comfortable with longer forms—but once in a while he can knock one out of the ballpark. To mix a metaphor.

THE ÆGYPT SERIES

.

GENRE TROUBLE, OR JOHN CROWLEY'S UNFINISHED SYMPHONY

James Hynes

FOR THE MOST part, the American novelist John Crowley flies under both the commercial and critical radars, as invisible to most readers as he is to most critics. You don't have to look very hard to see why this should be. Despite their high literary gloss and intellectual sophistication, his first three novels were originally published as genre fiction: *The Deep* is a gothic fantasy reminiscent of Mervyn Peake's Gormenghast trilogy; *Beasts* is a science fiction romance about the genetic recombination of humans and animals, sort of a cross between *The Island of Dr. Moreau* and *The Wind in the Willows*; and *Engine Summer*, Crowley's most impenetrable work, is an after-the-apocalypse narrative. In an attempt to give it mainstream credibility, some admiring critics have called his next book, *Little, Big*, a magic realist novel. But *Little, Big*, his best-known work and arguably his masterpiece, is unequivocally a fantasy novel, albeit a highly idiosyncratic one. Much of the book reads like a straight literary narrative—it is as compelling a por-trait of a long marriage as any I know—but it is based on the Sufi fable *The Parliament of the Birds* and uses the themes and arche-types of Northern European folklore. In other words, it is a long, gorgeously written, picaresque family saga, in the last 50 pages of which all the major characters, with one heartbreaking exception, turn into fairies.

There are some exceptions to his critical invisibility: he's been championed by Michael Dirda of the *Washington Post*; Harold Bloom has officially canonized three of his novels (*Little, Big, Ægypt*, and *Love & Sleep*) in one of the lists in *The Western Canon*; and various other reviewers have compared his later novels *Ægypt* and *Love & Sleep* to the work of Thomas Mann and Robertson Davies. Count me in: I've read *Little, Big* four times now, shamelessly weeping each time over those last, extraordinary 50 pages, and over the years have purchased and given away 15 copies of it (when I could find it—it is inconsistently in print). When "You'll love this" isn't recommendation enough, I have proceeded to claim (as I'm claiming here) that *Little, Big* is an Important American Novel that bears comparison to such works as *One Hundred Years of Solitude* and Nabokov's *Ada*.

Still, Crowley's career is an object lesson for any writer who wants to write serious fiction outside the lines, as it were: once you enter the labyrinth of genre, it may be impossible to find your way out again. It's all right, apparently, for a writer with an established literary reputation to venture into science fiction (Margaret Atwood's *The Handmaid's Tale*), the gothic (John Updike's *The Witches of Eastwick*), or fabulism (nearly anything by Salman Rushdie), but God forbid someone should try to create literature with the tools of the genre writer. Ursula K. Le Guin and Philip K. Dick have peeked over the edge of genre into the promised land, and lately Stephen King, by sheer force of will, it seems, has won an O. Henry Award. But even these authors are only grudgingly allowed at the garden party, whispered about when their backs are turned. They remain tainted, half-castes in some old melodrama of artistic miscegenation, trying to pass for literary.

I suspect that the genre/literary divide is not nearly as important to Crowley as it is to a reader like me, who feels the need to justify his love for fantasy novels to his literary friends. From his earliest work, Crowley has simply ignored the distinction; he is not so much undermining the border between genre and literary as he is acting as if it weren't there at all, except perhaps as a marketing consideration, moving back and forth across the border easily and at will, taking what he wants from either tradition, and shrugging off the critics from either side of the divide who don't want anybody trading with the enemy. And so, emboldened perhaps by the success of *Little, Big* among both fantasy and mainstream readers, Crowley has since embarked on an even stranger and more ambitious project, a four-volume series of novels, set both in the present day and in the late sixteenth century, and based in large part on Renaissance mysticism. While the books so far are entirely satisfying as narrative, the series is fundamentally a huge novel of ideas, an epic meditation on the search for gnosis, for an intuitive grasp of the interrelatedness of all things. The first of the series, *Ægypt*, was widely and respectfully reviewed, as was the second novel in the series, *Love & Sleep*. With the publication of *Love & Sleep*, Crowley's publisher, Bantam, made a full court press attempt to break him through, Cormac McCarthy-style, releasing all of his previous novels in handsome new trade paperbacks (the first three in one volume), but unfortunately the attempt didn't take. Now, six years later, only Crowley's new novel, *Dæmonomania*, the third in the Ægypt quartet, is in print, and it is being buried alive in the scifi/fantasy section of your local superstore. Thus, by the curious logic of our commercially driven literary culture, the most mediocre graduate of an academic writing workshop automatically receives the official imprimatur of "literary writer" along with his or her MFA, while John Crowley's lushly written and vastly more intellectually satisfying books are shelved, if they are in print at all, with nth-generation cyberpunks, vampire novelists, and Tolkien wannabes.

To be fair, Crowley doesn't make it easy on himself. Given the hidebound rules of genre vs. literary (hidebound at least for most of us, if not for Crowley himself), it's hard to peg these books.

For pages and pages at a stretch, these novels read as straight, mainstream narrative, a fact which is liable to disappoint the spectacle-hungry genre reader; yet there are occasional, not entirely unequivocal incursions of the fantastic and the fabulous—sightings of angels in a crystal ball; an Elizabethan wizard's photograph of the young William Shakespeare; werewolves—which are liable to put off the more fastidious mainstream reader. Furthermore, they are eloquently but densely written, requiring a level of concentration beyond that of the average literary novel, let alone the average genre book; gnosis is a compelling but complex notion, not easy to explain, and Crowley isn't attempting to explain it, really, but to evoke it as a storyteller. Adding to the difficulty is the unfortunately glacial pacing of each novel's release—seven years between *Ægypt* and *Love & Sleep*, and six between *Love & Sleep* and *Dæmonomania*. As someone who's just read all three one right after the other, it's clear to me that they are best reviewed as one immensely long and ambitious novel, but the recent "Books in Brief" notice of *Dæmonomania* in the *New York Times Book Review*, for example, reviewed it as a brilliantly written, but rather baffling fantasy novel by someone who is *also* the author of the Ægypt series; the reviewer expressed a confusion about the parallel storylines that could have been cleared up if he had bothered to read the first two volumes. In large part this is Bantam's fault, for not only has the publisher neglected to mention anywhere on the dust jacket of the book that it is the third in a series (probably for fear of scaring off readers), but it has not even kept the earlier books in print. The literary world is what it is, I suppose, and no doubt Crowley is even more keenly aware than I am of the huge risks he is running—of intimidating readers and baffling reviewers, of trying the patience of his publisher, of falling off the literary map altogether—but in the end, literary greatness isn't bestowed on the faint-hearted. However frustrating the pace of its creation must be to his readers, his publishers, and Crowley himself, the Ægypt quartet is—already, unfinished—an astonishing accomplishment.

Taken together, the three books so far tell, roughly speaking, two large, complicated, and thematically intertwined stories. One is set in the late Seventies in a fictional region of the Northeast called the Faraway Hills (very like the Berkshires, where Crowley lives) and centered around a writer and historian named Pierce Moffett. Having lost his position at a small college in New York, Moffett washes up in the Faraways, amid a network of Sixties survivors. These are not the highly ideological veterans of the Sixties who moved into academia and politics, but castaways of the *other* Sixties, the spiritual Sixties, the gentle dopers and vegetarians and New Agers who resettled in crumbling industrial towns in Massachusetts and upstate New York and opened tarot parlors and bookshops. Crowley's cast includes Brent Spofford, a Vietnam vet and an old student of Pierce's; Beau Brachman, the informal leader of a casually communal house and daycare center and a practitioner of astral projection; Mike Mucho, a psychologist at a private institution called the Woods and inventor of a pop psychology system called Climacterics; Rosie Mucho, nee Rasmussen, Mike's wife, who is divorcing him and sleeping with Spofford; Mike and Rosie's young daughter Sam; and another Rose, Rose Ryder, who is Mike Mucho's lover in the first book, and in the second and third volumes, Pierce's.

As Pierce enters into this shifting web of friends and lovers, he begins work on a book about what he calls the *other* history of the world, based upon his theory, from his studies in the Renaissance, that the world sometimes changes overnight:

> Did he really intend to suggest in his book that once-upon-a-time the useless procedures of magic had had effects, the lead had turned to gold, the dead had risen; but that then the world ("the world") had passed through some sort of cosmic turnstile and come out the other side different, so that now not only are the old magics inefficacious but *now they always were*? Was he going to say that?

He guessed he was. Certainly he was going to hint at it, utter it, assemble ambiguous evidence for it, hold his readers in suspense with a search through history for the proof of it, the one thing—event, artifact, place, word—that is still, indisputably, what it once was in the past age, as nothing else any longer is. Whatever it might be.

He was going to entertain the notion; oh more, he was going to fête it, he was going to wine and dine it; he was going to have his way with it amid the spilled cups and crushed fruit of an uproarious banquet. And he was going to father on it a notion more powerful than itself, a notion which would only be given birth to in his concluding pages: *only if we treat the past in this way, as though it was different in kind from the present, can we form any idea of how different from the present the future will be.* (*Love & Sleep*, p. 168)

Pierce is also hired by Rosie Rasmussen's elderly uncle Boney, the director of the Rasmussen Foundation, to edit the papers of a local celebrity, a dead and nearly forgotten historical novelist named Fellowes Kraft. In the central coincidence of a narrative full of coincidences (and that is in large part *about* coincidence), Pierce discovers in Kraft's old mock-Tudor home a last, unpublished manuscript that covers the same ground philosophically as his own prospective book. Indeed, much of Ægypt is given over to excerpts from Kraft's first novel, *Bruno's Journey*, about the Renaissance philosopher and alchemist Giordano Bruno; from *Bitten Apples*, his romance about the young William Shakespeare; and, most importantly and prolifically, from Kraft's last manuscript, a curious but exquisite philosophical romance centered around Bruno and the Elizabethan alchemist John Dee. This last work continues on through *Love & Sleep* and *Dæmonomania* (where, not knowing its provenance in the first two books, the *New York Times* reviewer was baffled by it), making up not quite half of the quartet so far.

Just as there is, according to Crowley and his character Pierce, another history of the world, there is another account of the Ægypt quartet. Apart from being an unusually lush, and leisurely, account of the lives of its modern and historical characters, the novels are based largely on the themes of Hermetism (after Hermes Trismegistus, its mythical prophet), the highly syncretic late-Classical philosophy combining elements of Platonism and Gnosticism, and the philosophical underpinning to alchemy. More particularly, Crowley is writing out of the variety of Hermetism that flourished during the Renaissance, when a fascination for magic and alchemy informed both literary culture and science; his main inspiration is the work of the English historian of Renaissance magic, Dame Frances Yates. Bruno enjoys quite a reputation these days as a martyr for science, but he was also a major, if not *the* major Hermetist of the Renaissance, disseminating its ideas and obsessions all across Europe, from Rome to Paris to London and back again. And while John Dee is mainly remembered as an astrologer and a crystal ball gazer, he was also an all-around natural philosopher, adviser to Elizabeth I, and in Kraft's novel, harried family man. Natural philosophy and magic were all mixed up in the Renaissance, and Crowley, in his quartet, is doing his best to mix them up again.

All of this compounds Crowley's genre trouble: spare a thought for the poor conglomerate publisher who is asked to market a wildly allusive and intensely erudite 1300 page unfinished novel with a cast of alchemists and hippies, based on Renaissance esoterica and issued one book at a time over 15 years. It would be easier if Crowley were taking the low road, writing a pop, New Age tract, another *Celestine Prophecy* (to which *Ægypt* and *Love & Sleep* have, very unfairly, been compared). Instead, he is writing rigorously about a subject many readers would consider inherently unreasonable, engaging the philosophy behind alchemy, the strange, rich, and surprisingly resonant early modern search for gnosis that Frances Yates explored in such books as *Giordano Bruno and the Hermetic Tradition* and *The Rosicrucian Enlightenment*. Thus the quartet is intellectually sophisticated, but in an idiosyncratic way. There is a slow, powerful forward momentum to the twin narratives, as Giordano Bruno, in the 16th century, heads unknowingly toward the stake, and Pierce Moffett, in the 20th, heads for a sort of spiritual auto-da-fé. As the modern day narrative has progressed from volume to volume, the hippie gentleness of *Ægypt* has darkened, with Pierce descending into an increasingly transgressive eroticism encompassing homoerotic fantasies with an imaginary adolescent son and real sadomasochistic sex with the troubled young woman Rose Ryder. Rose leaves him finally, following her former lover Mike Mucho into a frightening Christian cult known as the Powerhouse. Mike, in turn, is pursued by his ex-wife, Rosie Rasmussen, determined to keep custody of their daughter Sam. Meanwhile, the 16-century narrative, which was kept rigorously separate in the earlier volumes—a novel within a novel—begins in *Dæmonomania* to bleed into the present day narrative, the two of them stitched increasingly tight together by parallelisms of plot, character, language, and even props. Sam is diagnosed with epilepsy; epileptic seizures having once been considered trance states leading to visions and prophecies, her condition seems to tie her to the girlish angel Madimi who speaks through his crystal ball to John Dee in the historical sections. Indeed, this Sam/Madimi parallelism is reinforced by a time-traveling exchange of orbs, as a child's inflatable ball from the 20th century mysteriously bounces into John Dee's study, and Dee's own crystal ball is handed down through the centuries, through Fellowes Kraft to Boney Rasmussen, to end up as one of Sam's playthings, stuffed in her backpack.

All this is dramatic enough, as are various other subplots not mentioned here, but in a curiously oblique way, with the focus more on the spiritual struggle of each character (particularly the struggles of Pierce and the two Roses) than on their actions. Anyone reading these books purely for plot would quickly be discouraged; as lovely as the prose is, there are longeurs and repetitions, as Crowley, given the years between each book's release, is forced to recap stuff that a reader unwilling to start from scratch might have read years ago. There's also a fair amount of winking self-referentiality: Pierce's explanations of the intent and structure of his work-in-progress are meant to double as descriptions of the Ægypt quartet itself, and it's easy to come to the conclusion by the end of *Dæmonomania* that Pierce's, Crowley's, and Fellowes Kraft's projects are all one and the same. At a costume ball on the winter solstice near the end of *Dæmonomania*, Pierce has a funny encounter with a man in a mask—"Masks always make us oracular. The one this fellow wore was a realistic human face, a pleasant tired older fellow with crinkly eyes and a shock of molded white rubber hair. Pierce supposed he ought to know the face"— who can only be Crowley himself. They have an ingeniously misdirected conversation, as Pierce thinks they're talking about the masked man's failed production of Marlowe's *Doctor Faustus*, while the Crowley figure is clearly talking about the book in the reader's hands:

> "I came to believe," the man said, and crossed his legs, ready for a chat, "that Marlowe must have been an awful shit."
>
> "Oh?"
>
> "Yes. I think of him as a totally amoral person who liked to arouse people, just because he knew he could. Get them to riot and go on rampages. His plays did, you know. Against Jews. Catholics. Whomever he could turn a crowd against."
>
> "Magicians."
>
> "Oh yes. Poor old Doctor Dee. And I don't think for a minute he cared anything about the Devil or God's justice. He was like a punk rock star today, with a swastika tattooed on his forehead, getting kids to go mad and commit suicide." He lifted his drink to his mouth, and drank, or pretended to. "A genius, though. Unlike your rockers. There's the difference."
>
> Who was that mask? Pierce knew he had seen the face it was modelled on, in some special context; the boyish snub nose, the hair that had once been sandy. "What happened?" he asked. "To your production?"

The man sighed hugely, and for a long moment looked around himself, the expression on his false face altering as the light took it differently. Then he said:

"Well I've failed. I failed. Yes I think that's evident now." He said this with what seemed great anguish. "The conception was just too huge, the parts too many. No matter how long it was let to go on, it got no closer to being done."

"It's a corrupted text," Pierce said. "I believe." There was, he now saw, another bentwood chair beside the man, exactly like the one he sat in.

"I so much wanted it to *knit*," the other said. He interlaced his own fingers. "Past and present, then and now. The story of the thing lost, and how it was found. More than anything I wanted it to *resolve*. And all it does is *ramify*."

"You take this party, or ball," he said, lifting his glass as though to toast it. "I mean it's hardly the *Walpurgis-nacht* that was promised for so long."

"Well," Pierce said. "I mean."

"The all-purged night; the all-perjurers'-night. The transmuting revels, the night machinery out of which we all come different. Wasn't that the idea? 'Where nothing is but what is not.' What is not yet, or is not any longer."

"Ah," said Pierce . . . [*Dæmonomania*, p. 394]

Yet this self-referentiality is not the usual postmodern giddiness, but part of the quartet's rigorous structure, which is liable to seem strange to a modern reader. The Hermetists communicated their beliefs through highly allusive prose; and Crowley's lyricism is certainly allusive, occasionally maddeningly so—I sometimes wondered if the books' intended demographic was simply Harold Bloom—even down to the titles of each volume. *Ægypt*, with its fussy little ligature, refers not to the real country, but to the mythical Ægypt of Hermes Trismegistus; *Love & Sleep* is a sly abbreviation of the *Hypnerotomachia Poliphili*, a curious Renaissance volume about architecture and sex whose title can be translated as "The Struggle of Love in a Dream"; and *Dæmonomania* is also the title of an early modern witch-hunting manual. Not for nothing, in *Ægypt*, does Pierce struggle through an English translation of the *Soledades* by the early 17th century Spanish poet Gòngora, whose name became a watchword for complicated imagery and arcane mythological allusions. It is Crowley's way of warning the modern reader, *pay attention.*

But the Hermetists also communicated by emblems, dense, complicated illustrations inspired (mistakenly) by Egyptian hieroglyphics. These emblems, deliberately obscure, were meant to be instruments of gnosis, intended to enter the eye and go straight to the heart, bypassing the reasoning mind entirely, opening the viewer to the infinite web of connections between him and the cosmos. This, I think, is how Crowley intends us to read his work. The structure of the Ægypt quartet is largely symbolic: taken together, the three volumes are best read as a sort of modern alchemist's emblem book. For the Hermetists, and for Crowley in these sublimely eccentric novels, gnosis is a dual process—knowledge of one's true self on the one hand, and a direct, unmediated knowledge of the divine on the other—but these two brands of knowledge are not sought serially, one after the other, but simultaneously, with the implication that, after all, knowledge of oneself and knowledge of the divine are the same thing. Taken as one huge work, divided into twelve sections named after the Houses of the Zodiac (which are not, as Crowley carefully explains, the same thing as the signs of the Zodiac), the Ægypt quartet is a series of tableaux, or emblems, in which love and desire and death and identity are held to the light and examined in all their facets.

These tableaux are not necessarily discrete set pieces, either, but can be plotlines or situations that run through all three books, and must be extracted in the reader's imagination and looked at whole. A single example will have to suffice (it would take another book to tease out all the complexities of these novels; dissertation writers, take note). One of the Hermetists' articles of faith is the interconnectedness of all things (whatever its scientific validity, this is the metaphor at the root of astrology, that we are connected to the stars and they to us in subtle and mysterious ways). This can be a powerfully erotic idea, at least as Crowley expresses it, and perhaps the chief characteristic of the vast web of interconnectedness in these novels is their eroticism. Over the course of the books, nearly all the major characters are sexually involved with all the other major characters, in a web of astonishing complexity. Rosie Rasmussen and Mike Mucho are married, and produce their daughter Sam; Mike leaves Rosie to have an affair with Rose Ryder, and Rosie Rasmussen starts an affair with Pierce's former student Brent Spofford. But Spofford too once had a brief fling with Rose Ryder, and on one memorable occasion, Mike Mucho, Rosie Rasmussen, and Rose Ryder all ended up in bed together. Enter Pierce Moffett in *Ægypt*, in which, in a sly authorial sleight of hand too complicated to explain here, he and the reader come to confuse the two Roses, thinking that they're the same person. Both the reader and Pierce are surprised to discover at the end of the book that there are two Roses; it takes a second reading to see how Crowley does it. Subsequently, in *Love & Sleep* and *Dæmonomania*, Pierce becomes Rose Ryder's lover, and then, when she leaves him to follow Mike Mucho into the Powerhouse cult, Rosie Rasmussen and Pierce end up in bed together. As soap operatic as this may seem in description, what it resembles when extracted from the three books and held up to the light is a complicated alchemical emblem of intertwined bodies, with a powerfully allegorical, if mysterious, purpose. Because of the deliberate conflation of the two Roses in the first book and the fact that the two women sleep with all the major male characters and even with each other, the implication seems to be that they are the same woman in some metaphorical sense, or perhaps facets of the same woman. There is even a third Rose, sort of: Julie Rosengarten, Pierce's ex-lover and current literary agent in New York, who, it turns out in the third book, knows the New-Ager Beau Brachman, and together Beau and Julie are watching over Pierce, without Pierce's knowledge. (In a book as allusive as this one, all these Roses are, needless to say, a clear allusion to Rosicrucianism, a close relative of Hermetism.) And this does not take into account Pierce's eventual equation of Robbie, the imaginary son with whom he indulges in homoerotic fantasies, and Bobbie Shaftoe, the Kentucky girl with whom Pierce had his first sexual experience years ago, and who turns up late in *Love & Sleep* as a nurse's aide in the hospital where Rosie takes her daughter Sam for the treatment of her epilepsy. Bobby's father Floyd is a Kentucky hill man who roams the woods as a wolf in his sleep, mirroring a Bohemian werewolf in the historical narrative, who was the subject of another one of Fellowes Kraft's novels, *The Werewolf of Prague*, and whose real-life descendants many generations later come to populate the mining towns of Appalachia. Meanwhile the angel Madimi visits John Dee in the 16th Century and tells him to swap wives with his scryer, or crystal ball reader, Edward Kelley, which activity mirrors the interconnected sex in the Faraway Hills of the 1970s . . .

The masked man at the ball was right: none of this resolves, but it ramifies like hell. And that, perhaps is the point: Hermetism, and its parent, gnosticism, are not rigorous, rational philosophies, they are engines of revelation, meant to bypass the intellect, and this epic meditation on gnosis is constructed to become more complicated and ramifying the deeper you read into it; as Crowley put it in his earlier book, *Little, Big*, "the further in you go, the bigger it gets." The goal of gnosis may be a moment of perfect understanding, but that moment may not necessarily be simple, or explainable, or reproducible in anyone else. Alchemical emblems and Renaissance mystical prose are not supposed to make sense rationally, they are not analytical puzzles, they are not parse-able; rather, they are like a Western version of Zen koans, logical impossibilites that you are supposed to give yourself over to until you either get it, or you don't. At the very end of *Love & Sleep*, in a bravura passage of incantatory prose, Pierce, in a spiritual panic, imagines a messenger on his way—"or is it she?"—with a message that will save him:

> But will she come in time? Oh yes just in time; when-ever she comes is just in time; when we have despaired for the thousandth midnight of any such a one ever com-ing from anywhere, she will arrive, in a tearing hurry, breaking into or out of the last spheres of air, fire, water, earth as though throwing open the successive doors of a long corridor, down which she rushes, her hair streaming and her brow knit, her hand already beside her mouth to call into the ear of our souls *Wake up*. [*Love & Sleep*, p. 502]

Given the gloriously odd ambition of these novels, it's no won-der that the books come across as well-crafted but impenetrable to anyone who tries to read them for the usual literary reasons—plot, character, suspense—and why they are next to impossible to review as independent volumes. Lest this sound daunting, and pointless, and terminally odd, it's useful to note how fruitful this subject mat-ter has already been for a number of indisputably literary novelists: Marguerite Yourcenar sympathetically depicts a alchemist named Zeno, based on Paracelsus, in her masterpiece *The Abyss*; Peter Ackroyd performs one of his reliably mysterious interpenetrations of two widely distant historical periods in *The House of Dr. Dee*; and Lindsay Clarke uses alchemy for an extended meditation on gender in his splendid novel *The Chymical Wedding*. If Crowley is being obscure, he's in good company, and his books bear com-parison with any of these—indeed, they may very well be the most ambitious, mysterious, and rewarding of the lot.

Be assured as well that these books are also uncommonly and unfashionably beautiful, in their oblique but lyrical prose, in their overall architecture, and in the calm, deliberate passage of each extraordinary set piece. There are wonders in every volume: a great windstorm, hauntingly evoked, blows through both the 16th and the 20th centuries; John Dee really does turn lead into gold, only to have it turn to slime later on; and the twin werewolves, the Bohemian and the Kentuckian, rise from their bodies at night as wolves, battling witches at the gates of Hell in order to save the world. But there is also, if you find werewolves and transmutation off-putting, as keen and complex an understanding of difficult, troubled, and passionate characters as you are liable to find in any mainstream novel, set in a natural world that is evoked with extraordinary vividness.

A good novel must be note-perfect to succeed, but a great one can sprawl—must sprawl, if it is to encompass all the unseemly and unrestrained passion of its own ambition. The craftsmanlike novel is read the way an onion is peeled, one layer at a time, until you have nothing left; but with a John Crowley novel—well, the further in you go, the bigger it gets. Granted, half a million words on hippies and alchemists probably seems pretty big to begin with, but where Crowley's work does show its genre roots, what he does share with the best of modern fantasists and fabulists (Tolkien, Mervyn Peake, John Cowper Powys)—apart from sheer determination, in the face of critical and sometimes commercial neglect, simply to persevere—is a sense of spaciousness, of depth, of the boundlessness of his imagination. What he also shares with these writers is the ability to give the reader the feeling that at any point in these novels you could make a sharp left turn from the narrative and just keep going, there's that much world and story and mystery out there that he's simply not bothering to show you. It's a majestic folly, to spend all these riches of language and imagination and erudition, all this effort and all this time, to create a work of art that will, I hope, in its final volume, lead Pierce Moffett, and maybe his author, and maybe even me, to a moment of perfect understanding. *Wake up.*

THE ÆGYPT SERIES
John Clute

The three long reviews that follow represent one reader's history of response to John Crowley's Ægypt Series as it has evolved between 1987 and 2000. I have made some cuts to eliminate undue repetitions. I have also tinkered a bit with the content, when it seemed wise to make things clearer than I could at the time; but this tinkering is minor. I have also restored a passage or two. The journal responsible for publishing the original version is listed after each piece. I thank them.

1

Beginning *Ægypt* is not half the battle; it is very nearly the whole war. John Crowley's fifth book, the first part of a projected quartet, is much less a novel than a series of portals. Full of beginnings, plot spirals that return us to beginnings, and sudden vistas that signal even bigger beginnings to come, it does in fact literally begin several times—with an Author's Note that becomes part of the text: then a Prologue in Heaven after Goethe's *Faust*; followed by a Prologue on Earth to balance the first prologue; and continued by more than one chapter of initiation. And each beginning—each portal—remains open. Nothing is resolved. The last pages of *Ægypt* close on nothing.

It is a dizzying experience, achieved with unerring security of technique, in a prose of serene and smiling gravitas. Crowley's history as a published writer—his first three novels were released as genre science fiction, and his current publishers released the prize-winning *Little, Big* as a trade paperback with a dimity cover—has not been of the sort to generate a wide reputation, and it will be of great interest to learn if he can reach a welcoming public with this daunting anomaly of a book, this gaping portal that leaves us staring into a deeply strange world.

Just what this book is—just what *Ægypt* will become when complete—may be almost impossible to say. In conventional generic terms, the first volume is neither fish nor fowl, neither fantasy nor mainstream, while at the same time it adroitly mixes both modes together. The text contains discourses with angels, traversings of the heavenly spheres along routes mapped out by Renaissance magi like Giordano Bruno and John Dee, and a weaving of threads of preternatural coincidence; but Crowley parenthesizes this material by presenting it in the form of passages from a series of children's books. These magical tales, written by the late Fellowes Kraft, have haunted Pierce Moffett (who is the continuing protagonist of the series) from early childhood. The Prologue in Heaven, which recounts John Dee's first sight of angels, and his first intimation that out of infinite smallness or largeness a Sagittarian visitor was approaching our sphere to transform it utterly, is from one of Kraft's texts. And the Prologue on Earth shows Pierce, as a child, already haunted by Kraft's life of Giordano Bruno, the magus, mathematician, astrologer and scientist who helped create the modern world while searching backwards through time for Ægypt. The finger of Giordano Bruno (1548-1600)—as with all innovative thinkers on the cusp of paradigm shift, like Leibnitz, like Newton—points both ways.

Pierce Moffett's name reflects his nature, for he is both penetrant and woolly, rather like *Ægypt* itself. From childhood he has longed to inhabit a world he could recognize as being intended, pregnant with meaning, animate; and this yearning—this sense of desiderium, for he is sure that somehow he has missed inhabiting that world, he is sure that "once [,] the world was not as it has since become"—informs his every moment. As an adult he becomes a historian, looking for a version of the world that might account for the nature of things, but in vain. Victim and master of a poignant yearning heterosexuality, he falls uncontrollably in love with several women, each time with a view to seeing the universe entire. Signs and portents of some imminent transformation multiply around him—or perhaps he breeds them, perhaps Pierce Moffett is himself the visitor to our sphere who will bring the world alive, turn it into what it has always been.

The Manhattan Pierce inhabits for much of his life, like the Urban Fantasy Manhattan of *Little, Big*, or of Jerome Charyn's numerous fables of New York, or of Mark Helprin's *Winter's Tale* (1983), is very much a storied isle, drenched in the story of itself, a site for sore eyes, like a fount. It is not merely a city. It is the City, and one only leaves the City in order to search for the Golden Age. So when Pierce finally leaves Manhattan, it is to write a book about the meaning of the world, which he hopes to call *Ægypt*, a book which will open the Book on the world; and it is only appropriate that in Blackbury Jambs, his new hometown somewhere west and north of the City, probably in the lee of the Catskills, he finds a world far more drenched with implication than the slightly anodyne pastoral old-hippie escapism it first seems to represent.

This part of rural New York State has long been dominated by the Rasmussen family, whose charitable Foundation owns the nearby home left to it by Fellowes Kraft. Pierce soon meets Rosie Rasmussen, whom he has confused with another Rose—Rose Ryder—so that he cannot tell which "sister" he has instantly fallen in love with. Learning of his interest in Kraft, Rosie asks him to examine an unfinished manuscript left in the house. Pierce soon discovers that Kraft's unfinished tale of the meeting of John Dee and Giordano Bruno was to have been called *Ægypt*, and that in all essentials it was the book Pierce hoped to write. But here the ingenious assemblage of beginnings stops, and the volume ends.

The portrait of Pierce Moffett, gangling, vulnerable, sharp and sheepish, is lovingly comprehensive (he is a kind of portmanteau of Smoky Barnable and Auberon, *Little, Big*'s two viewpoint characters). The inhabitants of Blackbury Jambs sing through their lives like escaped children, for that is their pastoral destiny; but at intervals seem altogether human, too. The narrative itself, which spirals through time and space rather like a maze that Pierce must penetrate, startles the reader again and again with the eloquent rightness of the web of coincidences which structure it. And in moments of sudden realization, when Pierce sees for the first time something he had always inwardly known, the universe of *Ægypt* seems to talk itself awake. But what this artful (and sometimes arch) opening of portals will amount to, we can only guess.

As Crowley makes clear in his Author's Note, the spirit of Dame Frances Yates (1899-1981) of the Warburg Institute permeates his text, and it is to her that *Ægypt* owes its central thrust, for at the heart of Yates' revolutionary analysis of late 16th century intellectual history stands the figure of Bruno himself, whose defense of Copernicus's heliocentrism has traditionally been thought a proof of his essential modernity. But for Yates, Bruno's heliocentrism points rather to the figure of Hermes Trismegistus, a Gnostic Greek whose esoteric writings the Renaissance mistakenly thought to be pre-Christian, and to originate in Egypt.

Though it might seem impossibly intricate to the unlearned eye, the universe Bruno understood Hermes to describe was a single living entity which, in all humbleness and love, could be *understood*. To that end, he transformed the Lullian Art of Memory into a kind of holy pun. His Theatre of the World—his Ægypt—was intended both to show forth and to embody a triumphal unity of human and universal soul. His Ægypt wore the spiritual (and actual) countenance of the universe. It was a universe in which nothing (Kraft and Pierce long to believe) was illusion.

At times most movingly, at other times rather doggedly, *Ægypt* embodies the sense that it is itself meant ultimately to read as a Theatre of the World. Future volumes will undoubtedly weave Bruno and Pierce closer together; more interestingly perhaps, the text may also accompany Queen Elizabeth's astrologer John Dee to Bohemia, where he attempted—reading the signs of the times—to bring about a new order, a realm of the sun. He failed. *Ægypt* is set about a decade ago; as future volumes move towards the millennium, an utterly new world might well become visible, born anew. The quartet would be its Theatre.

—*The New York Times Book Review,* 3 May 1987

2

We continue to begin. *Love & Sleep* continues to open doors that open into other doors that open into other doors. It is a recursion of portals of quite astonishing complexity, while generating at the same time—it is a sensation not evident in the dawn pages of *Ægypt*—a sense of profound bondage. To get at the nature of the bondage depicted here, it might be useful to visualize a universal man, the one drawn by Leonardo da Vinci (after Vitruvius), an image we know well. A naked man stands within a rectangular frame, itself encompassed by a circular frame, which conveys (even to a modern onlooker) the sense of a mathematical (perhaps Platonic) expression of the ideal anatomy; the man extends his limbs to the edges of the rectangle within the circle: as though da Vinci were indicating that man is the measure of all things; or (to a modern onlooker) that all things measure man. The man's arms and legs are each depicted twice, so that his outstretched fingers and his feet make contact with both the rectangle and the circle. The man himself gazes towards us. He is not smiling. His gaze is archaic; he could well be the Sagittarian archer who is becoming Pierce (or Perceval) Moffett (or whom Pierce is becoming), for it may be that he is approaching us from some other sphere at so great a speed that the geography (or geometry) he traverses is a form of time; but no: not really: he is caught in amber, in bondage to the portal.

Pierce Moffett's bondage to the Story of the world in which we live—and which has not yet become the different Story only desiderium will tell us is different, because we will ourselves have become Shadows or dictates of that different Story—seems far more deeply and more profoundly mortal in this second volume of the Ægypt Series, whose first installment seemed autumnal on first reading; though now, on rereading, it gives off a springtide aura. But the spring—the season, the unleashing, the leap, the burgeon, the flow—is held in the fastness of the true autumn of *Love & Sleep* like the photographic negative of the open door you rush towards in the dream, but which shrinks (or shrinks you) as you approach.

The—as it were—mundane story of the Series does not here, in other words, advance much in time. The first third of the book is devoted to Pierce's Catholic childhood in a coalmining town in Kentucky; as a piece of writing it is more sustained (and more melancholy) than anything Crowley has yet attempted, but tends to convey (to a non-Catholic) not a lot of more than the grim iron gaze backwards so typical of Catholics of a certain age when they think about their childhoods. The second third is basically spent on Giordano Bruno and John Dee, or at any rate these figures as encountered in the works of Fellowes Kraft, whose children's books had (we now learn) enthralled Pierce in Kentucky, and who (we remember) spent his last years and died in the Arcadian polder which encases Blackbury Jambs; and who willed his burden of goods to the Rasmussens. The final third carries Pierce, and Rose Ryder and Rosie Rasmussen, with whom he is increasingly involved, past the death of Boney Rasmussen, Rosie's great-uncle and the central landowner in the area, whose home is in fact called Arcady, in whose fields one of Pierce's close friends grazes, as a matter of fact, sheep.

There is a huge amount to say, or very little, at this stage of Ægypt. It is superbly crafted, but it is not a text that flows, or is intended to; nor does it end. If a central thrust of the novel of fantasy is the movement of escape from the bondage of being who you are, then *Love & Sleep* represents an intake of breath before the thrust of Recognition, before the change of Story into what Tolkien might have called healing but which we could call catharsis, or aftermath: the intake of breath that augurs the uncasing of our mortal flesh: the suspended gaze upon the palace of memory, made of angels, as it prepares, like some heavenly cardsharp trompe l'oeil, to reveal who we are: for the universe of Neoplatonism (which the novel inhabits and explicates) is an infinity of angels, but we sleep. *Love & Sleep* is a novel which holds its breath (as, reading it, we hold ours) in order to awaken, but does not. There is a sense throughout the text that its characters (some of them do) or that even its author (now over 50) might well die before the breathing out. The book is a prison of memory, a Gnostic Hell: not a palace, not yet; a deeply melancholy book, and a brave one to write: because it stops short, short of the well of spring. What Pierce will bring to us, when he awakens, is daunting to await.

But hurry.

—*The New York Review of Science Fiction* No. 79, 1994.

3

The dog logo on the side of the bus says it all. As John Crowley notes (though typically he does not quite say what we are *quite* certain he intends us to think he means), it is the famous Greyhound Bus logo, and the greyhound it depicts is either pursuing or fleeing. Inside the bus we find Pierce Moffett—protagonist of this novel, just as he was of its predecessors—and he too is either pursuing or fleeing. Or both.

And so *Dæmonomania* begins to unfold, back and forth, over the years and through the hearts of its cast, whom we already know and love from the previous volumes. In its beckoning ambivalence it is a beginning entirely typical of John Crowley, author of *Little, Big*, probably the greatest fantasy ever written by an American; it is a beginning which points both ways: back to the mirror of the past, whose Shadows of similtude beckon imperatively; towards the portal into the next Story, which may be shut. Pierce's Great Year, which began with the spring pyrotechnics of *Ægypt* and aestivated through *Love & Sleep*, has now inched into the heavy days of fall. It is the Season of Revels, when Misrule takes the throne. When a party is given in the small Adirondacks city of Blackbury Jambs, 400 pages into this greatly complicated tale, its celebrants will be masked, and at least one mystery guest appears whose face would burn Pierce to death if the mask came off. His message (if hearkened to) could burn *Dæmonomania* to ash.

Pierce Moffett, however, has a long way to progress (or to retreat) before meeting the masked stranger. He has boarded the Greyhound on page one, in a state of "insupportable dread," to visit his lover Rose Ryder, who has left Blackbury Jambs to join a loathsome Christian cult in the great nearby city of Conurbana (which in real life could be anything from Scranton to Newark). But nothing anywhere in *Dæmonomania* moves in a straight line, and no sooner does Pierce enter his Janus-faced transport than we leave the Greyhound for 300 pages of backstory. We are reintroduced to the community of Pierce's friends, many of them kin to one another, with whom he lives in Blackbury Jambs, a place he retreated to at the revolving-door multiple beginings of *Ægypt* in order somehow to come to terms with his haunting conviction that "There is more than one history of the world," and that, somehow, he has (or, like a Theatre of Memory perhaps, *is*) the key that will change things utterly.

Pierce is a scholar of Hermetic texts, which he scours for clues to the nature of our modern desert of a world. He continues in this volume to examine obscure documents that purport to tell the true story of John Dee, the (historical) magus who entranced Queen Elizabeth with speculations and predictions; he inhabits the life of Giordano Bruno, who argued that the world turned around the sun, but whose conviction that the atoms which knit the universe together are in facts angels singing seemingly substrates the entirety of the Ægypt Series.

But all angels are fallen angels. Dee's and Bruno's sense that a new history had just begun has led Pierce nowhere. The universe—the Story we now ourselves inhabit—is still darkened in the pages of *Dæmonomania*, occluded, incoherent, broken. Caught here in what another religious tradition might well call Hell, we cannot understand who we may have been in the happier clime occultly visible, deep within the abysm of the world; or who we may become, in the blinking of an eye, when the gates open again, and a new history of the world begins.

All patterns of knowledge and investigation and intuition seem both true and false to Pierce; but increasingly the latter. He continues his work in the library of the dead Fellowes Kraft, whose papers have, throughout the Ægypt Series, been leading him deeper and deeper into a state where he can understand nothing: not this world, nor the prior world, nor any world that may come. It is still 1979 (those readers who guessed that the Series was designed to close with the Millennium are almost certainly wrong: there is only one volume to go). The flower children—whom we saw at the beginning of *Ægypt* still floating in their Catskills niche for trust fund babies—are now, as the year closes, dead or caught up in child custody disputes. The lives that once seemed livable in Blackbury Jambs—*Ægypt* was a book which rang with the sound of gates opening, endless possibilities awaiting an answer which would surely come soon, surely by now—have now turned to ice. Pierce's love affairs flounder. Grief and depression—Crowley is a masterful guide through the Laocoon coils of melancholia—coat the world. *Dæmonomania*, whose beauties and insights are compulsively gripping, is at the same time wracked with utmost misery. For the world seems to have been deserted by gods and angels alike.

The world of the book cannot therefore be seen clear. This is the argument of the book; and the ultimate reason for Pierce's fumbling, icy melancholia. It is also the problem with the book. *Dæmonomania* is a tangle. It is about bondage—the bondage games of Pierce and his lover, through which he attempts rather suffocatingly to bonsai reality into an accounting of Story; the Gnostic occlusions of the eye and mind which block any egress from our mortal prison; the bondage of transformations stalled in the leap, so that we are stuck halfway through the gate into light; dæmonomania itself, which is here defined as our obsession with fallen angels, or the obsession of fallen angels with us. But *Dæmonomania* is also a tale caught in its own trammels.

Like the Golden Ass who appears throughout, Crowley's astonishing, congested new novel awaits deliverance. If it is a scherzo— to invoke another paradigm pattern of four—then it is a frozen scherzo: the torrent of music stone stalled, so terribly sharp in the sudden silence of its absolute immobility that it cuts flesh. The great long tale of the Ægypt Series has stopped in the darkness before the dawn, the mouth of telling locked wide shut. The masked guest at the party held at the height of the Season of Misrule, who sounds very much like the author of a tale called *Dæmonomania*, confesses as much. "I so much wanted it to *knit*," he says, speaking with "great anguish." Pierce flinches from seeing his terrible face.

What would be truly terrible would be for it all to end here. We hope there will be time for all of us to finish the trip. There is one more volume to come. Sooner or later, the Ægypt Series is going to have to let its people go.

—*The Washington Post*, 8 August 2000

ASTROLOGY AND THEMATIC STRUCTURE IN THE ÆGYPT NOVELS OF JOHN CROWLEY

Don Riggs

IT IS DANGEROUS to write about a novel series that is only three-quarters finished, particularly a series such as John Crowley's *Ægypt, Love & Sleep,* and *Dæmonomania,* in which an event that takes place in the third novel, for example, will suddenly cast an event in the first novel in a strikingly different light. However, as a dominating theme of the series is change, and one of the qualities very consciously embraced is that of intertextuality, I will add my observations to the ongoing intertextual mix, fully expecting reversals in the next text. Pierce Moffett's history professor, Frank Walker Barr, near the end of *Ægypt,* lectures on certain literary works "which set up for themselves a titanic plot, an almost mathematical symmetry of structure, and never finish it; never need to finish it, because . . . the pattern has already arisen satisfyingly within them" (361), so a thematic structure has been made available to the reader who is able to accept it. Of course, I do want the fourth novel to come out; I do want to see what happens to Pierce and Rose and Rosie and Sam and the rest!

I am, of course, aware of the current theoretical stance that all writing is of its very nature intertextual (Allen, 1); however, Crowley, through both his Author's Note to each novel and constant references within the texts themselves, emphasizes the centrifugal aspect of his texts. Crowley notes his indebtedness to scholarly sources for his exploration of, for example, the Renaissance esotericism of John Dee and Giordano Bruno, and his character Pierce Moffett (a Sagittarian as Crowley is himself) is constantly reading in sources that can be located in the actual world of hard-copy libraries and rare book rooms. Similarly, Fellowes Kraft, whose historical novels have inspired Pierce from his childhood, is himself a fictional character and his works are fictions within the fictional world of Crowley's novels, but they themselves have actual sources, some of which Pierce tracks down and reads—or reads "in," as Pierce says to Rosie about the *Hypnerotomachia Poliphili* (*L&S*, 275).

Crowley at times teases us with these references; for example, while a novel of Kraft's refers to G.R.S. Mead's *Thrice-Greatest Hermes*, it has been "unfindable" to Pierce (*Æ.*,186), and Crowley's Author's Note indicates that he himself has used Walter Scott's edition of the *Hermetica*. His use of John Dee's diaries is thus accurate except insofar as the texts are "not now what they once were" (*Dæ.*, Author's Note). Pierce checks an early 20th-century biography of Dee to see if Kraft's narrative of Dee's meeting with Bruno was derived from that text or was invented; I tracked down the same edition of that biography and found that, no, Bruno was not reported as having met Dee; he is only mentioned in relation to continental alchemy contemporaneous with Dee: "Bruno was still alive, developing his theories of God as the great unity behind the world and humanity" (Fell-Smith, 83. See also Yates, *Giordano Bruno and the Hermetic Tradition*). I would suggest that Crowley's special adaptation of the intertextual process is directed specifically at scholars of the esoteric, and at those scholars who, in Wallace Stevens's words, most want what they read to be true—or, which is equally interesting, to be deliberate departures from the originals. Crowley will be hired to design a special circle in Hell for the source-influence scholar.

The structure of the novels is not only centrifugal in relation to other texts, it is also centripetal in relation to itself. Pierce Moffett is struck with the idea to divide the book he is writing in sections named according to the traditional Latin names for the mundane houses of astrology. For the unwary reader who made it to page 301 of Ægypt without figuring out what the book's three sections—Vita, Lucrum, and Fratres—are about, this is a revelation. As Pierce writes, "Somewhere tell story of how twelve [houses] came to be . . . but save this till late; let reader ponder, Vita? Lucrum? What's up, etc." (Æ.,301) But Pierce is shown to be an unreliable narrator: he decides that, in his book, Giordano Bruno will die in the eighth section/house, Mors, while in Crowley's Dæmonomania Bruno is not executed until the ninth section/house, Pietas. Of course, Pierce may not be unreliable, since his book is not Crowley's; the reader, however, may easily make that assumption.

If Pierce Moffett is a figure of John Crowley, he is only one aspect of Crowley, and constantly is used both as a key to the novels' structure, and as a decoy, providing the reader with false leads, as Pierce himself has both marvelous insights and rude awakenings. One event that throws Pierce and the system of astrology in high relief in relation to the recurring motif of the key—the literal key, but also signaling its metaphorical quality in relation to the apprehension of a truth—occurs in the second section of Ægypt, "Lucrum." Val, the local astrologer of Blackbury Jambs, the small town to which Pierce moves from New York City, is having a debate of sorts with Beau Brachman, the yoga teacher. Val accuses Beau of thinking that "this stuff [astrology] is bullshit" but Beau remonstrates, and Val corrects herself, saying that he thinks "the whole thing is a big prison" (225), to which Beau agrees, referring to the entire astrological system as heimarmene, which he says means both "fate" and "prison." This discussion is interrupted by Pierce, who tries to insert a key in the door of the room they are in; the key doesn't fit, and Beau says, "Come in . . . It's not locked" (226). Pierce has mistaken the building, but, the reader comes to realize over the following two novels (600 pages), that room and the discussion being held in that room at that moment, hold the key to the whole question underlying Pierce's life. His (literal) key does not fit that door, but that door doesn't need a key to unlock it; Pierce's hermeneutical approach is inappropriate for that discussion; nevertheless, that discussion would unlock the maze within which Pierce wanders.

Seventy-six pages after the preceding incident, Pierce realizes—aha!—that he can structure his book after the astrological mundane houses. He wonders about the significance and the ordering of these houses at this point, noting that *Mors*, or Death, is not the last house, but only the eighth—the last house is *Carcer*, or Prison. Pierce asks himself, "Why are we left at the end in prison?" (301) and reflects on Bruno's incarceration before his being burned at the stake. The answer to that question, however, was given 76 pages earlier, in the discussion between Val and Beau, when Beau says that the entire astrological system, "Destinies. Stars. Signs. Houses" is "a big prison" (225). Beau Brachman (=Brahmin) is the Gnostic figure for whom the entire system of planetary spheres and archons—the entire Hermetic system of correspondences studied by Pierce and applied by Val—is to be broken through and discarded in the soul's ascent to merge once more with the divine, which is referred to in some Gnostic texts as "the Depth" (Pagels, 321). Enlightenment is free—the door is open—but Pierce, like Perceval, has not asked the right question (has tried the wrong key).

I should point out that Beau Brachman's position on astrology has nothing to do with its efficacy; rather, Beau's point of view is that all of material reality is illusory in relation to Brahma, or the Depth, which is to say the Divine from which all reality was created and to which it all returns. After Beau, in the conversation with Val, has characterized the whole astrological structure as *Heimarmene*, or "where you're stuck," he asks the astrologer if she can deposit his daycare-center's checks for him at the bank.

"'Capricorn,' Val said, pointing a gunlike finger at him" (226); scrupulous care of material possessions is a focus for natives of that sign, which evidently is Beau's. They're both right; in this series, the cosmic machinery that bestows qualities and abilities on people works, but it is a trap. Note, for instance, Val's repeated nicotine cravings in Beau's "no smoking" apartment.

The image of the spiral is Crowley's resolution of the cyclical and linear views of history: things recur—for example, the "New Age" in the 16th-17th century cusp recurs in the "Dawning of the Age of Aquarius" of the 1970s—yet their recurrence is marked by difference. The metamorphosis of astrology provides a striking example of this. As contemporary astrologer Joseph Crane writes, "'Traditional astrology' is not one school or set of ideas but constitutes fifteen hundred years of changing assumptions and cultural contexts" (i). Pierce notes that Val has come by her understanding of the astrological houses through reading "magazines mostly . . . and . . . experience, she says, more than anything; but look how her descriptions match the ones Robert Fludd gives in his astrology, in about 1620" (Æ., 299). Pierce finds that "Val's descriptions were, well, *nicer* than the seventeenth-century mage's, more meliorative, always conceiving difficulty and obstacle as growth and struggle on a higher plane" (Æ., 300). This development in late-20th-century astrology, both in the novel and in social reality, reflects the influence of Dane Rudhyar, among others (Rudhyar, 4); what Pierce is observing is the fact that one facet of the astrological houses is traditional and, for the most part, unchanging, while the cultural context evolves together with attitudes towards fate, karma and free will.

Crowley's choice of Latin names for the astrological houses provides an engaging example of intertextual consistency and fluidity. Neither Pierce nor Crowley states explicitly which text of Robert Fludd has provided these names. Following a false lead, the overzealous literary scholar (myself) researching the "key" motif finds that Robert Fludd's *A Philosophicall Key* has absolutely no mention of astrological houses. This false lead, probably unintentional, illustrates the labyrinth of intertextual relations occasioned by following nonexistent hyperlinks (the labyrinth being another recurring motif that I will not discuss here). The text available to me, Tractatus II Part X Book IV Chapter iii of Fludd's *Tractatus Secundus De Naturae Simia seu Technica Macrocosmi*, gives "Vita" and "Fratres" for houses 1 and 3, as does Crowley, but the other seven keywords (representing the sections of the three novels now in print) differ—the basic meaning is the same, but the specific terms are not. For example, where Crowley uses the term "Lucrum" ("moneymaking"), the Fludd text I saw used "Substantiis, Divitiis, Possessionibus," "Uxor" is "Nuptiis, Mulieribus, Litibus et Contentionibus" etc. (678-79). Perhaps Crowley/Moffett had access to a different text by Fludd, perhaps Crowley condensed a long string of words into one, or perhaps "passage time," the subtle and generally unnoticed shift in the world posited by Crowley (through the writings of Fellowes Kraft and Pierce Moffett), has caused these words to change. It is a very minor, particular example of the intertextual tension between exact appropriation and creative reconfiguration.

These novels are filled with nested structures: a matrushka doll near the end of the third novel neatly places Rosie's daughter Sam in the work: "[a] little angel" (*Dæ.*, 332-34); the image of the crystal within which John Dee and Edward Kelley gaze recurrently throughout the three novels is described at the very outset of the first novel as containing vast spaces within it—in fact, containing the All, an example of the microcosm that contains the macrocosm (*Æ.*, 5-7); the planetary crystal spheres of the Ptolemaic universe constitute a series of nested structures (*Æ.*, 260, 317), that same set of nested structures is seen, transformed by time, by John Dee as mechanized at the dawn of the Enlightenment (*Æ*, 170), and, recalling the Whole contained within the tiniest concentric part of Dee's crystal, the cosmic structure is internalized through Giordano Bruno's mnemonic system (*Æ.*, 362-6). An additional nested structure is the set of historical novels by Fellowes Kraft, which is being studied by Pierce Moffett, who is in turn writing his own alternative history, which in turn has the same organizational structure—following the astrological houses—as the series of Crowley novels which we are reading. The references—both in Pierce's research and in Crowley's Author's Notes—to esoteric texts and historical studies themselves nest the novels intertextually.

Literary theorist Graham Allen states that, for contemporary critics, reading "becomes a process of moving between texts" (1). Crowley states of *Ægypt*, "More even than most books are, this is a book made out of other books" (*Æ.*, Author's Note), and implicitly invites (or challenges) the reader to move between his texts and others mentioned in them. Wolfgang Iser points out that the difference between person-person relationships and text-person relationships is in the availability of means to fill in the gaps left by the schematic nature of conversations and literary writing; people can ask questions of each other to provide clarification, but individual readers must resort to their own imaginations and to background research to help "fill in the aspect" in literary texts (108-9). In Crowley's novels, the reader is provided with references to other texts, but these texts do not always provide the reader with the "right key." Instead, they often open doors to mazes overlapping those traveled by Pierce Moffett.

These novels encourage certain habits of reading in the susceptible reader. They engage ways of comparing life outside the book with that inside—synchronicities, or meaningful coincidences, however unrealistic such occurrences may be. To the extent to which the series of nesting structures set up by the novels includes nesting the novels in the reader's own life, then the habit of reading set up by the novel can be translated into a habit of perceiving the same thing in "real" life. One such synchronicity—and I point out that Carl Gustav Jung first aired his concept of "synchronicity" in a dissertation on astrological relationships between married couples—occurred to me at the turn of the millennium (cf Abbott,

65ff.). On the evening of December 31, 2000, shortly past sunset, I noticed the evening star: a glance at the ephemeris indicated that it was Venus, in 25 degrees of Aquarius, about 45 degrees above the sun which, in 9 degrees of Capricorn, had just slipped below the western horizon. Not long past midnight, quite early on January 1, 2001, while weaving home on foot, I noticed Jupiter, retrograde in 2 degrees of Gemini, about 97 degrees east of Venus. The following evening, the evening of January 1, I came to the following passage in *Dæmonomania*:

> John Dee lifted the face of his mirror to the sky, caught within it the rays of . . . Venus, just then following the sun toward the west, effulgent, brightest object in the fading heavens . . . [and, later when] Venus had fallen far toward the west and her beams struck this tower at too oblique an angle, John Dee smacked his knees, arose from his stool, and consulted his ephemeris; he looked east to where Jupiter, jolly giant, had risen: as sovereign against melancholy as his beautiful blue daughter. (180-181)

I do not wish to claim a "privileged reading" of the text, nor do I wish to suggest a fatalistic or cause-effect relationship between the personal observation and the event described in the text. Rather, I want to point out that the consciousness developed in me as reader of these novels led me to a heightened receptivity to synchronous occurrences, among which was the observation of Venus and Jupiter, which therefore struck me with particular force when I read of Dee's observations soon after. The series of novels sets up and sets in motion series after series of interlocking structures crossing the boundaries between past and present, history and fiction, microcosm and macrocosm. The reader is challenged to continue reading outside of the novels, both in other novels and in scholarly literature, to pursue a constant re-reading of earlier events within the novels, to read the earlier events within the context created in the subsequent text(s), and, I would assume, to read the outer, intertextual relations within the context created in Crowley's novels.

WORKS CITED

Abbott, Edwin A.
Flatland: A Romance of Many Dimensions. New York: Penguin, 1998.

Allen, Graham.
Intertextuality. London: Routledge, 2000.

Crane, Joseph.
A Practical Guide to Traditional Astrology. Orleans, MA: Archive for the Retrival of Historical Astrological Texts, 1997.

Crowley, John.
Ægypt. London: VGSF/Victor Gollanz, 1988.
Dæmonomania. New York: Bantam, 2000.
Love & Sleep. New York: Bantam, 1994.

Fell-Smith, Charlotte.
John Dee. London: Constable, 1909.

Fludd, Robert.
Tractatus Secundus De Naturae Simia seu Technica Macrocosmi historia in partes undecim divisa editio secunda. Frankfurt: de Bry, 1624.

Iser, Wolfgang.
"Interaction between Text and Reader." *The Reader in the Text*. Ed. Susan R. Suleiman and Inge Crosman. Princeton, NJ: Princeton, University Press, 1980. 106-119.

Pagels, Elaine.
The Gnostic Gospels. New York: Vintage Books, 1989.

Rudhyar, Dane.
The Astrological Houses: The Spectrum of Individual Experience. Seba-

stapol, CA: CRCS Publications, 1986.

Yates, Frances Amelia.
Giordano Bruno and the Hermetic Tradition. Chicago:The University of Chicago Press, 1964.

PIERCE MOFFETT THE ASS:
APULEIAN AND BRUNONIAN THEMES IN JOHN CROWLEY'S *DÆMONOMANIA*
Sondra Ford Swift

In a pivotal scene in John Crowley's *Dæmonomania*, third in a projected quartet of novels, the protagonist, Pierce Moffett, is shown making a mask for a winter masquerade party. He intends to create a head like a chessboard knight's, but, apparently against his will, "the delicate length of temple and nose had come out blunt and ignoble . . . and the ears, lovingly crafted and successful in themselves, were just too big" (377). The horse has begun to become an ass. Accepting "that none of it was his choice anyway: or all of it was, and this was it," Pierce not only completes the sculpture but recognizes the implications of the image he is to don. Recalling a passage from the ever useful *Dictionary of Deities, Devils and Daemons of Mankind* and later, in a dream, Giordano Bruno's *Cabala del Caballo Pegaseo*, Pierce reflects upon the difference between the ass protagonist of Apuleius's 2nd century C.E. *Metamorphoses*, or *The Golden Ass*, and that of Bruno's 1585 work. The difference, as Bruno's ass itself spells out in Pierce's dream, involves the fact that Apuleius's Lucius is a young man who becomes an ass and painfully regains his humanity to become a priest of Isis; in contrast

Onorio, Bruno's hero, begins as an ass and remains essentially an ass, raised in that form and given wings like Pegasus's, but undertaking a series of human incarnations in the service of Hermes-Mercurius. As Pierce recalls, "Braying and kicking, or mild and patient, Onorio again and again is turned back from Heaven's cool shores and the prospect of green fields, to embody down on earth the *coniunctio oppositorium* . . . and to show us what it means to know and suffer" (379).

Dæmonomania ends with, first, the escape into the streets of "the Christmas ass" which had carried Bruno himself to the stake, and, second, a passage from Book Ten of *The Golden Ass* in which Lucius feels "in [his] darkest hour" hope that since it is spring, he will soon regain his human shape (451). It is thus conceivable that, at least on one level, not only the plot of *Dæmonomania* but those of the two previous novels, *Ægypt* and *Love & Sleep*, as well turn upon the difference between Apuleius's ass tale and Bruno's. After all, as Graham Sleight observes in a review of *Dæmonomania*, "it's so deeply wedded with the events and structure of its predecessors that it's no more a novel . . . than the bottom quarter of the Mona Lisa is a painting" (1). The importance to Crowley's structure of Apuleius's novel may come as a surprising idea, however. The ex-Dominican magician and mnemonician Giordano Bruno (1548-1600), if not his ass, is of course prominent from the beginning of the *Ægypt* series; he shares top billing with John Dee, the English magus (1527-1608), in Fellowes Kraft's fictional reconstructions of history, especially in the one Pierce has been editing. But Apuleius's presence is perceived once we have been alerted: Lucius's inquiries into magic lead to his transformation into an ass; Pierce too inquires into such matters, and he too becomes an ass—although in a Brunonian sense, not in a literal one. Again, both protagonists experience trouble with the erotic. Furthermore, Lucius can regain his human shape only by eating roses; eventually, after he has experienced many troubles, roses are vouchsafed him by the goddess Isis. Although Isis or her equivalent has apparently not yet manifested, roses are all too prominent in the *Ægypt* series, budding promisingly on an old bush outside Pierce's window (*Love* 158) and spilling over various lawns. Roses are especially prominent in the names of women. There is Julie Rosengarten, the editor of a book Pierce is writing on an alternate history of the world, one in which magic prevails; more important, there are so far two women by the name of Rose—the red-haired Rosalind (Rosie) Rasmussen, the director by default of the foundation for which Pierce is editing Kraft's novel, and the dark Rose Ryder—and in a crucial scene in *Ægypt* , Pierce makes the mistake of confusing the latter with the former. Thus begins his descent into the obsessive, sadomasochistic relationship with Rose Ryder that takes up much of both *Love & Sleep* and *Dæmonomania* and that, as erotic melancholy that stifles creativity, could be called a kind of asshood. In all three of Crowley's novels it is Bruno, not Apuleius, who supplies the immediately ascertainable complexion of Pierce's dilemma. That complexion consists of three elements: Bruno's concept of "asininity"; the importance of change, metamorphosis; and the role of images in the arts of memory and magic.

Asininity is the first element to consider. Apuleius himself, adapting an earlier story in Greek, had drawn upon associations the ass had in his time: its use as a beast of burden; its reputation for curiosity, stubbornness, and sexual vigor; and, most important, its association with the Egyptian god Set, the brother and killer of Osiris and thus the enemy of his wife Isis, Lucius's redeemer (Schlam 28, 40; Griffiths 24-26). As a magician and philosopher, Apuleius was probably also aware of the ass's connections with the malefic planet Saturn and its involvement with melancholy (von Franz 47). By the time Bruno wrote his *Cabala,* not only had *The Golden Ass* long been taken as an allegorical treatment of Apuleius's own transformation from feckless youth to philosopher (see Gollnick 17-19), but the creature itself had acquired Biblical sanction; it had been, after all, the beast Christ had ridden in his entry into Jerusalem. Bruno himself was very fond of the story in

Numbers 22 of the proud prophet Balaam and the angel who spoke through Balaam's ass (deLeon 128-30). As Frances A. Yates and Nuccio Ordine have shown (257-6l; 1-49), the image of the ass had become by the Renaissance rich with paradox: it could be an emblem of fleshbound ignorance or the wisdom of the simple and patient, or somehow both at once or capable of turning into the other. Thus in his *De incertitutidine et vanitate scientiarum* (1516), Cornelius Agrippa of Nettesheim, Bruno's predecesssor in magic, had written that the Hebrews had associated the hardworking, patient ass with the Kabbalistic Sephiroth of Chokmah (Wisdom) (382) and denied "that *Apuleius* of *Megara*, euer bene admitted to the holy mysteries of *Isis*, if first he had not of a Philosopher ben tourned into an Asse" (383). Bruno himself distinguished between what Ordine terms "negative asininity" and "positive asininity." In general, as Crowley's Bruno tells a startled Rudolf II in *Dæmono-mania*, negative asininity is the "condition of the Age of Gold, when men were asses" (199) and knew only Idleness, which he had personified in his *Expulsion of the Triumphant Beast* (1585). "Little did our first parents see that from the time they plucked the fruit of Knowledge, nothing would be the same again; they had unleashed Change, and with it Pain, and Toil" (*Daemon* 199). In Bruno's world, change and toil are good. Negative asininity is everything that resists change and toil, and with them, as Bruno tells the Emperor, "Evolution. Transmigration. Parturition. Metamorphosis" (199; see also Ordine 65). Negative asses, as Ordine quotes from *Cabala*, "wrapped their five fingers into a single hoof, so that they could not pick the forbidden fruit of the tree of knowledge as Adam did . . . " (66). Positive asininity, in contrast, is characterized not only by acceptance of change, toil, and humility, for the sake of the civilization they make possible, but by the capacity to achieve divinity through reason. After Bruno cleared the heavens of unsatisfactory images in his *Expulsion of the Triumphant Beast* (1585), he raised "abstract Asininity" to the seat Ursa Major had once occupied (see Ordine 6). Furthermore, in the infinite universe

Bruno is postulating, the positive ass's achievement of divinity is tied to his acceptance of metempsychosis, of changing into an infinite array of shapes including the non-human. For this acceptance, as Karen deLeon Jones points out, it is necessary to have been an ass as Bruno's Onorio had been, directly in union with Wisdom: "Onorio represents the life after revelation; he represents the manipulation of the secret of nature that is true magic" (95).

That said, precisely how do Apuleius's Lucius and Crowley's Pierce fall into asininity, negative or positive or both? In both cases, regardless of what St. Augustine would think (see *The City of God*, Chapter 8), magic itself is not the problem; neither is the investigation thereof. Rather, the problem lies within the investigator; both Lucius and Pierce are unable before their transformations to take magic as seriously as they might: that is, not only as an intriguing possibility but as a reality that would affect them personally and involve personal responsibility; furthermore, both protagonists have trouble perceiving what we might call the "big picture," the transcendent context in which magic belongs. Thus, regarding *The Golden Ass*, Nancy Shumate points out that "in this book magic is ultimately the chief symbol of the epistemologically slippery nature of the world as a whole" (47). Lucius, before he journeyed on business to Thessaly, had never realized this "epistemologically slippery nature"; however, as he approaches the area, famous for its witches, he "steps into a sort of twilight zone, where a whole range of 'knowledge' commonly considered firm is thrown into doubt; where cherished premises and assumptions are overturned; where fiction and truth are indistinguishable; where, in short, his acquired epistemological apparatus is no longer adequate to interpret the text of the world" (44). However, despite the stories he hears along the way of witchcraft and its dreadful effects, despite his inspection of a statue of Actaeon's transformation into a stag, despite even a brush with animated goatskins, Lucius fails to appreciate such as challenges to his interpretation of reality, much less as warnings of what might happen to him. They merely excite his "gee whiz" curiosity about the wonders of magic. As Marie-Louise von Franz points out, he feels as little personal involvement with them as he does about his sexual relationship with Fotis, the maid working for the family he is boarding with (30). For him the relationship is merely a game; the stories he hears and the images he sees are just stories and images. Thus, when Fotis invites him to see her mistress change herself into an owl, Lucius is all too willing to try such a transformation; he doesn't consider the possible consequences. However, Fotis brings the wrong ointment, and the young aristocratic dilettante begins his life as a human being trapped in an ass's body, experiencing all the brutality of the Roman world. That world becomes increasingly nightmarish, ending with the imminence of death with a criminal woman in the arena. It is then that Lucius, having escaped and run to the Gulf of Corinth, has the vision of Isis that promises his restoration to manhood and provides what Shumate calls his "metaphysical anchor" (314) in the slippery magical world. She gives him meaning and structure for it all. She also gives him what we might call a "positive ass" job, as a priest serving both herself and her husband Osiris. However, as Carl C. Schlam points out, Isis is just as magical as the witches Lucius had experienced; "there is no absolute division between magic and religion in the world presented in the *Metamorphoses*" (122). Isis is, simply, at the upper, transcendent end of the continuum. Hers is the benevolent grace of a goddess rather than the malevolent mischief of a witch (Schlam 122).

Similarly, Crowley's Pierce Moffett has difficulty with taking magic seriously and personally; by the end of *Dæmonomania*, he has not yet found a "metaphysical anchor" like Lucius's. Pierce has epistemological troubles in general; as is shown in *Love & Sleep*, he was capable even as a child of half denying, half forgetting things he had done, such as taking his dead aunt Opal's engagement ring (20-21) or setting forest fires (12-15). Playing at the "Invisible College" with his Kentucky cousins, he "knew it had only been a game, a game's dangerous and thrilling extension into somewhere beyond pretend but still a game, they were all only kids and not knights really: and yet it was *as though* it weren't a game but a true story he was caught within . . . "(*Love* 127). Such confusions and denials persist in his adult investigations of magic; "as if," he will insist to Boney Rasmussen's questions about the Fellowes Kraft novel of alternate history Pierce is to edit (*Ægypt* 330). Indeed, intrigued by the way in which the details of Fellowes Kraft's books dovetail with both emerging childhood memories and his old professor Frank Barr's suggestion that "there's more than one History of the World" (*Ægypt* 73), Pierce has already outlined for the literary agent Julie Rosengarten the scheme for a book about successive world ages, in one of which—the Renaissance—magic was real. He insists he's writing the book because "it's a fascinating story, a kind of intellectual mystery story" (*Ægypt* 194) and reminds her of "the one great drawback of practical magic . . . It didn't work" (197). Recognizing the wish to believe he is denying, excited by the prospect, and knowing far more than Pierce does about magic, Julie muses:

> Old Pierce . . . He thinks he's so sharp, so unfooled: like a color-blind person, undeceived by color. What he could never see is that those powers he was just talking about weren't wandering around in the world free like mutts waiting to be adopted; they were the creations of souls, created between souls, they were creation itself, and bringing themselves into being was the use they had. If you can create such power in your life, then it's your duty to create it. If you are somehow granted it, it's not for no reason. That's what evolution is. (*Ægypt* 198)

Indeed, like her friend Beau Brachman in Pierce's new hometown of Blackbury Jambs, Julie senses that a "passage time" between world ages is imminent. As that passage time approaches and magic presumably once again becomes possible, Pierce does indeed venture, if only half consciously, into magic, and in doing so, fulfills Julie's concerns. First, he seems to half create, half invoke a "son" for himself, whom he names "Robbie"; this Robbie, who becomes more and more tangible, turns out by the end of *Love & Sleep* and the beginning of *Dæmonomania*, to have been a real spiritual entity, Eros himself, whose mission clearly had been to bring Pierce and Rose Ryder together (*Love* 481; *Daemon* 28). Robbie leaves on the very night of the stormy autumnal equinox that seems to blow the new world age in. Even before that, but increasingly afterwards, Pierce tries out on Rose the magical, erotic binding techniques he learned from Giordano Bruno's *General Account of Binding* (1585). As he explains to Rose,

> Well I don't really know how *they* did it. But I don't think it was so different from what we do all the time. We can't think without images, and images have no power to work in us unless we are moved by them. What moves us most is love. Erotic power, erotic energy, desire. One magician said: *Love is magic, magic is love.* Giordano Bruno. He believed you gave life and power to the images you cast with love. (*Love & Sleep* 405)

Unfortunately, things go wrong. First, interpreting Bruno's instructions rather too literally (see Couliano 87-102), Pierce goes beyond trying to manipulate Rose's imagination to subjecting her to acts of sexual bondage; he goes so far as to photograph her bound and to display the picture in a frame decorated with dog leashes (*Daemon* 58, 138). Second, realizing that he is losing Rose to a Christian fundamentalist group called the Powerhouse, Pierce—Saturnian by nature—falls into what he himself recognizes as erotic melancholy, *amor hereos* (*Daemon* 366); he is soon no longer able to wash his clothes and take care of himself, much less work on his book. Third, he comes to regret his magical manipulations: "All magic is bad magic. He thought this thought for the first time. To do magic you must take power over others, and you must believe you can do what can't be done, and make others believe it too. All magic is bad magic" (158). He is in a very pronounced state of negative asininity.

Pierce's situation is ironic. All the time, even when he has denied them or forgotten them, he contains within himself the memories that could redeem him. As Jennifer Stevenson says, he is one of the Crowley "characters [who] feel literally inhabited by their memories" (11). The book which he had drawn upon in childhood, Alexis Payne de St.-Phalle's *Dictionary of Deities, Devils and Daemons of Mankind*, reinforced by a comic strip called "Little Enosh," seems to have imprinted in good Brunonian fashion powerful magical images upon his memory; among these, from the cover of the book itself, is John Dee's "Monas Hieroglyphica," which Pierce adopted for his "Invisible College" and indeed stamped on the bodies of its members. That book shows up in the Blackbury Jambs library; Val, the town's astrologer, is used to consulting it. Pierce has difficulty at least twice recognizing the Monas glyph. Once, as he is exploring Kraft's library, he finds a copy of Charlotte Fell Smith's biography of Dee; when he sees the Monas on the cover, he cannot remember either it or "drawing it on his cousins with a Scripto, or on the flyleafs of his lost books" (*Love* 239). Again, just after Robbie has entered his life and just as he is looking for Rose in the library, he has a near collision with Val. Val happens to be carrying the St.-Phalle book, but he recognizes neither it nor the glyph on the cover. The narrator thus comments:

> And if he had taken it from her, and in wonder opened it, would it not very likely have fallen open (in that age of the world, when Coincidence was so strong a god) right to the page from which Val had read to Rosie in the Volcano—that verso page where Plato was quoted on Eros? *He is not to be confused with the beautiful beloved, though men often make this mistake; rather his appearance presages the appearance of the beloved. He is the spirit who inspires love, who makes love unrefusable* . . . And wouldn't he have known then what had

seized him, known it was already past escaping, and thus perhaps have escaped? (*Love & Sleep* 402)

The implication in both passages is that recognitions, of Eros or of potent images, are not possible in the world age in which Pierce is living. In the first situation, the narrator observes that "memory in that age did not hold such things very well, or only some memories did; nor did the things themselves always awaken when they were looked at long and steadily enough . . . " (239-40). About the second passage, the comment is that "That age was passing. Val's arm was over the hieroglyph of the Monas stamped on the book's cover, and Pierce didn't see it, and this time it didn't call to him" (402).

By the end of *Dæmonomania*, it seems that the age Pierce has been living in has passed, just as the world Bruno and Dee lived in passed, and the reality of magic with it. By the winter solstice of 1979 the shamanistic Beau Brachman has gathered all "the creatures of the passage time" and will "separate those persons who will continue from the very same persons who will not, and then *turn back* with the ones who will not, away from the what-is-to-be, toward the what-has-been" (435). What will happen to Pierce in the new dispensation? Will he emerge from the melancholy that characterized his negative asininity, and how? Most important, will his emergence affect or be affected by the new order? There are some clues. In the alternative 1588 of Kraft's novel, the Emperor Rudolf seems to have broken out of his own melancholy by finally realizing the truth of Bruno's lesson:

> What had that Italian said, that uncowled monk. Toil destroyed the Age of Gold, and created injustice, and want, and inequity. And only more toil could correct this.
>
> He must not be still, any more than the productive seasons could stand still. Not even Winter stands still, but nourishes Spring in his old cold heart. He must

work, and not for himself; roll up his sleeves and humbly
toil. God had not taken from him the strength of his
hands by anointing his head. (*Daemon* 300).

Since the Emperor has already caused change in the external
world by moving the positions of the seasons and elements in his
Neue Saal (298-99), he has presumably aided in the shift from old
world to new that Dee had helped inaugurate with the winds granted him by the spirits of his crystal (*Love* 460-76). Similarly, in his
world, Pierce receives strong suggestions that he must be capable
of action. Thus, when Pierce tells Beau Brachman, "I feel like I've
somehow uncovered an awful secret evil that pervades the world"
and "The worst thing is how it seems to be my fault somehow,"
Beau replies to the first statement with "Maybe because you have"
and the second with "But that doesn't mean you're not supposed
to fix it" (*Daemon* 392). Later in the same scene, a masked man
who might be the ghost of Fellowes Kraft tells him of his difficulty
finishing a story: "Well at a certain point invention flags, you see;
you begin to repeat, helplessly. You keep coming upon the same few
conceptions over and over, greeting each one with glad cries, yes!
Yes! The way on! Until you realize what it is, oh here I go again, the
same story again, as ever . . . It'll have to be you that does it. Somehow, I don't know how. If you don't make a contribution, haven't
I labored in vain? Not to speak of your own sufferings . . . You'll
have to do it . . . I'm so sorry" (394-95).

By the novel's end, Pierce seems prepared to act, to finish what
he has been admonished to finish. He has some ideas about how
to continue Kraft's novel. Furthermore, he plans to leave soon for
Prague, where he will search as the Rasmussen Foundation has
directed him, for an object left behind in the transition from the
magical 16th century to the non-magical age that followed. There
is a clue that there might be an Isis, and transformation, waiting
for him. Earlier, in *Ægypt*, just after he has first come to Blackbury
Jambs, he saw emerge from a lake three young women: "a dark, a

light, a rosé; three graces" (124). Pierce's friend Spofford indicates vaguely that his friend Rosie is one of them ("Well, she's here"), thus making it possible for Pierce to mistake the dark-haired Rose Ryder for the red-haired Rosie Rasmussen. One wonders not only why the light-haired girl has never figured in the three novels so far but also if she will appear in the fourth. The three girls were, after all, de-scribed as "graces"; the emblem of the Three Graces was a power-ful one in the Renaissance, appearing on medals, in paintings, and in memory theaters as a sign of the plenitude and circularity of the universe (Wind 31-56, 100-110; Yates 74-75, 81-82). Furthermore, the colors of the three girls correspond to the colors Isis is wearing when Apuleius sees her in his dream. Thus, in P. G. Walsh's transla-tion, Isis "wore a multi-coloured dress woven from fine linen, one part of which shone radiantly white, a second glowed yellow with saffron blossom, and a third blazed rosy red. But what riveted my eyes above all else was a jet-black cloak, which gleamed with a dark sheen as it enveloped her" (219-20). Marie-Louise von Franz associates these colors with the colors that manifest in the alchemi-cal process—*nigredo, albedo, rubedo, citrinitas*—and reminds us that *nigredo*, the black stage, is the "death," the "putrefaction," the alchemical matter must endure before any other transformation can occur. Von Franz also reminds us that the *nigredo* of metals is equivalent to the Saturnian melancholy afflicting people (143). We think not only of Pierce's love melancholy focused on by the dark-haired Rose Ryder but also of the latter's disguise as Night at the masquerade party Pierce attended as an ass; we think also of "Una Knox," Boney Rasmussen's mysterious heiress, whose identity as "One Night" Pierce finally figures out at the same party. It is pos-sible then if the novel *Dæmonomania* describes Pierce's negative asininity as a *nigredo*, alchemical transformation will eventually occur for him and his Isis figure will appear. In the meantime, we can only wonder, "Who among those Graces was the blonde?"

WORKS CITED

Agrippa, Henry Cornelius.
Of the Vanitie and Uncertaintie of Artes and Sciences. Trans. James Sanford, 1569. Ed. Catherine M. Dunn. Northridge, CA: California State University, 1974.

Apuleius.
The Golden Ass. Trans. P. G. Walsh. Oxford: Oxford University Press, 1995.

Augustine.
The City of God. Trans. Marcus Dods. New York: The Modern Library, 1950.

Bruno, Giordano.
Essays on Magic. Trans. and ed. Richard J. Blackwell. Cambridge Texts in the History of Philosophy, ed. Karl Ameriks and Desmond M. Clarke. Cambridge: Cambridge University Press, 1998.
The Expulsion of the Triumphant Beast. Trans. Arthur D. Imerti. 1964. Lincoln: University of Nebraska, 1992.

Couliano, Ioan P.
Eros and Magic in the Renaissance. Trans. Margaret Cook. Chicago: The University of Chicago Press, 1987.

Crowley, John.
Ægypt. New York: Bantam Books, 1987.
Dæmonomania. New York: Bantam Books, 2000.
Love & Sleep. New York: Bantam Books, 1994.

deLeon-Jones, Karen Silvia.
Giordano Bruno and the Kabbalah: Prophets, Magicians, and Rabbis. Yale Studies in Hermeneutics, ed. Joel Weinsheimer. New Haven: Yale University Press, 1997.

Gollnick, James.
The Religious Dreamworld of Apuleius' "Metamorphoses": Recovering a Forgotten Hermeneutic. Editions SR 25. Waterloo, Ontario: Wilfrid

Laurier University Press for the Canadian Corporation for Studies in Religion, 1999.

Griffiths, J. Gwyn, ed. and trans.
Apuleius of Madauros, The Isis-Book (Metamorphoses Book XI.) Leiden: E. J. Brill, 1975.

Ordine, Nuccio.
Giordano Bruno and the Philosophy of the Ass. Trans. Henryk Baranski in collaboration with Arielle Saiber. New Haven: Yale University Press, 1996.

Schlam, Carl C.
The "Metamorphoses" of Apuleius: On Making an Ass of Oneself. Chapel Hill: The University of North Carolina Press, 1992.

Shumate, Nancy.
Crisis and Conversion in Apuleius' "Metamorphoses." Ann Arbor: The University of Michigan Press, 1996.

Sleight, Graham.
"*Dæmonomania* by John Crowley." *The New York Review of Science Fiction* March 2001: 1, 8-9.

Stevenson, Jennifer.
"Memory and the World of John Crowley: Technology and the Art of Memory." *The New York Review of Science Fiction* July 1998: 1, 8-11.

Von Franz, Marie-Louise.
A Psychological Interpretation of "The Golden Ass" of Apuleius. 2nd ed. Irving, TX: Spring Publications, Inc., 1980.

Wind, Edgar.
Pagan Mysteries in the Renaissance. New Haven: Yale University Press, 1958.

Yates, Frances A.
Giordano Bruno and the Hermetic Tradition. 1964. Chicago: The University of Chicago Press, 1991.

"THE WORDS OF MERCURY ARE HARSH...":
LOVE'S LABOUR'S LOST IN ÆGYPT
Matthew S. S. Davis

SIT DOWN, SORROW is the title of Fellowes Kraft's autobiography. It would seem to be taken from Shakespeare's *Love's Labour's Lost* (1592-1595?), and Crowley later provides a full apparent passage from which it originates:

> "Welcome the sour cup of prosperity!
> Affliction may one day smile again: and until then,
> Sit down, sorrow."

But something is wrong. The full quote should be:

> "I suffer for the truth, sir: for true it is I was taken with Jaquenetta, and Jaquenetta is a true girl; and therefore welcome the sour cup of prosperity! Affliction may one day smile again; and till then, sit THEE down, sorrow."
> (act 1, scene 1, the final speech; CAPS my own)

Serious emendation has occurred: the original passage is prose, not verse, and the proffered quotation is wrong. The only instance to be found of "Sit down, sorrow" is in the same sham-versification as the epigraph to chapter 14 ("The Castle of Trebona") of

323

Charlotte Fell Smith's *John Dee* (1909). We know from *Love &
Sleep* that Fellowes Kraft owns a copy of this work. Chapter 14
recounts the final weeks of Dee and Kelley in Bohemia, and the last
times they call upon Madimi. Though the two men appear to have
access to divine wisdom and the means of creating worldly wealth,
neither of these has brought happiness, as the two men are emotionally fatigued. As we know, this is the crux echoed throughout the
novel: whether characters have the luck, strength of character and
foresight to effect a wide change in their world and themselves.

The quote itself delineates an apprehension of the possibility
of change through a progression and reconciliation of apparently
contradictory images and circumstances. Its expression of morose
accommodation reflects the emotional trend and narrative progress of the novel toward failure. Although the quote only appears
specifically in the consciousness of Rosie Rasmussen due to its suggestive use by Fellowes Kraft, it also entails a burgeoning relevance
to the major themes of the novel. For Kraft, the particular chapter
and its epigraph evoke the Prague Spring Revolution of 1968, yet
one more failed opportunity, as per his own failure to find his Ideal
Friend. Rosie, reading Kraft's autobiography, finds that it reflects
her own forlorn state, having forgotten why or how she loves, and
evokes a wider fixless state of modern life. There is also a hint of
post coitum triste, the disillusioning inadequacy of sexual experience, wherein expenditure is also loss. We may also choose to see
in the quote a direct expression of one of the novel's major fantastic
themes: the invocation of avatars, divine embodiments and person-
ifications of abstract ideas and emotions. In the territory of Ægypt,
sorrow is not merely sadness: the melancholy personality under the
sign of Saturn is best equipped for those leaps of the imagination by
which the world will be reshaped. The overwhelming impression of
sadness in the novel relates to this presiding genius of melancholy, a
sorrowful dissatisfaction that, handled correctly, may be the impetus to a vision of a better world.

Given the connotative weight of these few quoted words, an

uninformed reader might be misled into thinking that *Love's Labour's Lost* might be one of Shakespeare's more sombre plays. But
even as associations of loss and estrangement flash through Rosie's
mind, she alerts us that "it was the source rather than the quote
itself that was significant." Indeed, the currents of *Love's Labour's
Lost* run deeper in Ægypt than these few ripples. *Love's Labour's
Lost* is contemporaneous with and engages the late 16th century
Neoplatonic ideas and Hermeticism in literary form that Ægypt
explores. Hermeticism and Neoplatonism both have their origins
in Marsilio Ficino's 15th century revival of Plato and 3rd-6th century
Platonic philosophies of a universe populated by supernatural enti-
ties, where man is an equivalent spiritual being, who in his wisdom
can affect the operations of a universe whose external reality is
only a fallen representation of eternal essences. Hermeticism em-
phasised the opportunities of magic for man's unfettered mastery
of his world. Neoplatonism harmonised the Platonic absolute with
the Christian God, and instead sought means to approach this ideal
state. Sixteenth century writers found in a work like Castiglione's
"The Courtier" a model by which they could have a lived experience of Neoplatonism, through courtly standards of behaviour, the
idealised love of an idealised woman, and transcendent literary
symbolism. To understand how Ægypt stands in relation to *Love's
Labour's Lost* we must examine the models that both Shakespeare
and Crowley utilize.

Embellished rhetoric, in this period, was not, as many modern
readers find it, a bombastic obstruction, but was in fact the signal
means of embodying and conveying knowledge and wisdom. Following the Italian lead of authors like Pietro Bembo and Castiglione, 16th century European writers, mostly centred around the
court, sought to find a suitable courtly diction that would equal
the heights of their classical predecessors. In their study of classical literature and learning they found their model: an ordered and
measured style, stately, sweet and resonant; in its measures could
be found a mirror of universal harmony. From this study arose a

concern with form, metre, and the accurate and intricate contrivance of rhetorical figures and tropes. This style of lofty sentiment, sweet rhythm, elaborate description often derived from classical mythology, and high-flown oratory now seems highly affected to modern readers—especially since its emphasis on didacticism at the service of rhetorical moral diatribes frequently surmounted and obscured the ostensible narrative. This embellished eloquent style of the late 16th and 17th centuries is generically known as Baroque, but in English prose it was identified as "Euphuism," after the novel *Euphues* by John Lyly (1578), while in Spain it was known as "Gongorism," for Luis de Gongora y Argote, author of *Las Soledades* (1611-13).[1] The reliance on metaphorical and metaphysical resources of sound and imagery stems from Neoplatonic theories of literature, where sheer linguistic technique developing conceits of Petrarchan complexity would raise an author's writings to a realised spiritual plane beyond the mundane. As poets like Sir Phillip Sidney were fond of demonstrating, "poet" meant "maker," and imitation was not a passive process, therefore in his imagination an author could approximate the powers of God. Through allegory and iconography the poet could represent a higher truth, could even body forth the cosmic harmony.[2] The development of a literary work through antithesis and parallelism is the result of the synthesis of Christian and Neoplatonic thought; this ensured a belief in the simultaneity of all events, past, present, and future in the mind of God and presented time as a manipulable element of literary structure. Formal rhetorical elements worked to contain uncertainty as the author represented new heights of perception, as opposed to the former reliance upon empirically chronological habits of narrative.[3] The acknowledged intent of all these oratorical techniques and apparatus was to lead the reader inward to deeper self-study, and for him to recognize how these representations are both within and without him, as is Crowley's intent and conscious modern deployment of them in Ægypt. In Frank Walker Barr's final lecture, Crowley makes it quite explicit that he is drawing upon

Elizabethan storytelling techniques of repetition to induce meaning.[4] Ægypt's very formal elements of themes, scenes, characters
and their thoughts repeating throughout is what makes Crowley's
work so refreshing and involving, and yet it is also part of the older
tradition within which he works.

It is therefore little wonder that Crowley should turn to *Love's
Labour's Lost*, a play written in imitation, examination and
parody of Euphuism. *Love's Labour's Lost* satirizes the verbosity
of Euphuism, mocks its style and content, and applies Euphuism's
reliance on antithesis and parallelism to the mechanism of its own
sophisticated, contrapuntal stagecraft. Of all Shakespeare's plays,
Love's Labour's Lost has probably the least action. It is a comedy
of contemplation, proceeding by the appearance and reappearance
of its characters and themes in different but very formal combinations. This description serves well for Ægypt, but closer examination reveals an even more detailed sequence of consonance between
the two works. While we have been overtly nudged to see *Las
Soledades* as bestowing some form on Ægypt, greater narrative
similarities can be found with *Love's Labour's Lost*.

In the play a group of scholar/knights retreats from the world,
makes vows of celibacy and forswears love so that they may con-
centrate on the studies that will bring them fame and triumph over
death and time. Of course the real world breaks in upon them
when they fall in love. Their experience with desire leaves them
compromised and their vaunted intellectualism is humiliated and
mocked when they each are made to woo the wrong maiden. As
the play ends, they are set challenges for the forthcoming year that
will be tests of character rather than intelligence. Such a description
adequately encompasses both Pierce Moffett's and the novel's conception of himself and also the events that occur to him within the
frame of Ægypt. Most critics point out that that the movement of
the play is about leaving off self-deceptions in a world of enclosed
artificiality to enter into a wider perspective of reality.[5] Of course,
this is a fundamental narrative pattern, and since in its philosophi-

cal form as "gnosis" is what Ægypt is all about it cannot really be argued that Crowley is drawing particularly upon this element. But this aspect is certainly more advanced than what one would expect to find in a comedy. And that it is a comedy is important, with its connotations of springtime and the pastoral.

In his treatment of Blackbury Jambs and the Faraway Hills, it is evident that Crowley is imbuing these locations with the qualities of Elizabethan pastoral. The works of Lyly and Gongora draw upon Classical Greek romances for their plots and atmosphere; so given these resonant models Crowley works to ensure throughout Ægypt the continuation of this tradition and to evoke pastoral modes. As Pierce is considering Gongora's *Las Soledades*, Crowley brings into sharp focus an array of pervasive allusions to the pastoral by having Brent Spofford write a letter to Rosie at Arcady: Arcadia is the traditional setting of pastorals, both a genuine place in Greece and an ideal country of the imagination, and was the title of Sir Phillip Sidney's major work; the shepherd wooing his Rosalynd (Rosie's full name) is the scenario of Edmund Spenser's "The Shepherd's Calendar"; and that Spofford should ask how to spell "idyll" evokes the original *Idylls* of Theocritus. Pastoral is a form of writing with a rustic setting: it advocates a simplicity of life and thought with affecting treatments of love, loss, the transcendent value of literature, and contrasts the corruption of the city against the innocence of the rural.

What pastoral had become through the centuries was a playground for sophisticates, a wishful trope re-imagining the complexities and apparent fruitlessness of life. But it also had a deeper significance; though its conventions might seem to have crystallized into a system of convenient symbols, it embodied a tradition of the first and ideal golden age. For the refugees of the Sixties and Seventies that populate the Faraways, their own attempts at pastoral living reveal their nostalgia for a golden age, simpler possibilities and a retreat from the complexities of a world that keeps moving. Pastoral presents a hopeful retreat where the courtiers, knights and warriors of the 16th century (or the Vietnam veterans of the 20th, such as Spofford) could invert the sense of fruitlessness in their contemporary life at court and instead find a full realm of expression for the ideals expressed by Castiglione. For 16th century courtiers, the court was the world and Arcadia offered a new structure for this world, with aristocrats as simple shepherds and where courtly love became the new organizing principle and consolation against death and failure.

For a pastoral comedy, *Love's Labour's Lost* has an advanced quality of knowingness, recognizing the pain that is often sublimated into soft reveries in generic pastoral writing. Shakespeare introduces the true emotional agonies that love and death entail. Acknowledging genuine mortification and bringing cyclicality into the lives of its protagonists transcends the obvious literary artificiality of its plot and characters. The original intellectual vows that lead to farce repeat themselves as an experience of some pain, tying the protagonists' development in the forthcoming year into a more complicated and emotionally resonant reality, as in Ægypt the awareness of the forthcoming year and its tribulations is the burden that must be borne so that final self-awareness may possibly be attained. The duping of the suitors into wooing the wrong women entails genuine confusion rather than mere comedy. The breaking of their vows and quibbling over their consciences is made ridiculous when they are gulled into making suits to the wrong women, but there is pathos in their predicament. Mockery is made to hurt. A debate of conscience is valid even if the basis for judgement is wrong, thus Pierce's self-recriminations are valid even when he has confused the two Roses at the Full Moon picnic.

The deeper pain arises from the pitfalls awaiting both the protagonists of *Love's Labour's Lost* and Pierce because of their shallow understanding of the courtly tradition in which they are trying to live. In each case they are more interested in having wisdom than in the processes by which that wisdom is achieved. Wisdom is gained in the Neoplatonic tradition through an involving love that

leads from the earthly to the divine.[6] In *Love's Labour's Lost* and
Ægypt, both in their studies and their romantic entanglements it
is the men's regard of self that defeats their ostensible aims. Their
studies and lives are egotistical quests after renown and self-satia-
tion, and when they fall in love they do not see the person, only a
means to the excitation of their own emotions. They are deluded
sensualists who are little able to see in their women a means to self-
fulfillment or a path to the higher wisdom. Instead they hoard the
Promethean fire for themselves, with their sensuous rhetoric merely
a celebration of its own power rather than a tool of effecting change
(as a character Bruno is open to criticism of vanity and self-infatu-
ation). The narcissism of these men is the root of their inadequacy
with their respective paramours.[7] The ladies in *Love's Labour's
Lost* can so easily fool their suitors since the men are so barely
aware of the women as individuals. This also holds true for Pierce
in his amorous experiences since his overconceptualising rarely
confronts the actuality of his lovers and, authorial legerdemain
aside, is one of the principle reasons underlying his confusion of the
two Roses. When the women in these fictions actually assert their
identities and demands no wonder the men are so confounded. The
danger posed in both works is of having more language or facility
of ideas than genuine experience. In the arena of Ægypt thoughts
and representations of thoughts are as real as characters, and we
must expect the characters themselves to confuse and elide this difference.

Crowley overlays characters, images and concepts to achieve
his effects, and then rewards readers for detecting his parallels
and antitheses by inviting them deeper into the operations of his
novels. Like Dr. Dee's Monas, where an apparently sufficient and
complete icon is instead a whole sequence of intricately and close-
fitting symbols and meanings, the attentive reader by picking up on
just one detail may be able to follow paths that were obscured or
covered, thereby encountering previous figures and themes in new
guises and combinations to discover more of the missing history

of Ægypt. Pierce is superimposed upon the young Shakespeare. *Love's Labour's Lost* unites Rosie and Fellowes Kraft in the same emotional space. Shakespeare is used to introduce the 16th century world and John Dee.[8]

Strangely, Giordano Bruno does not seem a part of this web of connections and never appears to even touch it. Scholars have ever been eager to connect Shakespeare to Bruno, these two towering 16th century writers of mutability, prolific multiformity, and the ever changing self. Almost all of this Bruno-Shakespeare scholarship has centered on *Love's Labour's Lost*, where Bruno's ideas and his character are represented in Shakespeare's art.[9] Frances Yates, the grand dame of Ægypt, most assiduously drove this line of scholastic inquiry. It begins with the traditional identification of the play's pedant Holofernes with the writer John Florio. Florio (1553-1625) was the son of an Italian Protestant émigré, an accomplished linguist who translated Montaigne, compiled an Italian/English dictionary, and was a significant conduit for Italian learning in English. Florio introduced Bruno to English society during his 1583-85 visit to England, both in person and then by including Bruno as a character in his book of dialogues, *Florio's Second Fruits* (1591). Florio introduced Bruno to the respective circles of Sir Phillip Sidney and Sir Walter Raleigh. Bruno dedicated several of his books to Sidney, a former pupil of Dee, and it is thought that Bruno's *De gle Eroici Furori* (1585) (*Heroycall Furies*, or Heroic Frenzies) may have had significant influence on the Sidney school of sonneteering.[10] Bruno would also have been well received by Raleigh, another protégé of Dee, since Raleigh was acquainted with some of the hermetic texts and much interested in astronomy.[11] The phrase "school of night" in *Love's Labour's Lost* has frequently been identified as a reference to Raleigh's "school of atheism[12]." His group's association with study of scientific and astrological learned occupations, as mirrored in the play, was then mocked as part of the developing Counter-Reformation that would eventually result in the death of Bruno and the overthrow of Bohemia.[13]

Using the points of Holofernes-Florio and the "school of night/ atheism," scholars have therefore triangulated that Berowne in *Love's Labour's Lost* is Shakespeare's representation of Giordano Bruno. This identification has been longstanding, not just for its homophony, but also because of Berowne's extensive use of celestial imagery, his celebration of a vivifying divine love, his extensive use of eye and visualisation imagery, and his fiery logic-chopping intellect. Even if Shakespeare never met Bruno, he may well have known Florio since Florio tutored Shakespeare's patron, the Earl of Southampton; furthermore, Bruno was established in London as a literary influence and as a personality of forceful eloquence. Shakespeare was certainly acquainted with those works in which Florio kept the fires of Bruno burning. *The First Fruits of Florio* features the phrase "It were labour lost to speak of love,"[14] and in the play he quotes an aphorism from *The Second Fruits of Florio,*[15] the book that recapitulates much of the content of *Heroycall Furies.*[16] In that work, Bruno rejected Petrarchism and courtly love with its emphasis on the love of worldly women, instead lauding love of an ideal as an inspiration to knowledge and truth.[17] Berowne largely recapitulates those arguments in *Love's Labour's Lost,* IV, iii, 285- 361, while IV, iii, 337-42 may also echo Bruno's *Spaccio della bestia trionfante (The Expulsion of the Triumphant Beast)* where the gods speak of love in the constellations.[18] Finally, as Bruno debates much on the nature of the sonnet and includes instances of his own in *Heroycall Furies,* so Shakespeare also mocks Petrarchism and courtly love, and includes sonnets in *Love's Labour's Lost.*[19]

While all of the above indicates that Shakespeare knew of and was willing to avail himself of Bruno's work and thoughts he would have been almost certainly antipathetic to the man himself. Bruno was a heretical Catholic, while Shakespeare appears to have been a Catholic with a small "c." Shakespeare abided by the old Ptolomeic celestial system, and did not share Bruno's Copernicanism and ostensible pantheism. They moved in separate circles of patronage. Florio's *Second Fruits* revived the animosity between Bruno and

English pride with the reminder that in *The Ash Wednesday Supper* Bruno had ridiculed the mediocrity of English learning. It is likely that Shakespeare's response was to mock pedants and false forms of scientific enquiry in *Love's Labour's Lost* in ways that approximated those of Bruno and his English associates. The play acts out the conflict between the Italian Renaissance's concern with man's intellectual nature and English Humanism's focus on man's moral nature. Bruno's character in the *Heroycall Furies* stressed that infatuation not overcome reason, but Shakespeare finds love a humanizing force even for his Bruno character. In short, Shakespeare's comedy satirizes Copernican fanatics and inspired Saturnian melancholics, using Bruno's own conception of love at the expense of Bruno's perceived arrogance.[20] In *Love's Labour's Lost*, Crowley finds a fictionalized portrayal of Bruno against which he may measure his own portraiture.[21]

Ægypt sets a scene for the free play of ideas, where intertextuality, life experience, and fantasy all abut the same lines. Words in Ægypt occupy not only a place on the page but also in the worlds of fact and the imagination. At the instant of recognition the perceiver effects a change both within himself and that which is perceived, the external world. Whether all of the paths above were precisely those taken by Crowley is debatable, but having been carved out by the imagination they now exist for others to follow and expand. Any new means of observing and evaluating ought not to be discounted and when the journey is made by the mercurial engines of thought then even the harshness and length of the way crossed ought to be worth the pains taken as we follow "after the songs of Apollo".[22]

APPENDIX

Berowne's speech, *Love's Labour's Lost*, IV, iii, 285-361

'Tis more than need.
Have at you, then, affection's men at arms.
Consider what you first did swear unto,
To fast, to study, and to see no woman;
Flat treason 'gainst the kingly state of youth.
Say, can you fast? your stomachs are too young;
And abstinence engenders maladies.
And where that you have vow'd to study, lords,
In that each of you have forsworn his book,
Can you still dream and pore and thereon look?
For when would you, my lord, or you, or you,
Have found the ground of study's excellence
Without the beauty of a woman's face?
From women's eyes this doctrine I derive:
They are the ground, the books, the academes,
From whence doth spring the true Promethean fire
Why, universal plodding poisons up
The nimble spirits in the arteries,
As motion and long-during action tires
The sinewy vigour of the traveller.
Now, for not looking on a woman's face,
You have in that forsworn the use of eyes
And study too, the causer of your vow;
For where is any author in the world
Teaches such beauty as a woman's eye?
Learning is but an adjunct to ourself
And where we are our learning likewise is:
Then when ourselves we see in ladies' eyes,
Do we not likewise see our learning there?
O, we have made a vow to study, lords,
And in that vow we have forsworn our books.
For when would you, my liege, or you, or you,
In leaden contemplation have found out
Such fiery numbers as the prompting eyes
Of beauty's tutors have enrich'd you with?

Other slow arts entirely keep the brain;
And therefore, finding barren practisers,
Scarce show a harvest of their heavy toil:
But love, first learned in a lady's eyes,
Lives not alone immured in the brain;
But, with the motion of all elements,
Courses as swift as thought in every power,
And gives to every power a double power,
Above their functions and their offices.
It adds a precious seeing to the eye;
A lover's eyes will gaze an eagle blind;
A lover's ear will hear the lowest sound,
When the suspicious head of theft is stopp'd:
Love's feeling is more soft and sensible
Than are the tender horns of cockl'd snails;
Love's tongue proves dainty Bacchus gross in taste:
For valour, is not Love a Hercules,
Still climbing trees in the Hesperides?
Subtle as Sphinx; as sweet and musical
As bright Apollo's lute, strung with his hair:
And when Love speaks, the voice of all the gods
Makes heaven drowsy with the harmony.
Never durst poet touch a pen to write
Until his ink were temper'd with Love's sighs;
O, then his lines would ravish savage ears
And plant in tyrants mild humility.
From women's eyes this doctrine I derive:
They sparkle still the right Promethean fire;
They are the books, the arts, the academes,
That show, contain and nourish all the world:
Else none at all in ought proves excellent.
Then fools you were these women to forswear,
Or keeping what is sworn, you will prove fools.
For wisdom's sake, a word that all men love,
Or for love's sake, a word that loves all men,
Or for men's sake, the authors of these women,
Or women's sake, by whom we men are men,
Let us once lose our oaths to find ourselves,
Or else we lose ourselves to keep our oaths.

It is religion to be thus forsworn,
For charity itself fulfills the law,
And who can sever love from charity?

NOTES

[1] The name "Euphues" was introduced into English by Roger Ascham in *The Schoolmaster* (1570), as influenced by the Italian courtly tradition, to mean a man well made for learning and able to use it best.

[2] Sidney, Sir Phillip. "Defence of Poesy," *Selected Writings,* edited by Richard Dutton. London: Carcanet, 1987, pp. 106-8.

[3] Nelson Jnr., Lowry. "Gongora and Milton: Toward a Definition of the Baroque," *Comparative Literature*, Volume 6, Winter 1954, pp. 53-63.

[4] *Ægypt*. New York: Bantam, p. 360.

[5] Palmer, D. J. "The Early Comedies," *Shakespeare: A Bibliographical Guide*, edited by Stanley Wells. Oxford: Clarendon Press, 1990, pp. 83-105.

[6] Auden, W. H. "Love's Labour's Lost," *Lectures on Shakespeare*, edited by Arthur Kirsch. London: Faber & Faber, pp. 33-43.

[7] Bloom, Harold. "Love's Labour's Lost," *Shakespeare and the Invention of the Human*. London: 4th Estate, pp. 121-147.

[8] There is a lunatic fringe (Graham Phillips and Martin Keatman *The Shakespeare Conspiracy*, 1994) which argues that the William Hall sent from England in August 1593 to meet Edward Kelley in Bohemia is in fact William Shakespeare, but I note this only to indicate the border separating inspired interconnectivity from sheer bloody stupidity.

[9] Gatti, Hilary. "Appendix II: Bruno-Shakespeare Criticism," *The Renaissance Dram of Knowledge: Giordano Bruno in England*. London: Routledge, 1989, pp. 171-188.

[10] Buxton, John. *Sir Phillip Sidney and the English Renaissance*. London:

Macmillan, 1954, pp. 162-67.

[11] Yates, Frances A. *The Occult Philosophy in the Elizabethan Age*. London: Routlege Kegan & Paul, p. 145.

[12] Persons, Robert. *Responsio ad Elizabethae Edictum*. 1592.

[13] Yates, Frances A. *The Occult Philosophy in the Elizabethan Age*, London: Routlege Kegan & Paul, p. 145.

[14] Yates, Frances A. *A Study of Love's Labour's Lost*. Cambridge: Cambridge University Press, 1936, p. 34.

[15] Yates, Frances A. *A Study of Love's Labour's Lost*. Cambridge: Cambridge University Press, 1936, p. 24.

[16] Yates, Frances A. *A Study of Love's Labour's Lost*. Cambridge: Cambridge University Press, 1936, p. 109.

[17] Yates, Frances A. *A Study of Love's Labour's Lost*. Cambridge: Cambridge University Press, 1936, p. 105.

[18] Yates, Frances A. *Giordano Bruno and the Hermetic Tradition*. London: Routlege Kegan & Paul, 1964, p. 356.

[19] Yates, Frances A. *A Study of Love's Labour's Lost*. Cambridge: Cambridge University Press, 1936, p. 11.

[20] Yates, Frances A. *The Occult Philosophy in the Elizabethan Age*, London: Routlege Kegan & Paul, pp. 150-153.

[21] In a letter Crowley has revealed that it had been his intention to return to Shakespeare, with Bruno his rival for the love of Aemilia Lanier (the Italian woman A. L. Rowse conjectured as the Dark Lady of Shakespeare's sonnets) and *Love's Labour's Lost* as his revenge on Bruno.

[22] *Love's Labour's Lost,* V, ii, 922.

BLACKBURY JAMBS, AND OTHER MISUNDERSTANDINGS

Graham Sleight

AS PIERCE MOFFETT explains to Julie Rosengarten when pitching her his book on Renaissance magic, the ideas of magi like Bruno, Dee, or Marsilio Ficino were founded on a colossal misunderstanding. The *Corpus Hermeticum*, which was brought to Florence around 1460, and which they believed to date from the era of Moses, actually comprised much later writings from an Alexandrian Gnostic sect of the 2nd or 3rd century after Christ. Frances Yates, the historian who provided so much of the background for the Ægypt sequence, explains how this misdating happened:

> We can understand how the content of the Hermetic writings fostered the illusion of the Renaissance Magus that he had in them a mysterious and precious account of most ancient Egyptian wisdom, philosophy, and magic . . . The scraps of Greek philosophy he found in these writings, derived from the somewhat debased philosophical teaching current in the early centuries A.D., confirmed the Renaissance reader in his belief that he had here the fount of pristine wisdom whence Plato and the Greeks had derived the best they knew. (Yates, 1964, p.6)

In short, Ficino and his contemporaries were seeing in the *Corpus Hermeticum* what they wanted to see, rather than what was actually there. But arguably this misunderstanding of the origins of the Hermetic writings produced a much richer intellectual ferment than would have been the case if they had been dated correctly. Misunderstanding seems to cluster around the stories with which Ægypt concerns itself, as Pierce himself writes when discussing an anecdote about the production of gold:

> "Now it may be," he typed, "that every other recorded instance of gold made by fire—there are hundreds of them, almost all seeming to be variants on a few themes, like old comedy plots—maybe every one is false, the product of mendacity or wishful thinking or the accumulating errors of multiple transmission, history's game of Telephone that always pushes anecdotes towards clarity, wonder, or exemplum." (*Dæmonomania*, 40)

That's a pretty despairing point of view for a historian to take. If history is a game of Telephone, the truth distorted at every stage, then how can one meaningfully find out about "the past"? If "the past" is constantly distorted or misrepresented, it makes all the more difficult Pierce's quest to explain to his readers what is the one thing we inherit from it which retains the powers it once had. The fact that the text is studded with examples of people (especially Pierce) one way or another *getting the story wrong* only emphasizes the problem.

This device is present right from the start—beginning with Pierce's meditation at the opening of Vita.1 on how wishes can go awry. The dæmon who granted Midas's wish fatally misunderstood the sense of what the king wanted, though it was scarcely its job to do so—as Pierce says, such creatures are necessarily "literal-minded, deeply stupid from man's point of view" (18). Pierce himself is quite prone to misunderstanding or mishearing others, beginning later in the same chapter, when he runs into Spofford and hears the name of the local river as the Blackberry. Much of the rest of his story in that first volume revolves around his confusion between Rosie Mucho and Rose Ryder—in one sense, the sort of benign comedic error which animates, for instance, Shakespeare's *Comedy of Errors. The Solitudes* (*Ægypt*) derives much of its sunny tone from the fact that Pierce seems to pay relatively little for the mistakes he makes—indeed, they bring him to a point where he seems to have possibilities both personal and professional stretching out limitlessly before him.

By the time of *Love & Sleep*, however, this device of misunderstanding has begun to be used in darker ways. In the Prologue, Pierce remembers, or thinks he remembers, taking in and raising a she-wolf when he was a child; setting fire to a forest to impress a woman; and knowing how to compress coal to make a diamond (5). From the narrative that follows of his Kentucky childhood, it seems that these are misrememberings of things that actually happened. (I say "seems" because the unreliability of narrative inevitably becomes an issue here.) It's far more understandable, at least, to hear that Pierce sheltered the feral child Bobby Shaftoe rather than a she-wolf. But there's ambiguity here: is Pierce's memory of the she-wolf a truth that has survived the passage-time? Similarly, how real is his son Robbie? Pierce seems to conjure him into existence by writing a heartfelt story about him (322), but—to put it mildly—the Robbie who arrives shoeless at his door is not what he was expecting. Again in this volume words themselves are subject to distortion, as in Bobby's informing Pierce about "fuckn" and the "Holy Spert" or Boney's evasive references to his old girlfriend "Una Knox." And it's impossible not to feel that there is some vast gap in comprehension between Pierce and Rose in their relationship.

In *Dæmonomania*, it seems as if the story itself is mishearing or misremembering itself. The first house in that book, Uxor, opens with a whimsical but dark-hued survey of this: "What was less noticed was that, here and there, effects were preceding their causes.

Not often, not consistently, or life would become unintelligible: just here and there, now and then, and trivial mostly" (12). But the slippages of reality which pervade *Dæmonomania,* and which leave Pierce more trapped than ever, are cumulatively anything but trivial. We can no longer, for instance, trust the manuscripts recording Dee's conversations with angels: "That, anyway, is what one scholar or investigator claims was there on that page, on a certain day some years ago, in the Manuscript Room of the old [British] museum . . . Maybe in that year it was. Maybe it still is" (118-19). Crowley tops this with what must surely win some kind of prize for Least Certain Author's Note ever committed to paper: "All extracts from the diaries, works, and letters of John Dee are quoted more or less *verbatim* except for those which are fictitious, or are not now as they once were" (453). Meanwhile, Rose seems and then seems not to have an abusive former husband named Wes (62, 397); Rosie's daughter Sam appears in Dee's glass (82); and Spofford denies (442) ever having owned the crook which he was unambiguously carrying when he met Pierce. The text is reasonably clear that so far as there's a reason for these slippages, they are a symptom of the passage-time signalled by the wind that blew through at the end of *Love & Sleep.* The world has, to some extent, become malleable; and those who wish to manipulate it to their own ends can do so. But that doesn't rob the slippages of their disturbing power. There's a sense even that the author can't control what's happening—the extraordinary imprecation at the start of Uxor's second chapter "listen to me and I will tell you" (19) raises a slew of questions all by itself. Who is speaking? Crowley? Why does he suddenly sound so desperate? *Dæmonomania* as a whole remains in the mind as a ghastly nightmare of uncertainty and lost possibility—the very opposite of the first volume.

The nightmare is nowhere darker than at the Halloween party at Butterman's, when Boney's daughter Val discovers how illusory Una Knox was; and when Pierce encounters a masked figure who tries to enlist him into the telling of a story he seems unable to complete himself (393-95). It's almost beside the point whether this masked figure is John Crowley or Fellowes Kraft (or both, or neither)—although certain cues (the sandy hair, the abortive production of *Faustus*) argue for it being Kraft's shade. The point is that Pierce doesn't hear what is being asked of him; or rather, if he hears, he doesn't listen. And it's certainly the case that the figure is a storyteller whose dire words describe a fatal incapability to finish telling the story that he had begun.

There is a sense in which all Crowley's major protagonists are the authors of the stories in which they find themselves, and that ultimate understanding for them (at the end of their stories) consists of seeing clearly the shape of that story—which is the book we readers hold. With Smoky in *Little, Big* or Rush in *Engine Summer*, it seems in the end that they have made the right choices. Their basic goodness shines through the stories that they have become. Their choices (especially the choices made for love) redeem the mistakes, like Smoky's infidelity. In a darker vein, Denys Winterset in "Great Work of Time" is utterly trapped by the net of events he has woven by serving the Otherhood. Even if he acted for the best reasons—one thinks of Huntington's powerful arguments that the Otherhood is a moral force (*Novelty*, 96-99)—he and they acted to control the fates of others. Given Crowley's preoccupation with authorship and how stories can be created or manipulated, it's inevitable that he should brush up against issues of control; and it's clear he deeply distrusts those who seek power over others' stories. It's difficult to think of another person or group in Crowley's work who attract such authorial savagery as the Powerhouse in *Dæmonomania*. Russell Eigenblick is treated comparatively benignly despite his questing for the Presidency in *Little, Big*: he is as much at the mercy of the Tale as anyone.

Pierce seems to make his choices for reasons both less good than Smoky's and better than Denys's. The three wishes he formulated at the start of the sequence have come true: he has good health, a trouble-free income from the Rasmussen Foundation, and love came to him in the longed-for form of Robbie/Eros, the precursor of Rose Ryder. There is a sense as *Dæmonomania* grinds to its awful conclusion that he is, like Midas, trapped by having had his wishes taken the wrong way. Doubtless the final volume which Crowley is now working on will cast a new light on what Pierce has been able to save as the passage-wind passed; and the one glimmer of hope at the end of *Dæmonomania* is that Sam has been rescued from the vile Powerhouse. But, in the end, Pierce has imposed his will on the world as any storyteller (or historian) must and has reaped the consequences. One of the fundamental issues addressed by Ægypt is how we impose shape on one-damn-thing-after-another to create stories and histories for ourselves. And the message these examples repeatedly provide is that to write or read or hear a story is necessarily and inevitably to get it wrong.

Harold Bloom, the literary critic and an acknowledged influence on Crowley, describes the relationships governing literary influence in strikingly similar terms. In his 1973 book *The Anxiety of Influence*, Bloom argued for a theory of poetic history (or, equivalently for him, poetic influence) founded on misunderstanding:

> Poetic influence—when it involves two strong, authentic poets—always proceeds by a misreading of the prior poet, an act of creative correction that is actually and necessarily a misinterpretation. The history of fruitful poetic influence, which is to say the main tradition of Western poetry since the Renaissance, is a history of anxiety and self-saving caricature, of distortion, of perverse, willful revisionism without which modern poetry as such could not exist. (Bloom, 1997, p.30)

The world we see emerging through the Ægypt sequence has, I am arguing, come into being by precisely the same means. This is not the place to go into the elaboration of Bloom's theory, but two observations seem to me especially important. Firstly, Bloom's theory is profoundly shaped, as is Ægypt, by Gnosticism: Bloom explicitly identifies himself with Valentinus, a Gnostic speculator of the same period as the *Corpus Hermeticum*. Secondly, Bloom prefers to describe the process of influence between poets as founded not on misunderstanding but misprision. Discussing this suggestive word's use in Shakespeare's Sonnet 87, he describes the particular weight it had for the author: "[It] implied not only a misunderstanding or misreading but tended also to be a punning wordplay suggesting unjust imprisonment" (p. xiii). Imprisonment, literal and metaphorical, is the dark heart of Ægypt. From Pierce binding Rose (or vice versa) to the alchemical processes Dee and Kelley employ, it is a motif which recurs in many of the most intense scenes of the series. One remembers also that Pierce first conceived of his novel ending with the house Carcer: Bruno jailed for nine years before his muzzled death. Pierce asked himself then why his scheme would leave his novel ending in prison, and we shall doubtless have to wait for the last volume to find out. As *Dæmonomania* ends, Pierce seems about to leave for Europe, like Hamlet for England, to seek some escape from the constraints around him. If he does, perhaps he will be as changed as Hamlet in the last act.

One last perspective on misprision and constraint may be useful. In a brief but dense entry on the term Bondage in the *Encyclopedia of Fantasy* (1997), John Clute argues for its relevance, in a particular sense, to fantasy fiction. In naturalistic fiction, the constraints the author works under in describing the world are, self-evidently, those of the real world: a novel in which, say, cars run on water is necessarily not naturalistic. Similarly, in science fiction (at least in theory) writers are bound by the laws of nature and extrapolative rigor in outlining their future societies. But if, in a fantasy, there is only one weapon which can kill the dragon terrorizing the land, and that weapon can only be fetched from the mountain at the edge of the world, no-one imposes that constraint upon the characters but the author; and the imposition and lifting of such bondage is (Clute argues) a fundamental movement of fantasy fiction. No constraint, in fantasy, is accidental. Clute describes his sense of the relevance of this notion to Ægypt in the reviews collected elsewhere in *Snake's-hands*. It will be clear from what I've said that I share this sense and feel it's deeply related to the persistent misprisions that I've been describing. The passage-time has unknit the ties that link cause and effect in the mundane world—hence the instances of the world misunderstanding itself in *Dæmonomania*. The movement into a non-naturalistic realm has created possibility and so also constraint, freedom and so also bondage. Misprision is, repeatedly and obsessively, the tool with which the books attempt to comprehend that realm.

Frank Walker Barr, perhaps the sanest observer in the sequence of the processes at work in history, runs into Pierce in a misprisioned Floridan Egypt at the end of *Love & Sleep*. At one point, Pierce expresses his deep sense of what it is to be misunderstood: "He experienced the madman's awful bind: having to ask for help, from people who cannot conceive the spiritual difficulty you're in; and realizing that they can therefore give you no help; and so sinking deeper into darkness before their kind puzzled faces" (492-93). This striking moment, like so many others, shows the emotional force that misprision acquires in Crowley's hands. Story after story, nested in each other in Ægypt, can only look for kind puzzled faces to misunderstand them. Perhaps, as readers, that's the best we can do.

REFERENCES

Bloom, H.
(1997) *The Anxiety of Influence: A Theory of Poetry* (Second Edition). New York and Oxford: Oxford University Press.

Clute, J. and Grant, J., ed.
(1997) *The Encyclopaedia of Fantasy.* London: Orbit.

Yates, F.
(1964) *Giordano Bruno and the Hermetic Tradition.* Reprinted 1991, Chicago: The University of Chicago Press.

TIME IN ÆGYPT

Alice K. Turner

MONTH	PIERCE	ROSIE	OTHER
The Prologues			
Mar	(1952) Pierce Moffett, age 9, wakes up.		(1582) Dr. Dee writes about the angels that Kelley sees in the crystal.
Vita = Life (Aries) "I am"			
Aug '78	Arrives at Faraways, meets Spofford; at Full Moon party meets Rose.	Loses rearview (don't look back), moves to Boney's with Sam.	
Lucrum = Wealth (Taurus) "I want"			
Sep '78	Pitches Julie book idea.	First sees crystal; divorce preliminaries; Boney offers job.	(Mar 1582) Dr. Dee meets Kelley, first shows crystal; Kelley sees Sam in glass.
Dec '78	Takes Blackbury Jambs apt., money from Sphinx, book sale; visits Axel at Xmas.		Spofford's lamb dream; consults Val.
Mar '79	Moves to Jambs.	Court appearance with Mike Mucho.	Beau's magic carpet ride; foresees Pierce climbing Mt. Randa, trouble at The Woods.
Fratres = Friendship (Gemini) "I think"			
Apr '79	Starts journal, encounters Rose.		(Apr 1582) Dee and Kelley at Glastonbury.
May '79	Encounters Rosie; job offer from Rosie; begins Kraft's book.	Croquet party, meets Pierce, offers him job.	(1582) Madimi shows Bruno to Kelley and Dr. Dee.
Jun '79	Balloon festival; finally gets Rose/Rosie straight.	Divorce degree nisi comes through.	
Prologue: to the Summer Quaternary			
Dec '79	Climbs Mt. Randa with mismatched shoes. Visits Winnie in Florida.		
Genitor = Parenthood (Cancer) "I hold"			
	(Autumn 1952) starts forest fire in Kentucky.		Bobby's Grandpap says salamander burned forest.

Dec '79	Visits mother Winnie in Florida.		
	(Feb 1953) Meets "feral child" Bobby for first time.		
Jun '79	Book proposal to Julie; visits father Axel 6/20.	Reads Life of Bruno.	

Nati = Children (Leo) "I command"			
Jun '79	Wishes for love; Sphinx calls; picnic; Robbie appears.	Boney to Intensive Care; Sam sleepwalks; picnic on Mt. Merrow.	(Jun 15, 1583) Bruno & Dee meet in England; Madimi warns Dee of Bruno, promises winds. Beau's "movie" (284).
July '79	7/4 sex with Rose, fireworks.	7/4 visit to absent Cliff, Val comes; 7/5 Boney dies.	(Sep 1583) Bruno goes to see Dee, Dee already gone (to Europe).

Valetudo = Sickness (Virgo) "I suffer"			
Jul '79	Pallbearer; offered Foundation fellowship. Rose "seeing things." Buys first bonds (scarves), uses them on Rose.	Boney's funeral; asked to be Foundation Director. Second look at crystal (Sam sees).	(Aug 1583) Kelley seems to have his own version of Robbie; Madimi appears as near-naked woman
Aug '79	Gets driver's license; applies to stay at Winterhalter cottage.	Sam's first fit; an ear infection.	Wind, wolves, Madimi seems to speak directly to Dee
Sep '79	Big wind at equinox 9/22	Woods people appear. 9/21 Sam's first big fit (after seeing Dee in glass).	Bobby commits two murders; Sister Mary Philomel lets something out of the chest; Ray cures a woman of devils.
Dec '79	Visits Winnie.		

Prologue: to the Autumn Quaternary			
Dec '79	Gets on bus to Conurbana.		

Uxor = Marriage (Libra) "I wed"			
Sep '79	9/22 Rose flips car during equinoctial wind; Robbie departs. 9/23 Val's party. Pierce moves into Winterhalter cottage. Buys old frame. Sex with Rose gets intense, takes photo. Gives her money for study; she departs for Conurbana.	Visits Butterman's with Allan; Sam recognizes "ode house." Takes Sam to Little Ones. Begins to fear The Woods. 10/25 Spofford and Cliff leave for Dakota and wolves.	Ray focuses on Sam; Mike acquiesces. Sam and Dee see each other in the crystal. (1584?) "Ben" tells Kelley to swap wives. (23 May 1587) Kelley has his last visitation. Sam's rubber ball bounces into Dee's room.

Mors = Death (Scorpio) "I desire"			
Oct '79	Rose speaks in tongues. Barnabas College taken over by The Gospel Speaks.	10/30 Sam goes to Little Ones hospital for 3 days.	(1587) Madimi speaks to Dee, gives him wind power; he lets it go. (15 Jul 1587) Dee adopts wolf boy.
Nov '79	Goes to Woods outreach in Conurbana; meets Mike.		Bobby and Grandpap in hospital.

Pietas = Religion (Sagittarius) "I see"			
Nov '79	Calls Rhea for help. Rose recalls Mal Cichy. Pierce flubs proposal. Sleeps with Rosie.	With Sam visits Pierce in new house. Loses custody of Sam through error. Takes foundation directorship. (Boney freed.)	Dee releases wolf boy. Beau and Julie confab in NYC.
Dec '79	12/22 At the ball, is given his directive by Beau, by JC/Fellowes Kraft. Drives off, through hallucinations, to Conurbana and Bobby. Gets lost, goes home, finds out where Sam is from Rose. Climbs Mt. Randa. Goes to visit mother in FL. Rose goes to Peru. Pierce sings with Sam.	Gives ball 12/22. Spofford returns. With Beau, Cliff, Spofford and Val, goes to rescue Sam.	(1593?) Dee sells crystal (date seems wrong). Dee dies near winter solstice. (1979) Beau makes a U-turn. Beau exchanges himself for Sam; takes away "those whose time is now past or passing." Sister Mary Philomel opens a box
Regnum = Rule (Capricorn) "I have"			
Benfacta = Success (Aquarius) "I hold"			
Carcer = Prison (Pisces) "I know"			

Notes

House: The common astrological signs of the zodiac do not accurately correspond to the *houses* of the horoscope computed by Val, the astrologer of Blackbury Jambs. John Crowley uses Val's system to organize the Ægypt series.

Month: There is some good evidence that the events of these three books actually took place three years earlier, in 1975 and 1976. (See *Dæmonomania* 333; *Love & Sleep* 479, in the Bantam editions.) However, at the end of *Dæmonomania* we get the unambiguous date of 22 December, 1979, and if we backdate from this point, then the wind blew in 1979 and Pierce first visited the Jambs in 1978.

Readers are encouraged to draw their own conclusions and prepare for the possibility of further changes to come in the final volume.

JOHN CROWLEY ON THE ÆGYPT SERIES
(Interviewed by Alice K. Turner, August 2000)

I NEVER ANTICIPATED how long the Ægypt series would take to write, nor how long a book it would be (for it is really one long book, divided into four volumes). It started as solely a historical novel, about Giordano Bruno and John Dee and the history of magic. About 1969, I discovered the books of the historian Frances A. Yates, which was where I started to read about this stuff. She influenced my earlier books too: In *Little, Big* there are the researches of Ariel Hawksquill, and even in *The Deep* there are sets of fortune-telling cards that are largely based on descriptions of "memory images" I found in her book *The Art of Memory.*

And so the research for Ægypt goes back that far. I first encountered Bruno in *The Art of Memory* and then found Yates's book *Giordano Bruno and the Hermetic Tradition* somewhere around 1970, a book that I've read over and over again. Dee I got originally from Frances Yates also. At first, the book had more English connections—I had Shakespeare as a character, and the Irish rebellion under Hugh O'Neill, and Irish fairies fighting Elizabethan magicians, all of which had to be let go. (Shakespeare still shows up, in the form of a novel by Fellowes Kraft, my fellow crafter of weird tales.)

Then somewhere around 1981, '82, I read Hans Jonas's book

351

about Gnosticism, *The Gnostic Religion*, and that was the next step. Jonas's view of the Hermetism that influenced Bruno is very different from the Renaissance one, but they seemed to go together. The sense of an earthly world surrounded by sphere upon sphere of powers, not friends to man, reaching out to a divine sphere which is our souls' origin; the idea of a tragic fall that actually preceded the creation of the physical universe—these were very potent ideas for me, as I have found them to be for others.

At that point, then, I had a story, and a mythic structure, though it may not be entirely clear to readers yet. Maybe it'll never be clear! But I hope the book is amusing enough without it's being absolutely clear.

The idea of a modern aspect to the story only came after I'd been working on it for quite a while. I had thought of a single volume, some 600 pages long, but once the modern part of it occurred to me, I had to put the huge matter I had evolved into some sort of structure, as much for my own uses as for readers' convenience, and I hit on the structure of the twelve houses of the zodiac. You can divide up twelve houses in a number of ways; six houses in each of two books, say; but I realized soon enough that two weren't going to be enough. Three? Well, traditionally the houses of the zodiac are divided into four sets of three—four "quarternaries" consisting of three houses each—so, in a cavalier way, I thought I'd connect to that and write four. How I could take such a decision without really realizing I was committing decades of my life to it I don't really know!

When you think about it, there are, though, at least four separate stories going on that could take up four longish books. There's Pierce Moffett's story, that's the principal one which mostly takes place over the course of one year, from spring to spring, say 1978 and 1979, though some of it is set earlier. There's John Dee's story set back there in the 16th century, there's Bruno's story at the same time. And the story of Rosie Rasmussen and her daughter Sam, which goes alongside Pierce's and connects at points. But actually,

I had supposed the book would continue the historical story for a couple of decades longer, and involve many other characters, events and wonderments. I thought surely I'd have room for it. And now I see that I don't!

The four novels rest on the premise that any world is possible. It's up to us to decide what world it's going to be. Down to its physical laws. During certain periods that recur irregularly in human history, we go through a "passage time" when the world can change into anything the souls that inhabit it can form and choose and create. Pierce formulates this idea on his own (with the help of hints in the work of Fellowes Kraft) and though he doesn't really believe it himself, he convinces Julie Rosengarten, his literary agent and ex-girlfriend, that he wants to write a pop-science-magic book that will describe and assert this possibility: that at certain periods in the history of the world, at crux points, we can actually decide what world we're going to create. Now in the 60s and 70s a lot of people *did* think they were creating new worlds to choose among. At that time, in little towns like the one in my books, there were people who really did believe in a kind of magic. It seemed to be a crux time, and not only to me.

Which I relate to Renaissance magic. In the late 16th century Giordano Bruno, heretic runaway monk, and John Dee, practicing magician and alchemist, felt themselves to be at a crux, a passage time. They felt the world was changing. And it really was. The sun was actually shifting its position, for one thing! Magic practices well attested in their day don't work any more now. Well maybe our world is changing too . . . or maybe not! The fact is, in this conception, *there would be no way to tell*, for after the change is over, you can't determine that it ever happened. Once the passage time is past, you can't find evidence that there was a time the world was open to other possibilities. Those other possibilities are all a dream. *This* is the one that got chosen, this is the only reality there is. And that's where we stand right now. You can look back at the Renaissance—or at the 60s or 70s—and say, well, that wasn't going to happen, all those utopias, that magic. *This* was going to happen.

The last book of the series (as yet untitled) will be set in the present, 2002 or so, and will be looking back from the world we brought into being after the struggles and adventures of the passage time—a world which no longer contains all the possibilities that were alive for a moment then.

And that's the world we live in right now—Isn't it?

Think of Prague, in Czechoslovakia—in a sense the capitol city of the series. There was a moment in the early 1600s when Prague seemed to be full of magical possibilities. The same in 1968, the "Prague Spring," part of that weird world-wide imaginary revolution that so moved and influenced people of Pierce's (and my) age. Now in the last book, we're going to hear from Fellowes Kraft, who was in Prague in 1968, and conceived his own scheme of history there, the one Pierce adopts from him. By the time Pierce is thinking up his own book, though, the possibilities of the Prague Spring seem gone, and Prague has been in a frozen state under Communism since 1968—changeless. But then we will see the world my characters (and all of us) have created during their passage time— the world in 2002, or whenever. And Prague is free and a different place, and not the only one. Who would have expected the huge, vibrant changes in Prague of the last few years?

So this scheme underlay much of the writing of the first two volumes of the series. *Dæmonomania*, the third book of the series, is somewhat different from the first two. Reality is beginning to slip as we get deep into the "passage time." We begin to see that in a passage time not only the future but the past can be—must be!—recreated by being reimagined. The deepest laid secret of the book is that there is a sense in which we are making up the world as it goes on. Pierce imagines his lover Rose Ryder running away from her ex-husband in upstate New York, taking a train to the city, and being drafted to star in the soft-porn movie at which, readers of *Ægypt* will remember, Pierce met the Sphinx, his former girlfriend.

Later Rose remembers the same scene. Did Pierce alter the past by what he imagined? Can she remember being there because of his dream?

The fabric of reality gets thinner and more manipulable. Hints get stronger, possibilities get larger. Bruno and Dee and the magic doctors of the Renaisance can bring magical ancient Ægypt into being, cause it to be, even though it never really did. They brought into existence the immortal Egyptian brotherhood which keeps showing up, which takes care of Bruno, which adopts Dee's secrets, which comes down to the present or sends its messenger through time to the present.

A central question that readers have to decide is whether the angel Madimi is telling the truth, or is right about the world. She says there is supposed to be a wind that blows in the passage time when change is possible and another wind that blows it out again and brings in the new age. Two winds. She explains this very carefully to the Polish count when they're talking in *Love & Sleep*. Readers who have got this down are probably going to be trying to decide, well, was the Armada wind the one that blows it in or the one that blows it out? There's one wind that blows in the present day, the one that blows in the autumn equinox. So you could say that the whole intervening time is some sort of passage. But that doesn't seem right. What the reader may begin to suspect is that this is not true, this whole system, with winds and passage times, it may not be so at all. Madimi is not the most reliable source!

Pierce postulates, at the end of *Ægypt*, another wind. He says he can imagine a wind that blows away the magic world. He imagines it happening around 1620, the time of the Battle of the White Mountain, when the Protestant Palatine who was elected king of Bohemia, the Winter King, and his English wife were defeated by the reactionary Catholic forces under Archduke Ferdinand, which started the Thirty Years War. This forms the tragic ending of Fellowes Kraft's novel. Then you could say there was a wind that began with the Armada and ends in 1620 when it blows away all that magic stuff. From then on, you've got nothing but this awful war and the things that come after. This comes at the point where Pierce, having read Fellowes Kraft's manuscript for the first time, is sitting and thinking about the suggestion that he finish the book.

The book has other schemes too, in which reality is shown to be softening or loosening. Bobby Shaftoe, the Kentucky girl whom Pierce knew as a boy, seems to be a witch who is a werewolf's granddaughter; she and her grandfather seem descended from a world or world-view contemporaneous with Bruno's and Dee's, where in pastoral societies witches, male and female, held periodic battles with other witches or—in some societies—were pursued and captured by werewolves, in order to ensure a good harvest. Her grandfather remembered something of this ancient struggle; Bobby less. But she looks at Rose Ryder at one point and says to herself, *Is she of my kind?* She's not sure in the end. So there is a possible interpretation of the Rose-Pierce relationship as a witch-werewolf relationship, just as earlier the child Pierce did actually pursue Bobby, the child witch, and attempt to save her, and failed at it. And maybe he's been doing that with all the women in his life who get away from him in the way that they do. And maybe Rose, in a certain sense, is the last chance he's going to have of making this pursuit come out right. He does pursue her, she gets away and she joins up with the witch side of life, represented by the religious cult, the Powerhouse, and their promise that you can have whatever you want if you pray for it: witches have this insatiable hunger, and the promise of Honeybeare's Powerhouse cult is that God wants you to have all that stuff.

Certainly it's the case that Pierce's pursuit of Rose Ryder is the nexus of all the forces which in the passage time can change the world: what might be called the arts of desire. (Not a bad title!) Among those arts are alchemy, the witch/werewolf dramaturgy, prayer and theurgy, magic, and sex.

The nexus of sex, magic, and power is central to *Dæmonomania*, indeed to the whole story. There's a moment in *Ægypt* when

Pierce reflects on the men Rose has been with: he fears that the men she has been with are men who really want power and not sex. They use sex as a way to get power. Pierce, however, uses power as a way to get sex. Power frightens him. He doesn't know how to deal with it. In the very first chapter of *Ægypt*, when he's wishing his wishes, he says, "No, not power." But whatever power is guilty of, Pierce feels, sex is not. Sex, soiled and chained and even bought and sold, is innocent. Maybe it's a generational thing, but that's something that I am liable to feeling, even though I know better. Pierce doesn't know better, maybe, but I do!

Little, Big was about sexual innocence, about innocence in general, about an Edenic world. Novels that are Edenic have this quality, that original sin has not happened, so everything that everybody does, no matter how urgent or serious or even criminal it seems, is harmless. People can behave in certain ways, act out certain kinds of sexual dramas, even kill, but in an Edenic world these things are essentially harmless. I try to reverse that in the series: this is a fallen world, where sex turns out to be a burden, a guilty secret, something inflicted on us by the gods, the archons who rule the world. A very Gnostic idea.

Pierce, though, has no conception of this. Initially, in the sex games he plays with Rose Ryder, Pierce thinks he can pretend to be something he's not. He thinks it's like wearing a mask, that behind it he can do things that he couldn't do otherwise. Because of that mask he can't truly be loved, therefore he can't cease to be loved. It's very self-protective. He gets in much deeper than he expected because, as is continually said by the Renaissance magicians in the book, magicians have to be careful not to get themselves caught in their own devices. Which is just what happens to Pierce. Which he should have known! Pierce is not a very good historian, but he's a much worse magician.

Pierce, like Dee's assistant Edward Kelley, invites possession beyond the point where he can manage it. It overwhelms him, though he thought he could avoid it. If, without wisdom and the proper protections, you try to fool around with the powers and use these powers for your own ends, then they will get you. Because they are real powers, and they come to inhabit you, and then you're sunk. That's what happens to Kelley and it's kind of what happens to Pierce too. The sum of it all is his little imaginary son, Robbie, who appeared in *Love & Sleep*, whom Pierce thinks is the creation of his sexual feelings, somehow the embodiment of them, or the satisfaction of them. But no, no: we see in *Dæmonomania* that he's the power who's come to make sure that Pierce is stuck, chained fully and firmly down by the powers that he's invoked. In fact, he's the greatest of all the powers: Amor, Eros.

Throughout this book, power is regarded as conscious, as a person. All powers, sexual powers, understandings, knowledge, all of these things are persons who can talk to you and seem to have insides of their own. When Honeybeare's people are speaking in tongues, they are indeed possessed by powers that Honeybeare invokes and can implant in them. At the same time they are the "psychological" realities we are familiar with. For people like Pierce and Rose Ryder (she in religious ecstasy, he in paranoid dread) it is *as if* the powers of the spirit, of sexuality, of imagination, are persons: but *exactly* as if.

Almost everything in the series exists on more than one level in this way. There is a level in which the Powerhouse is an ordinary, commonplace little pseudo-Christian cult, and at the very end that's what Pierce knows it to be—which may be one of the indications that the passage time is over. On another level, the cult leader, Ray Honeybeare, is an actual demon, a representative on this earthly plain of higher powers, and Mike Mucho and the rest of the cult members are actually possessed. They get hold of Sam, Rosie Rasmussen's and Mike Mucho's child, as part of a messy divorce dispute: but they have also seized the embodiment of eternal Sophia, the suffering deity whose suffering makes the universe, who has appeared in a multitude of forms throughout the ages, and who must be saved.

Beau Brachman, guru and baby-sitter of Sam, also is a power: in fact Beau is the only one we see wielding magic or mystic powers in the modern part of the book. Beau is at once an ordinary guy who's taking care of people in his little house and at the same time a kind of Bodhisattva who's returned to earth to help everybody along. Beau's friend Cliff, who hardly appears, is one of them too. (We might not be done with Cliff yet.) These are beings who are acting the part of powers. They are at the same time ordinary humans and beings who have a mission to save the world—if they don't save Sam, the Sophia of our time, from the dark forces, the world is going to cease to evolve, the work of the passage time won't be completed, we won't be able to survive. So they are going to do that, but at the same time they're just good men who have enough psychic or spiritual energy to stand up to Honeybeare and take Sam away from him. Beau is a kind of Gnostic saint, somewhat apart from the real world.

The central mythology of Ægypt is Gnostic. One of the central Gnostic conceptions is that human beings are part of God. They retain a divine spark that is no part of physical creation. God didn't make the bad world we live in, which is an illusion projected by the angels, demons, gods, and other intermediary powers who rule over us on a daily basis, and who are in fact farther removed from God than we are. We have forgotten this, and must remember it—that's *gnosis*. The gods can do what they want with us most of the time because we think they're so ancient and powerful, but in fact we're more powerful than they are. When we move toward being like them, mimic them, we are in fact debasing ourselves. To subject yourself to the archons is to not understand your own divine origins. (This is not an orthodox Judeo-Christian idea; indeed one of the archons that we are better than is Jehovah himself: *Jove Jehovah Jaldaboth*, as the lost Gnostic radio station WIAO in *Dæmonomania* calls him.)

So in a passage time, for a moment, the universe is arranged in such a way that human lives are reflections or embodiments or manifestations or versions of the powers beyond them. After the passage time is over, they're not, though they may think they are. Or they seem like they are, or they can talk themselves into believing they are. But they aren't, they're just ordinary human beings with delusions or obsessions. In the passage time though, not only are they the earthly manifestations of beings like Jehovah, Sophia, Eros, and the witch/werewolf opposition, beings with these stories to act out, but they do act them out. One minor one who appears briefly in *Dæmonomania* is Mal Cichy. He is the producer of the soft-porn film, the guy on the train that Rose runs into when she runs away from her husband, if she ever really does. And Beau meets him as an insatiable orgiast in the '60s sex club called MM, presided over by another manifestion of Sophia. And he's the guy dressed in the devil suit at the Rosie Rasmussen's Christmas party at Butterman's castle—which automatically makes him *not* the devil, because Rosie's command to her guests was, *Come as you aren't!*

So the world progresses forward as a real world and in the passage time it fingers out into all these other possibilities and dangers and then if we're successful it reassembles itself as real—but a few things aren't there any more when it comes back together again. Beau's role, at this point, is to shepherd some of the other no longer necessary powers out of the world that will be.

Pierce, when he is a child, thinks that his job is to rescue Bobby, then later to rescue Rose Ryder. And he thinks he fails at both. But his real job, the job of all of us in this book—and readers get into it too!—is not to rescue either of those, who can't or don't need to be rescued, because they're witches or whatever, but to rescue Sam. The critical point for Pierce is when Beau comes to him after the Christmas ball and asks him to go after Rose Ryder once more to help find Sam, who has been taken away by Honeybeare's cult. He says no, I don't believe in any of that stuff, I can't do it any more—but then he says all right, I'll have to go and do it. And he does his duty. In the course of Pierce's pursuit of Rose, and only *because* of his pursuit or her, he finds the one piece of the puzzle he needs to contribute. He finds out where Sam has gone.

Bobby says, urging Pierce to follow Rose, speaking as a witch for just one moment, "We'll steal the world if you let us." By that, at that moment, she means herself, Honeybeare, all the witches or demons, whether in the cult or not. She says: there is a "we" and I'm one of them. She knows that Pierce can't rescue Rose, but she also knows that he has to keep following. The world falls apart if werewolves don't follow witches and chase after them. And though Pierce fails, loses his way, goes off on the wrong road and never catches her, he has learned one thing in his pursuit—where the cult has taken Sam—and he can then tell Rosie and Beau. Which is what he has to do.

That's what my characters do: Smoky, Pierce. They play their parts. They say, I don't believe in any of this stuff, I don't get it, I'm outside this game, but I'll do it. And they do. It is in a way like Camus's version of Existentialism, except that Existentialists live in a world totally without magic possibilities. I present people who do not have an innate sense of magic possibilities, who feel themselves to be immune to it, and I put them in these magic situations. And they all say, all right, I'll try, I'll do what I am asked to do. I don't understand it, but I'll do it anyway. Pierce finds Sam through the hallucinations of his journey, because he is willing to follow Rose into the darkness.

Rosie herself has such a moment: when she has the strength to hold her masked ball on the castle island, and dresses herself as her great-uncle Boney. Somehow this act is enough to free Boney from the limbo in which he's stuck, and his spirit can begin its journey to the upper realms. And the book says of her efforts that we act on earth as best we can, and do what it seems that we must, and in doing so sometimes we accomplish redemptions (and defeats) in other worlds that we can know nothing of. And that's what happens to Pierce. At a certain moment, he has come to this actuality and he has to perform an act of rescue, without knowing that he's doing it. But he does it.

In the Sixties when I was smoking dope and taking drugs I had the revelation that I could write about imaginary worlds: that I don't have to write about this sometimes beautiful but at bottom godless, spiritless, existential world that I really in fact believe in. I found I could write about alternative worlds, that this was just fine. You don't have to make a choice, you can write about any kind of world. But this does not alter the existential situation we have within us.

So the adventures of my characters in my novels are existential, but I don't believe they are exactly moral. I believe that they are *aesthetic.* They are in a book, and the largest understanding these characters can ever going to come to is that they are in a book: not that they have rights and wrongs to deal with, actions with consequences, but that they are in a book. (Smoky Barnable, in *Little Big*, has this revelation at the last moment of his—fictional—life: he sees that the goal of the journey is in fact "back there," that is, back into the book the reader has just read.) Centrally, I am not a moral writer. I am not concerned in my fiction with what you should do or not do in life, or what's good or bad. I'm trying to explore the dilemma of characters who are creations in a book— which is in effect a Gnostic dilemma: souls who find themselves in a world that they suspect is not merely fallen or bad but entirely unreal, including their own histories and natures. In the *Ægypt* series, the characters, book by book, come closer and closer to realizing it—though perhaps they never quite can.

Dæmonomania was influenced by the computer, as well. I have always written my books in longhand because I never learned how to type. That's changed somewhat with computers, but I still do most of every book in longhand on long legal pads. Nowadays because typing and retyping and rewriting is so much easier, I do more of it on the computer than I ever used to do on the typewriter. I used to write a draft in pen, and then another draft in pen and then only when I had finally thought everything through, as far as

I possibly could, did I start typing. I would usually type only one draft, maybe retype some pages if I absolutely had to, but the idea of retyping things was just so appalling that sometimes I'd leave things as they were rather than retype.

Learning a new method of putting words on paper definitely changes your compositional methods. I think of Henry James halfway through his career when he began dictating to a "type-writer"—a typist—and she would type this up and give him a draft and he would go over it and correct it and change it and edit it and give it back. And it really changed his style. *Love & Sleep* was the first whole book I actually wrote with a computer, and my holograph manuscript was still quite complete. Now my manuscripts are scrappier, but they still exist. I love the word processor--it's a great thing! I'm still a slow typist, but I've finally learned to type with all my fingers instead of just two. I'm better in the morning than I am in the afternoons. I think a long time before writing, I don't generate huge numbers of drafts; in fact I find it nearly impossible to throw out something I've written. I'll put it in another book, or put it somewhere else, or spend huge amounts of time trying to shoehorn it in. It's a drawback since I'm very prolific and I don't need to do that, but I can't resist hanging on. I also tend to checkerboard as I write, instead of starting at page 1 and then writing on to the end. A scene, and then one later on, and then over to the side. This may be part of what makes these last books so interreferential. I write a scene and then next a scene that happens much later but that refers to the other scene or echoes or inverts it. Or I write a scene and then, next, a scene that foreshadows it earlier. It's a danger, because I know that readers can't read them in the same way as writers write them. I tell my writing students not to do that. Don't have a book assembled in your mind and then give out gradual scraps to the readers, assuming that they will put them in the right places, like a jigsaw puzzle with a big picture that you will have in the end. Readers don't read like that, because they don't have your big picture to plug these things into. Readers are just getting them sequentially, one at a time. So I warn against that, but I actually do it myself.

I'm trying to become a little more user-friendly, not only in methods. I've taken a break from the Ægypt series to write a book with very different ambitions (though it too deals with the powers and great angels). It's called *The Translator*, and will be out in a year. It's a love story about poets and poetry, and it takes place at a Midwestern university at the time of the Cuban missile crisis. It was a very refreshing project, and was written very quickly.

These books are only marginally science fiction, but that's always been problematic. My first book, *The Deep* created quite a stir in science fiction, though there were, from the beginning, people who thought it should have been published in the mainstream. This has been a paradox of my writing career, and I'm not the only one. You've got this genre you can be in and attract almost everybody's attention and they'll love and admire you and keep your books in print and there's a whole unit within this group who want them to be really good books, and know the difference between good books and bad books. They know the kind of book they like, and that there can be good ones and bad ones of that kind. Some people can read the bad ones and the good ones and they don't seem to make much distinction. They love 'em all. But then there is the reader who will say, "Your book was just the kind of book I like, but it was *also* really a good book and it was comparable to other kinds of book. And I have read other kinds of books, Nabokov and so forth, so I have a basis on which to judge. And I thought your book was really good." It's a kind of big frog in a small puddle kind of philosophy.

I've always felt a kinship with science fiction, though not entirely immersed in it. I was a little too late to be a New Wave guy myself but I was certainly influenced by New Wave SF as to the possibilities of the genre: Tom Disch (*334*) and Brian Aldiss particularly; Samuel Delany for extravagance, J. G. Ballard for restraint and melancholy. Ursula Le Guin for the possibility of feeling: not only

Left Hand of Darkness but the early books like *City of Illusions* and *Planet of Exile*, the first and still among the very few science fiction books that ever brought tears to my eyes; Joanna Russ, *Picnic on Paradise*. Those were the books I began with, after not having read science fiction since *Martian Chronicles* and Kornbluth and Simak.

I read *Lord of the Rings* and held it somewhat in contempt, its childish moralities and good-manners writing, and the epic inflation—"Wagner without music." But I read it all, and then on a rainy afternoon a couple of years later, with nothing to do, I began it again—and read it all again; and I still remember it.

At the same time I was reading the books with which in some ways I inwardly class—class, not compare—my own, in ambition and kind anyway: *V* and *The Crying of Lot 49*, *One Hundred Years of Solitude*, *Ada*, *Giles Goat-boy*.

Writers keep, in addition to their own lists of the Ten Best Books of all Time, Ten Books I would Least Like to have Missed, etc., another list, of the books they would most like to have written: my list includes *A High Wind in Jamaica* by Richard Hughes, *The Once and Future King*, Virginia Woolf's *Orlando*, Stevenson's *The Suicide Club*, Chesterton's *The Man Who Was Thursday*. I don't know what if anything to make of this list, but there it is for me.

Now I face the last book in the *Ægypt* series, which will also be shorter than the others, and different in tone and style. The problem will be to free these characters from the daemonic prison; they have (some of them anyway) discovered that in fact the lock is on the inside, not the outside, but now they have to turn the key. I want to suggest the possibility of awaking in the end from this strange Gnostic dream itself—to allow my characters at length to arise and go into the common day, into the spring and the rain and the beating of their hearts. Is that possible?

THE TRANSLATOR

.

LIFE AFTER ÆGYPT:
NOTES ON JOHN CROWLEY'S *THE TRANSLATOR*
Bill Sheehan

AFTER SPENDING NEARLY twenty years producing the first three installments of his dense, monumental work-in-progress, Ægypt, John Crowley returned to a simpler, more accessible narrative mode in *The Translator*, a lovely, unexpected novel that deals with poetry, politics, and angelic intercession in an earlier age of the world: the Kennedy administration.

Crowley's decision to interrupt his magnum opus and write a stand-alone novel was largely the result of a change in his professional circumstances. Following the publication of *Dæmonomania* in 2000, Crowley moved from long-time publisher Bantam Books to Avon Books, a subdivision of the HarperCollins publishing conglomerate. His editor at Avon, Lou Aronica (who had earlier been at Bantam), suggested that Crowley inaugurate this new relationship by writing something altogether different, something whose appeal would not be restricted to readers of the Ægypt series. Crowley, in need of a break from that massive, endlessly ramifying project, agreed, and offered Aronica the book that would become *The Translator*. (As it turns out, the book is actually published by William Morrow, another division of HarperCollins.)

This novel, about poets and poetry, originated in a remark

made by novelist and poet Thomas M. Disch. According to Crowley, Disch once noted that "Americans, though they don't read very much poetry, are fascinated by poets." Disch further stated that he had devised a solution to the difficulties implicit in writing fiction about an authentically great poet. The central problem—infusing the text with authentically great poetry—could be dealt with by creating a fictional poet who writes in a foreign language, and whose poems, therefore, only appear in translation. Galvanized by these interrelated notions, Crowley began to assemble the elements of a viable—and highly original—narrative.

The first of these elements was the choice of a protagonist: exiled Russian poet I. I. (Innokenti Isayevich) Falin, whose history reflects the larger history of twentieth century Russia, and whose character reflects the eternal, peculiarly Russian passion for poetry. The remaining elements came in what Crowley calls a "package," containing the setting (the American Midwest of the early 1960s), the central political events of that era (the Cold War, the nuclear arms race, the Cuban Missile Crisis), and a richly imagined metaphysical drama involving the existence—and possible intervention—of angels. With these building blocks firmly in place, the writing proceeded with astonishing speed, and Crowley—a notoriously exacting stylist—completed the entire novel in a little under a year. It was, he says, "the easiest novel I've ever written, at least since the potboilers of the seventies, *The Deep* and *Beasts*." But unlike those apprentice novels, *The Translator* is a mature, fully developed work of art.

The novel opens with a brief, portentous prologue set in Washington, DC in 1961. Christa (Kit) Malone, along with twenty other high school seniors, is waiting in a White House anteroom to meet the President. Kit and the others have had poems reprinted in a national anthology of young people's poetry called *Wings of Song* (a tip of the hat to Disch, author of a book of similar title), and have been granted a brief audience with John F. Kennedy as a reward. The prologue is notable for its vivid, economical portrait of the energetic young president, who charms the students individually and collectively and informs them that poets are "the unacknowledged legislators of the world." In addition, two key details emerge from the scene. Kit hears the name I. I. Falin—that of the exiled poet now teaching at an unspecified Midwestern university—for the first time. And the reader learns something that Kit herself does not yet know, but soon will: she is pregnant, a fact whose consequences will reverberate throughout the novel.

The narrative moves forward to 1993. Kit, now a middle-aged professor and respected poet, travels to Russia—to the newly rechristened city of St. Petersburg—to participate in a conference on the life and work of I. I. Falin. Kit, we discover, knew Falin for a time, and, in fact, began her own career by publishing her "Translations Without Originals," fifteen poems—"poems neither his nor hers, or both his and hers"—adapted from Falin's Russian originals, now long since lost. Kit has come to tell her Russian colleagues all she knows about Falin's life, and about his mysterious, unresolved disappearance in 1962. She carries with her a special gift for her host and sponsor, Gavriil Viktorovich Semyonov. The gift is a poem, written by Falin in 1962, but titled, significantly, "1963". The lines of this poem will likewise resonate throughout the text, acquiring an increasingly literal meaning as the narrative progresses.

"1963"

Child, never forget that this too is true:
So that justice in our cosmos may be preserved,
The angels that watch over our nations each have their opposites,
A left hand whose works the strong right hands don't know.
If a nation's angel is proud, then the other is shy
Brilliant if the nation's angel is dull
Full of pity if the angel shows none
Laughing if it always weeps, weeping if it cannot weep.

But so that order may also be preserved
(Which has always concerned the great ones more)
The nation's angel is the greater, older and more terrible,
And from his sight the lesser always hides.
Lost, pale and bare, he shivers and sings
And there is no reproach so stinging as his smile.

Along with the poem, Kit offers Semyonov her own reminiscences, which return us to the world of 1961 and to the dramatic center of the novel.

Back in that earlier world, Kit begins her undergraduate studies at the same Midwestern university where I. I. Falin now teaches. She is one semester behind her fellow freshmen, having spent the past several months in a Catholic retreat called Our Lady of Charity of the Good Shepherd. There, surrounded by other pregnant teenagers and censorious nuns, she gave birth to a boy born with "a grievous hole in his heart and an incomplete intestine." This child, the first of Kit's significant dead, lived for a few hours, was baptized, and died. Following her son's death, Kit descended into an acute depression, in the depths of which she nearly succeeded in killing herself.

Kit thus enters college trailing a painful personal history behind her. A major element of that history—one that led, albeit indirectly, to her unplanned pregnancy and subsequent breakdown—is her dangerously intense attachment to her brother Ben, who "abandoned" her to enlist in the army, and who now serves as a "military adviser" in a remote, unfamiliar country called Vietnam. By the time she enters college, Kit has become a lost, diminished soul, unable to connect with things that once sustained her, such as her abiding belief in the importance of poetry. Her condition is best described by the Russian prefix "bez," which—she will soon learn—means "without": i.e., without love, without faith, without hope. This is the state of her mind—and spirit—when she encounters Innokenti Isayevich Falin.

Kit's first encounter with Falin has dramatic, even magical, overtones. In the chaos of registration day, she loses an envelope filled with the semester's tuition money. Frantically, futilely retracing her steps, Kit returns to the building where registration took place. There, she notices a figure standing by a window reading, notices:

> . . . his galoshes, unbuckled. Then his hound's-tooth overcoat, collar turned up. His hair, thick black and upstanding but so fine it seemed almost to move in the random airs of the place, like undersea grasses.
>
> That long V of a face, at once gaunt and tender, merry and haunted.

She recognizes him from photographs, engages him in conversation, and then sees "the toe of his black rubber boot pointing at a paper oblong half buried in the sawdust." It is, of course, her missing money, brought to her attention as if, well, by magic. She talks with him further, sends him a poem she has written about her brother Ben, and soon finds herself enrolled in his upper-class seminar, "The Reading and Writing of Poetry." From this point forward, their nascent, increasingly impassioned relationship dominates the text.

In some respects, Kit and Falin seem like diametrical opposites. She is a young, fundamentally innocent woman whose life has been shaped by books, by the love of her family, and by the quotidian kindnesses of a privileged culture. He is a haunted, middle-aged survivor shaped by the massive strictures of a totalitarian regime. She has given up on poetry. He is virtually a monument to the power of the poetic impulse. They are, in a sense, like creatures living on opposite sides of the looking glass, each staring out at the Wonderland the other inhabits. In other respects, they complement—even complete—each other. Their intense, mutually redemptive relationship begins in the classroom, and then spills over into less circumscribed areas.

As a teacher, Falin is both passionate and charismatic, dedicated to the proposition that poetry is essential to the growth of the human soul. On the opening day of class, he "introduces" himself by reading a passage from Pushkin, and asks every student to recite—from memory—a particularly meaningful poem. The students respond with passages from Frost, Baudelaire, Emily Dickinson, Omar Khayyam and others. Poetry is, from the outset, an integral part of the fabric of this novel, and many poets—among them Eliot, Shakespeare, Swinburne, Keats, Pasternak, and A. E. Housman—add their voices to the text. One short lyric by Housman seems, in retrospect, to serve as a portrait, or metaphorical reflection, of Falin's own, otherworldly character, and of the role he will play in Kit's life.

> From afar, from eve and morning
>   And yon twelve-winded sky,
> The stuff of life to knit me
>   Blew hither: here am I.
>
> Now—for a breath I tarry
>   Nor yet disperse apart—
> Take my hand quick and tell me
>   What have you in your heart.
>
> Speak, now, and I will answer;
>   How shall I help you, say;
> Ere to the wind's twelve quarters
>   I take my endless way.

Crowley's painstaking, incremental portrait of Falin shrewdly mixes the quotidian, realistic details of ordinary life with hints, rumors, faint suggestions of the magical and arcane. Falin's origins—and, as we will eventually learn, his ultimate fate—are shrouded and obscure. At one point, Kit comes to think of him as "a being who didn't follow the laws of physics," and Gavriil Semyonov confirms this view when he describes Falin as a "master of invisibility," an art acquired in the prisons and labor camps of Josef Stalin's Russia.

> "He was strange and wonderful man," Gavriil Viktorovich said. "He had ability to appear suddenly behind or beside you when you had not seen him approach . . . . I asked him how he comes by this ability to appear and to disappear, and he told me it was easy, and I could do it too: I needed only to practice invisibility, as he had."

Increasingly fascinated by Falin, Kit begins to follow the poet around the campus, as though testing her own capacity to become invisible. Of course, Falin discovers her, and invites her for coffee at a local diner. In the course of their conversation, he reveals certain aspects of his history to her: his years in Stalin's gulags, the death of his wife in the siege of Leningrad, the subsequent death of his only child. Kit, haunted always by the memory of her own dead child, begins the process of forging a connection with this enigmatic, compelling figure.

Of course, Kit's relationship with Falin is only one aspect of her day-to-day life at the university. Her studies, which she treats with characteristic seriousness, and her friendships—with a sympathetic roommate from New York, and with members of various campus political organizations—occupy much of her attention. But her world changes, abruptly and for good, when word reaches her that her brother Ben—former object of her misdirected passion—has died in a military "accident" in the Philippines. In fact, Ben, stationed most recently in Vietnam, may have been one of the first American casualties in a clandestine, undeclared war. In the aftermath of Ben's funeral, she decides to drop Falin's class, but he convinces her to continue. In exchange, he offers her something he has so far withheld from everyone else: the story of his early life.

Falin's life began, in effect, at the age of six (or seven, or possibly eight). He came to consciousness in a railroad station in a nameless Russian city, alive and healthy, but with no prior memories. Taken in hand by "Teapot," a Russian incarnation of the Artful Dodger, he joined a group of roving "besprizornye," lost children without parents or homes, disenfranchised victims of the disastrous Revolution. These lost children constituted a world hidden within the larger world of Soviet life. (As always in Crowley's fiction, there is more than one history of the world, and more than one world contained within the larger, all-encompassing World.) Falin grew up in this gray, Darwinian society, surviving by learning the secret of invisibility, and by cultivating his innate gift for poetry. In time, he would create an imagined poetic cosmos, a world of endless, interconnected realms overseen by the faceless entities he thinks of as "the Gray Gods." Ultimately, after years of prison camps, and after years spent writing pseudonymous poems passed by hand from reader to reader, poems safely published only in foreign countries, he declared his identity in an open letter to Nikita Kruschev, "speaking truth to power." Shortly afterward, he found himself exiled to the world beyond the looking glass: America.

Under the influence of Falin's story, Kit makes the crucial decision to return to college for the summer semester, where she takes an intensive course in written and spoken Russian. Her ostensible goal: to prepare herself for a government career, possibly, she indicates, in the CIA. Her actual goal: to learn the language that will unlock the secrets of Falin's poems. By day, she works alongside dedicated cold warriors in the classroom and the language lab. By night, she works with Falin himself, "translating" his poems, an inherently impossible task that helps restore her commitment to poetry, which helps, in turn, to restore and rebuild her own divided soul.

In the final sections of the novel, various worlds—the public and private, the real and the fanciful—come together in an extraordinary series of linked events. In October of 1962, US reconnaissance planes discover the presence of Russian missiles in Castro's

Cuba, less than one hundred miles from the American mainland. The cold war mentality—defined by its belief in the MAD logic of Mutual Assured Destruction, and predisposed to incredible acts of brinkmanship and nuclear machismo—asserts itself both in Russia and the United States. As Kennedy and Krushchev face off like gun-fighters in a John Wayne epic, the stage is set for the Cuban Missile Crisis, and the possible end of the world.

Crowley's recreation of those days of crisis—days marked by escalating tension, waking nightmares, patriotic fervor counterbalanced by the occasional voice of dissent, and by the growing sense that a nuclear exchange has become virtually inevitable—is evocative and precise. Despite that sense of dire inevitability, the world, of course, survives. Krushchev backs down at the eleventh hour, and Kennedy agrees to refrain from mounting a second invasion of Cuba. As one participant puts it, when the crisis has passed: "Everyone knew who were the hawks and who were the doves, but today was the doves' day."

But Crowley's version of those events also carries with it the contradictory sense that the doves should *not* have carried the day, that the logic of history and the momentum of events should, by rights, have resulted in a different, vastly more tragic, conclusion. The bombs, he tells us, were supposed to fall, but somehow did not. Years after that momentous non-event, Kit looks back in undiminished surprise, and meditates on the extraordinary, possibly miraculous, reversal.

> it was true. The disaster we were all implicated in—all of us who should have known better and spoken out, all of us who were foolish and blind and didn't do what we should have done, and who knew it, too, and still did nothing, only waited in what we convinced ourselves was helplessness for it to happen . . . The final logic of this century, the century that believed in logic and history and necessity, the final spasm so long and well prepared: it didn't happen, and now seemed likely never

to happen. You couldn't tell, of course, and there were plenty of other things that could and did happen—she thought of Ben—but not *that* one, the worst one. And there ought to be someone to thank, someone to whom to be grateful.

As Crowley reveals—and as Kit comes eventually to believe—there *is* someone to be grateful to, someone responsible for saving the world: Innokenti Falin.

In the latter stages of the narrative, all of the odd, otherworldly aspects of Falin's life and character—his magical properties, his gift for invisibility, his sense of urgent but undefined purpose, his poetic conceit regarding the Angels of the Nations, with their eternally opposing natures—coalesce in an unverifiable notion that nevertheless seems to be true: the notion that Falin himself is a "lesser angel," and that he has played a part in the salvation of the world. With great delicacy and clarity of purpose, Crowley broadens and deepens his portrait of Falin, showing us a being who is both human and "other," who—like most of us—struggles continually to achieve a sense of his own fundamental purpose. At one point, Kit, convinced she is in love with Falin and determined to consummate that love, bluntly attempts to seduce him, with the following result.

> She tried to turn him toward her, nuzzling, her hands on his shoulders. He drew away and looked down at her
>
> . . .
>
> "Kit," he said . . . and seemed to ponder—not what to say but whether he would say it. "I do not think [this] is . . . what I am for."

Falin's sense of who he is and what he is "for" crystallizes as the nuclear exchange draws closer. He warns Kit that he will soon be going on an unspecified journey, if, as he puts it, he is "summoned." Once that summons has taken place, he informs Kit that he has made an "offer," and that the offer has been accepted. Shortly afterward, he drives away in his gaudy, all-American convertible, carrying with him the only copies of his Russian manuscripts. The next day, his car is discovered, submerged in a nearby pond. Falin is missing, and only his briefcase—emptied of poems—remains behind. In some invisible but adjacent realm of being, a sacrifice has been offered and accepted. In the wake of that sacrifice, disaster is averted, and the world continues on.

Does Falin save the world? Is he, really, the "lesser angel" of the beleaguered Russian people? Crowley supports the notion with sly hints and subtle allusions, but refuses to eliminate the aura of mystery that clings to Falin throughout. If he is an angel, he is a deeply human one, as his name—often mispronounced as "fallen"—implies. (Madimi tells us in the Ægypt Quartet: "All angels are fallen angels." There is no other kind.) Kit herself comes to believe in the reality of Falin's sacrifice. Looking backward from the vantage of more than thirty years, she discusses her beliefs with her aging, unfailingly open-minded father.

> " . . . no, of course [the war] didn't happen," Kit said, and she rose up and went to the window, as though to release her thought or her soul that way. "It didn't, it should have but it didn't. Because the lesser angel of one nation interceded. On our behalf. He made an offer; he offered himself."
>
> "The lesser angel," George said. "The *lesser* angel."
>
> She turned to her father, and his face wasn't sarcastic or mocking but only intent and listening, and she thought, How do I dare to tell this, how do I dare imagine it to be so, imagine believing it?

But she can imagine it and does believe it, impossible though it seems. With unobtrusive artistry, Crowley makes her uneasy belief seem both plausible and moving, placing it at the heart of a beautifully sustained novel in which the mundane and the magical, the ordinary and the numinous, exist together in seamless narrative harmony.

The Translator is, on its deepest level, about salvation. Seen in terms of the Little/Big dichotomy that permeates Crowley's work, it dramatizes that central theme on both the personal and universal levels. Falin, the exiled lesser angel, quite literally saves the world by interceding—bargaining—with the greater angel of the Russian nation. (In a chilling coda to the central story, Crowley indicates that the terms of the bargain might have required an additional sacrifice, one that took place on November 22, 1963. This unconfirmed possibility haunts Kit, and haunts the reader, as well.)

At the same time, Falin rescues Kit from the consequences of her own despair. When we first encounter Kit, she has lost her way, and has given up both on poetry and on the larger possibilities of life. By asking Kit to serve as "translator" for his own poems, by helping her to find a voice for those translations, Falin offers Kit a way of reconnecting with her dormant poetic spirit. As Kit will acknowledge in a conversation with Gavriil Semyonov, Falin himself, in the end, "is truly the translator."

> "I thought he needed me, that I was helping him save his poems from being lost. I thought he chose me because I would do it: I would do it as he wanted it done, would only help, and not put myself into what was his. And I didn't mind."
>
> "But was not so?" . . .
>
> "I think that he hoped he could pass on to me something he couldn't keep any longer. He wanted it for me."
>
> "You began then to write again."
>
> "Yes." . . .
>
> "Not his poems into other poems, then. Himself into . . . into another poet."
>
> "Sort of. Somehow." She stopped; she had not said any of this before. "Can you imagine how strange it is to think that?"

Crowley's deepest concerns—his metaphysical speculations, his reflections on language, his meditations on the nature of "translations" vs. "originals"—rest on a superstructure of realistic, thoroughly convincing detail. His portrait of American life in the early 1960s, an era that now seems fundamentally different from the present, rings absolutely true. As L. P. Hartley once noted: "The past is a foreign country: they do things differently there." Crowley recreates that foreign country with authority, fidelity, and affection. The other foreign country that haunts the narrative, Russia under its various regimes, possesses a similar—and similarly affecting—quality of genuine, felt life. By bringing a powerfully empathetic imagination to bear on his extensive historical research, Crowley translates the convulsions of a violent century into something vital, moving, and new.

In many respects, *The Translator*, with its relative simplicity of language and plot and its intense focus on 20th century history, represents a departure for Crowley, and even suggests a possible new direction for his fiction. Still, Crowley's work has always encompassed a number of recurring themes and concerns, and this latest novel is no exception. Many of his most characteristic obsessions are present in *The Translator*, retooled and modified to fit their new surroundings.

The concept of a "passage time," a period of infinite possibility that occurs between the end of one world age and the beginning of the next, is clearly central to the Ægypt sequence. In a somewhat less sweeping form, the same concept reappears in *The Translator*. The Kennedy years, as Crowley recreates them, are also a kind of passage time, a fluid period poised between the ideological certainties of post-war America and the traumas to come. The world of the passage time is, by definition, unstable, a condition that Kit, who sees the world as "real, solid, but somehow tentative, able to go either way," instinctively recognizes. It is also, by definition, a vulnerable time: Unless the world survives the threats and challenges of the passage time, the new age, whatever it is, will never materialize. In *Dæmonomania*, the threat to the world is represented by the abduction of Sam Mucho, incarnation of Sophia, the iconic feminine figure whose fate is linked—has always been linked—to the larger fate of the world. In *The Translator*, that threat takes a much less abstruse, much more direct form: the imminent prospect of nuclear war.

The Translator, in its way, also deals with the Art of Memory, a concern in virtually all of Crowley's work. In *Little, Big* and the Ægypt series, memory is both the seat of knowledge and the source of magic, a way of organizing and understanding the universe. *The Translator*, which is composed primarily of Kit's reminiscences, is itself an act of memory, and the narrative illustrates the importance of memory in a variety of ways. For instance, the students in Falin's seminar on "Reading and Writing Poetry" are graded entirely on their ability to memorize a large number of poems. As Falin tells them, "For a poem to live within a reader, reader must be able to say it in his own mind and heart." This idiosyncratic grading method reflects a profound—and profoundly Russian—historical principle. As Gavriil Semyonov says to Kit, poetry helped preserve the Russian soul, while poetry itself was often preserved by memory alone. Poets, he recalls,

> spoke the truth long after others ceased or were silent. And even when they themselves were silenced we could say truths they had said, in their voices, because we remembered their poems. [They] could be banned and burned but not plucked from memories.

Another element that recurs in this book is the notion, central to so many of Crowley's novels, that the characters are caught up not simply in their own dramas but in a larger narrative, an overarching Story in which they must play out their designated parts. *Little, Big* is probably the purest example of this peculiarly Crowleyan motif, but *The Translator*, too, tells the story of a Story. This Story is composed, in equal parts, of history, myth, and everyday circumstance, and Kit can sometimes discern its outline from her own position, deep inside the many-layered tale. Late in the novel, speaking to Falin about the bleakest moments of her life—her brother's death, her suicide attempt, her dead child—she glimpses that outline for the very first time.

> Sometimes she stopped [telling her story] . . . and slipped again into silence . . . [Falin] waited and said nothing till she went on. Telling it she saw that she believed it was all one story, a web knotted at every point, and that the center of the story was her own blind stupid willful wanting, black spider that had caused it all . . .

Later, as the novel's public and private dramas gain momentum, she will come to understand that "this story had taken her up, and was going to keep on till it was done, whatever it was." At one time or another, most of Crowley's protagonists come to a similar realization, yielding, in the end, to the dictates of a Story larger than their own.

The Translator is a luminous, beautifully composed book that shows us our world from a startling, wholly original perspective. To use what has become the common cliché in describing Crowley's work, the further in you go, the bigger it gets. Like Crowley's best, most characteristic fiction, *The Translator* expands our definition of fantasy, offering the moving, profoundly unsettling spectacle of characters confronting the hidden secrets of the universe, learning that the world is larger, deeper, and infinitely stranger than experience has led them to believe. When Auberon, in *Little, Big*, discovers the picture of a fairy buried in a faded stack of photographs; when Pierce Moffett glimpses the possibility that the world once worked in a different fashion; when Kit learns that the Angels of the Nations are—or may be—more than simply metaphors, the universe opens up to reveal a limitless array of possibilities, radiating outward in every direction beyond the fields we know.

THE FICTION OF JOHN CROWLEY:
A BIBLIOGRAPHY
Graham Sleight

*1962   "Holy Saturday." Typescript. Also exists as 1967 typescript.

*1964   "The Squire Completes His Tale." In *Pegasus*.

*1967   "Souvenirs." Typescript.

1975   *The Deep*. Garden City, NY: Doubleday. Reprinted 1987, London: Unwin Hyman.

1976   *Beasts*. Garden City, NY: Doubleday. Reprinted 1978, London: Futura.

1977   "Antiquities." In *Whispers*, ed. Stuart Schiff, Garden City, NY: Doubleday. Reprinted in *Antiquities* (1993a).

1978   "Where Spirits Gat Them Home." In *Shadows*, ed. Charles Grant, Garden City, NY: Doubleday. Reprinted as "Her Bounty to the Dead" in *Antiquities* (1993a).

1979a   *Engine Summer*. Garden City, NY: Doubleday. Reprinted 1980, London: Victor Gollancz.

1979b   "The Single Excursion of Caspar Last." In *Gallery*, December 1979. Reprinted, with minor revisions, as the first section of "Great Work of Time" (1989b).

1980   "The Reason for the Visit." In *Interfaces*, ed. Ursula Le Guin and Virginia Kidd. New York: Ace. Reprinted in *Antiquities* (1993a).

1981a   *Little, Big*. New York: Bantam. Reprinted 1982, London: Victor Gollancz. Reprinted 1990 with a new Foreword by the author, New York: Bantam Spectra. Reprint forthcoming, 2002, New York: HarperPerennial.

1981b   "The Green Child." In *Elsewhere*, ed. Terri Windling and Mark Arnold, New York: Ace Books. Reprinted in *Antiquities* (1993a).

1983   "Novelty." In *Interzone 5*, Autumn 1983. Reprinted in *Novelty* (1989a).

1985   "Snow." In *Omni*, November 1985. Reprinted 1986 in Terry Carr, ed., *Best Science Fiction of the Year 15*, New York: Tor. Reprinted 1986 in Gardner Dozois, ed., *The Year's Best Science Fiction, Third Annual Collection*, New York: Bluejay. Reprinted in *Antiquities* (1993a).

1987   *Ægypt*. New York: Bantam Books. Reprinted 1987, London: Victor Gollancz. Reprinted 2001 (with minor revisions) as an e-book by www.electricstory.com.

1989a   *Novelty*. New York: Doubleday Foundation.

1989b   "Great Work of Time." In *Novelty* (1989a). Reprinted 1990 in Gardner Dozois, ed., *The Year's Best Science Fiction, Seventh Annual Collection*, New York: St. Martin's. Reprinted 1991 as *Great Work of Time*, New York: Bantam Spectra.

1989c   "In Blue." In *Novelty* (1989a). Reprinted 1990 in David Garnett, ed., *The Orbit Science Fiction Yearbook 3*, London: Orbit. Reprinted 1991 in Michael Bishop, ed., *Nebula Awards 25*, New York: Harcourt Brace Jovanovich.

1989d   "The Nightingale Sings at Night." In *Novelty* (1989a).

1990   "Missolonghi 1824." In *Isaac Asimov's Science Fiction Magazine*, March 1990. Reprinted 1991 in Ellen Datlow and Terri Windling, ed., *The Year's Best Fantasy and Horror: Fourth Annual Collection*, New York: St. Martin's. Reprinted in *Antiquities* (1993a).

1991   *Beasts/Engine Summer/Little, Big.* Omnibus consisting of 1976, 1979a, 1981a. New York: BOMC/QPBC.

1993a   *Antiquities: Seven Stories.* Seattle, WA: Incunabula.

1993b   "Exogamy." In *Omni Best Science Fiction 3*, ed. Ellen Datlow, New York: Omni Books. Reprinted in *Antiquities* (1993a). Reprinted 1994 in Ellen Datlow and Terri Windling, ed., *The Year's Best Fantasy and Horror: Seventh Annual Collection*, New York: St. Martin's.

1994a   *Love & Sleep.* New York: Bantam Books. Reprinted 2001 (with minor revisions) as an e-book by www.electricstory.com.

1994b   *Three Novels.* Omnibus consisting of *The Deep* (1975), *Beasts* (1976), and *Engine Summer* (1979a). New York: Bantam Books. Reprint forthcoming under the title *Otherwise*, 2002, New York: HarperPerennial.

1996   "Gone." In *The Magazine of Fantasy and Science Fiction,* September 1996. Reprinted 1999 in Edward L. Ferman and Gordon van Gelder, ed., *The Best from Fantasy and Science Fiction*, New York: Tor.

1997   "Lost and Abandoned." In *Black Swan, White Raven*, ed. Ellen Datlow and Terri Windling, New York: Avon.

2000a   *Dæmonomania.* New York: Bantam Books.

2000b   *An Earthly Mother Sits and Sings* (chapbook, illustrated by Charles Vess). Minneapolis, MN: Dreamhaven Books. Reprinted 2001, without illustrations, in Ellen Datlow and Terri Windling, ed., *The Year's Best Fantasy and Horror: Fourteenth Annual Collection*, New York: St. Martin's.

2001   "The War Between the Objects and the Subjects." In *Embrace the Mutation: Fiction Inspired by the Art of J.K. Potter,* ed. William Schafer and Bill Sheehan, Flint, MI: Subterranean Press (in press).

2002   *The Translator.* New York: William Morrow.

       "The Love Song of Menelaus." Typescript.

*Undated.

The source for those entries marked with a * is the webpage for the John Crowley papers at the Harry Ransom Humanities Research Center, University Of Texas at Austin. The webpage address is http://www.hrc.utexas.edu/fa/crowley.john.html. Aside from material related to his fiction (including "Learning to Live With It," an early version of *Engine Summer*), the Crowley papers include a wide range of material related to his work as a filmmaker. Of the starred works, "The Squire Completes His Tale" and "The Love Song of Menelaus" are poems. "Souvenirs," which also exists in some manuscripts with the title "Souvenirs of Lord Byron," is an unproduced play.

The **Ægypt** sequence, projected to be a quartet, at present consists of the volumes *Ægypt* (1987); *Love & Sleep* (1994a); and *Dæmonomania* (2000a). John Crowley has indicated, in an interview with Gregory Feeley in *Interzone* 21, that his preferred title for the first volume is "The Solitudes."

This bibliography is based on original work by Michael Andre-Driussi, and I'm grateful to him and to John Crowley and Alice Turner for their help. Any corrections or comments can be e-mailed to me at grahamsleight@hotmail.com.

SCREENWRITING BY JOHN CROWLEY
Matthew S. S. Davis

CLOUDS [WNET-TV] Crow Indians near the site of Little Big Horn hold a rodeo. Shown as part of "American Dream Machine."

DECEMBER'S CHILDREN [Children's Asthma Institute and Hospital, Denver] Docudrama of children with asthma.

THE HARD CHARGERS [Time-Life Television] One-hour documentary about Southern stock-car racing. Narrated by William Conrad. Part of the series "The Alcoa Hour."

THE GREAT AMERICAN BALLOON JOURNEY [Time-Life Television] One-hour documentary/fantasy about a trip across America in a hot-air balloon. Narrated by Jean Shepherd. Part of the series "The Alcoa Hour."

ONE BY ONE [Leavall-Brunswick Inc] 1974?? Feature documentary of the International Grand Prix season. Narrated with on-screen appearances by Stacy Keach.

THE ERIE WAR [WNET-TV] 1977. Half-hour historical drama

for young people. Part of "Ourstory" series.

AMERICA LOST AND FOUND [Lance Bird and Tom Johnson / Media Study, Inc.] 1980. One-hour documentary on the America of the '30s.

HINDENBURG: SHIP OF DOOM [HBO] 1981. Docudrama recreating the final flight of the Hindenburg airship. Part of "Flashback" series.

THE WORLD OF TOMORROW [Lance Bird and Tom Johnson] 1981. Feature documentary on the 1939 World's Fair in New York. Narrated by Jason Robards.

NUCLEAR ENERGY: THE QUESTION BEFORE US [National Geographic Society] 1981. Wisconsin faces the promises and problems of nuclear power.

THE LAST PLAGUE [HBO] 1982. Docudrama recreating the great 1918 influenza epidemic in New York. Part of "Flashback" series.

NO PLACE TO HIDE [Lance Bird and Tom Johnson] 1982. Half-hour documentary. The bomb-shelter craze of the 1950s. Part of the PBS series "Matters of Life and Death."

THE SECRET AGENT [Jackie Ochs and Daniel Keller] 1983. One-hour documentary on the effects of Agent Orange, in Vietnam and back home. (Written with Laurie Block.)

AMERICA AND LEWIS HINE [David Allentuck and Nina Rosenbloom/Daedalus Productions] 1984. One-hour documentary on the work of the great social photographer. (Additional writing by Laurie Block and John Crowley.)

CURTAIN'S UP! BROADWAY & LONDON [RKO] 1985. One-hour television special about English and American theater, hits and flops, actors and companies. Hosted by Tony Randall.

ARE WE WINNING MOMMY? AMERICA AND THE COLD WAR [Cinema Guild/Better World Society] 1986. Feature documentary about the Cold War in America. (Written with Laurie Block.)

CAPITALISM--Market and Enterprise / COMMUNISM--The Path of Revolution / THE SOCIALIST IMPULSE [National Geographic Society] 1986. Historical educational series on the development of the economic and political "isms." (Written with Laurie Block.)

AMERICA'S CUP 1987: THE WALTER CRONKITE REPORT [James Donaldson] 1987. Feature documentary on the Australian race. Narrated and hosted by Walter Cronkite.

TO TASTE A HUNDRED HERBS/ALL UNDER HEAVEN [Richard Gordon and Carma Hinton/(Long Bow Group] 1987. Two parts of a three part film "One Village in China" portraying aspects of life in the traditional village of Long Bow, China. (Additional writing by Laurie Block and John Crowley.)

$10 HORSE AND A $40 SADDLE [Brian Dew] 1988. One-hour documentary on the life of Monroe Veach, trick-roper, saddle-maker, Westerner. A meditation on the idea of the West.

THE GREAT DEPRESSION [National Geographic Society] 1990. Educational archival film.

1917: REVOLUTION IN RUSSIA [National Geographic Society] 1990. Historical educational film. (Written with Laurie Block.)

FIT: EPISODES IN THE HISTORY OF THE BODY [Laurie Block/ Straight Ahead Pictures] 1991. Documentary feature/special on the history of the practice and meaning of physical fitness in America. (Written with Laurie Block).

PEARL HARBOR: SURPRISE AND REMEMBRANCE [Lance Bird, Tom Johnson/WGBH] 1991. Two-hour documentary on the events leading up to the Japanese attack on Pearl Harbor, and how that event has reverberated in the American consciousness ever since. Part of the series "The American Experience." (Written with Lance Bird & Tom Johnson.)

THE RESTLESS CONSCIENCE [Kohav Beller] 1991/93? Feature documentary explores the motivating principles and activities of a small group of individuals within wartime Germany who comprised the anti-Nazi underground. (Assisted writing)

THE LIBERATORS: FIGHTING ON TWO FRONTS IN WWII [Miles Educational Film Productions Inc] 1992. Part of "The American Experience," a series from WGBH in Boston. (Written with Daniel V. Allentuck & Lou Potter.)

"DEGENERATE" ART [David Grubin/Los Angeles County Museum of Art] 1992. 60 minute PBS special recreating the infamous Nazi propaganda displays of modern art.

NOBODY'S GIRLS [Mirra Bank/Maryland Public Television] 1995. Feature documentary about little-known Native American, Mexican-American, Chinese, and African-American women who lived in the American West in the last century.

THE GATE OF HEAVENLY PEACE [Richard Gordon and Carma Hinton/Long Bow Group] 1995. Three hour documentary about the events in Beijing in 1989, the occupation of Tienanmen Square and the massacre in the streets, set in historical context. (Written with Geremie Barmé.)

THE US-MEXICAN WAR: [KERA-TV] 1998. 3-hour series. (Assisted writing)

BEYOND AFFLICTION: THE DISABILITY HISTORY PROJECT [Laurie Block] 1998. A four-hour radio documentary series distributed on NPR. (Assisted writing)

BILLY THE KID [DVTV/The Learning Channel] 1998. One hour documentary. Part of the series "Gunfighters of the West."

IN SEARCH OF CHINA [Emma Morris/WETA/K2 Media] 2000.

SELECTED NON-FICTION
BY JOHN CROWLEY:
REVIEWS AND ARTICLES
Matthew S. S. Davis

"John Crowley," *The Faces of Science Fiction*, ed. by Patti Perret; 1984.

[*The Education of the Senses*, Peter Gay] *Philadelphia Inquirer*, January 15 1984.

[*Enderby's Dark Lady*, Anthony Burgess] *Philadelphia Inquirer*, June 10 1984.

[*Edmund Gosse: A Literary Landscape*, Ann Thwaite] *Philadelphia Inquirer*, September 2 1984.

[*Cider with Rosie*, Laurie Lee] *New York Newsday*, December 2 1984.

[*The Memoirs of John Addington Symonds*, ed. Phyllis Grosskurth] *New York Newsday* Feb 10 1985.

[*Lanark*, Alasdair Gray] *New York Times Book Review*, May 5 1985.

[*The Kingdom of the Wicked*, Anthony Burgess] *New York Times Book Review*, September 22 1985.

[*Cities and People: A Social and Architectural History*, Mark Girouard] *Philadelphia Inquirer*, January 26 1986.

[*The Little People*, MacDonald Harris] *New York Times Book Review*, March 2 1986.

[*From the Realm of Morpheus*, Steven Millhauser] *New York Times Book Review*, October 12 1986.

[*The Pianoplayers*, Anthony Burgess] *New York Newsday*, October 21 1986.

"Shakespeare's Ghosts," *Penguin Encyclopaedia of Horror and the Supernatural*, ed. Jack Sullivan, 1986.

[*Time's Arrows: Scientific Attitudes Toward Time*, Richard Morris] *Philadelphia Inquirer*, April 7 1987.

[*Little Wilson and Big God*, Anthony Burgess] *New York Newsday*, May 3 1987.

[*Winsor McCay: His Life and Art*, John Canemaker] *New York Newsday*, August 30 1987.

[*The Arabian Nightmare*, Robert Irwin] *New York Times Book Review*, November 15 1987.

[*Galileo Heretic*, Pietro Redondi] *New York Newsday*, January 10 1988.

[*The Confessions*, William Boyd] *Washington Post Book World*,

May 8 1988.

[*Labrador,* Kathryn Davis] *New York Times Book Review,* August 14 1988.

[*Any Old Iron,* Anthony Burgess] *Washington Post Book World,* Feb 12 1989.

[*Fragments for a History of the Human Body,* Parts I, II and III, ed. Michael Feher] *Washington Post Book World,* July 9 1989.

[*First Light,* Peter Ackroyd] *New York Times Book Review,* September 17 1989.

"The Labyrinth of the World and the Paradise of the Heart," *The New York Review of Science Fiction* #15, November 1989 (Paper presented in the Honors Colloquium, "Civilization," at Williams College, 1986).

[*Mary Reilly.* Valerie Martin] *New York Times Book Review,* February 4 1990.

"My T.H. White," Readercon #3 Souvenir Booklet, March 30-April 1 1990.

[*The Book of Evidence,* John Banville] *Washington Post Book World,* April 8 1990.

[*Cow,* Beat Sterchi] *New York Times Book Review,* July 8 1990.

[*The Mask of Nostradamus.* James Randi] *Washington Post Book World,* September 17 1990.

[*Pinto and Sons,* Leslie Epstein] *New York Times Book Review,*

November 4 1990.

[*Was*, Geoff Ryman] *New York Times Book Review*, November 1990.

[*Gerontius*, James Hamilton-Patterson] *Washington Post Book World*, May 5 1991.

[*Out of this World: Otherworldly Journeys from Gilgamesh to Einstein*, Ioan Couliano] *Washington Post Book World*, August 25 1991.

[*The Glorious Constellations: History and Mythology*, Giuseppe Maria Sesti] *Washington Post Book World*, December 1 1991.

[*Gospel*, Wilson Barnhardt] *Washington Post Book World*, April 18 1993.

[*Tintin in the New World*, Frederick Tuten] *Washington Post Book World*, July 4 1993.

[*The Fermata*, by Nicholson Baker] *Washington Post Book World*, Feb 20 1994.

[*Banished Children of Eve*, Peter Quinn] *New York Times Book Review*, April 3 1994.

"Read This", *The New York Review of Science Fiction* #71, July 1994.

[*Foxfire*, Joyce Carol Oates] *New York Times Book Review*, September 13 1994.

[*Shadow of a Flying Bird*, Mordecai Gerstein] *New York Times*

Book Review, November 20 1994.

[*Robert Louis Stevenson, a Biography*. Frank McLynn / *The Letters of Robert Louis Stevenson*, Vol. III. ed. Bradford A Booth] *Washington Post Book World*, Jan 8 1995.

"The Gothic of Thomas M. Disch," *Yale Review*, v. 83 , #2, April 1995.

[*Athena*, John Banville] *Washington Post Book World*, July 9 1995.

[*The Magician's Doubts*, Michael Wood / *The Stories of Vladimir Nabokov*, ed. Dimitri Nabokov] *Washington Post Book World*, Nov 19 1995.

[*In the Beauty of the Lilies*, John Updike] *Washington Post Book World*, February 4 1996.

[*Searching For Memory: The Brain, the Mind, and the Past*, Daniel L. Schacter] *Washington Post Book World*, August 11 1996.

[*Eros, Magic, and the Death of Professor Culianu*, Ted Anton] *Washington Post Book World*, October 20 1996.

[*The World of Edward Gorey*, Clifford Ross and Karen Wilken] *Washington Post Book World*, December 9 1996.

[*The Story of the Night*, Colm Toibin] *Washington Post Book World*, May 18 1997.

[*The Everlasting Story of Nory*, Nicholson Baker] *Washington Post Book World*, May 31 1998.

[*Wonders and the Order of Nature*, Lorraine Daston and Katherine Park] *Washington Post Book World*, October 18 1998.

[*The Arcanum: The Extraordinary True Story*, Janet Gleeson] *Washington Post Book World*, May 23 1999.

[*The Sharp Shooter*, Frederick Busch] *New York Times Book Review*, May 30 1999.

[*The Jew of New York*, Ben Katchor] *Yale Review*, v. 87 #3, July 1999.

[*Among the Believers: The Rise of Irrationalism and the Perils of Piety*, Wendy Kaminer] *Washington Post Book World*, October 17 1999.

[*The Last Life*, Claire Messud] *Washington Post Book World*, October 24 1999.

[*The Testament of Yves Gudron*, Emily Barton] *New York Times Book Review*, February 13 2000.

[*Being Dead*, Jim Crace] *Washington Post Book World*, June 11 2000.

[*Story of O*, Pauline Reage] *Washington Post Book World*, June 18 2000.

[*The Hill Bachelors*, William Trevor] *Washington Post Book World*, December 10 2000.

[*The Queen's Conjuror: The Science and Magic of Dr. John Dee, Advisor to Queen Elizabeth I*, Benjamin Woolley] *Washington Post Book World*, April 1 2001.

CONTRIBUTORS PAGE

Michael Andre-Driussi edited and published *Lexicon Urthus*, a reader's guide to Gene Wolfe's Book of the New Sun series. His fiction has appeared in *Interzone* and *Tomorrow SF*, among others.

William H. Ansley has a Masters Degree in Computer Science and works at a community college. He is co-founder of a website for children who read: http://www.inklesstales.com.

Brian Attebery is author of two books on fantasy and the forthcoming *Decoding Gender in Science Fiction*. Along with Ursula K. Le Guin and Karen Joy Fowler, he edited *The Norton Book of Science Fiction*. He teaches at Idaho State University.

Harold Bloom, Sterling Professor of Humanities at Yale and Berg Professor of English at New York University, is the author of more than twenty acclaimed books of criticism, the latest of which is *How to Read and Why*.

John Clute, novelist, anthologist and co-editor of *The Encyclopedia of Science Fiction* and *The Encyclopedia of Fantasy*, has won virtually every award available for criticism in the science fiction field.

Matthew S. S. Davis is a part-time librarian and full-time reader. These two aspects unite in his Thomas M. Disch website (http://www.michaelscycles.freeserve.co.uk/tmd.htm). He is currently compiling a checklist of Cyril Connolly's writings.

Thomas M. Disch is a prize-winning novelist, poet and critic. His most recent work of criticism is *The Dreams Our Stuff is Made Of: How Science Fiction Conquered the World.*

James Hynes is the author of two novels, *The Lecturer's Tale* and *The Wild Colonial Boy*, and a book of novellas, *Publish and Perish.*

Don Riggs co-edited *Uncommonplaces: Poems of the Fantastic* with Judith Kerman, and has published scholarly articles about the fantastic in literary and visual art in various journals. He teaches at Drexel University.

Bill Sheehan is the author of *At the Foot of the Story Tree: An Inquiry into the Fiction of Peter Straub*, which won the 2001 World Fantasy Special Award (Non-Professional). His essays, interviews, and reviews have appeared in *The New York Review of Science Fiction*, *Nova Express*, *Paradoxa*, and numerous other publications.

Graham Sleight works as a commissioning editor for a London publisher. He has published science fiction criticism in *The New York Review of Science Fiction.*

Adam Stephanides lives in Champaign, Illinois and has a Ph.D. in American History. His Dissertation is entitled "Tomorrow's Women and Yesterday's Men: Junior Novels and Social Change, 1946-64."

Jennifer Stevenson has written several articles on the work of John Crowley for *The New York Review of Science Fiction*. Her short fiction has appeared in science fiction anthologies *Women at War, Horns of Elfland, Fields of Blood*, and *Sextopia*.

Sondra Ford Swift teaches English at Old Dominion University and Saint Leo University in Norfolk, Virginia. An article of hers has appeared in the recent anthology *The Blood Is the Life: Vampires in Literature*.

Alice K. Turner has been for many years the fiction editor of *Playboy* magazine, and is also an anthologist and the author of *The History of Hell*.